DISHONORED AMERICANS

The Revolutionary Age

FRANCIS D. COGLIANO AND PATRICK GRIFFIN, EDITORS

Timothy Compeau

DISHONORED AMERICANS

THE POLITICAL DEATH OF LOYALISTS IN REVOLUTIONARY AMERICA

Dishonored Americans

THE POLITICAL DEATH OF LOYALISTS IN REVOLUTIONARY AMERICA

Timothy Compeau

UNIVERSITY OF VIRGINIA PRESS
Charlottesville and London

UNIVERSITY OF VIRGINIA PRESS
© 2023 by the Rector and Visitors of the University of Virginia
All rights reserved
Printed in the United States of America on acid-free paper

First published 2023

1 3 5 7 9 8 6 4 2

Library of Congress Cataloging-in-Publication Data
Names: Compeau, Timothy, author.
Title: Dishonored Americans : the political death of loyal-
ists in revolutionary America / Timothy Compeau.
Description: Charlottesville : University of Virginia Press, 2023. | Series: The
revolutionary age | Includes bibliographical references and index.
Identifiers: LCCN 2023027627 (print) | LCCN 2023027628 (ebook) | ISBN 9780813950457
(hardcover) | ISBN 9780813950464 (paperback) | ISBN 9780813950471 (ebook)
Subjects: LCSH: American loyalists. | Honor—United States—History—18th century. | United
States—History—Revolution, 1775–1783. | United States—Politics and government—1775–1783.
Classification: LCC E277 .C665 2023 (print) | LCC E277 (ebook) | DDC 973.3/14—dc23/eng/20230810
LC record available at https://lccn.loc.gov/2023027627
LC ebook record available at https://lccn.loc.gov/2023027628

Cover art: "Stamp Master in Effigy," John Warner Barber, *Interesting*
Events in the History of the United States, New Haven, CT: J.W. Barber, 1828.
(Rare Book and Manuscript Library, Columbia University)

For my parents

A Man's *honour* is his political life; and the moment he sacrifices it, he dies a political death—he is no longer a useful member of the community, but is truly a burden to society.

—*Spooner's Vermont Journal,* June 7, 1785

CONTENTS

ACKNOWLEDGMENTS   xi

Prologue   1

Introduction: Political Death   7

1. Dishonor   23

2. Captivity   49

3. Revenge   76

4. Loyalist Honor   106

5. Political Rebirth   137

Conclusion: The Loyalist Puzzle   173

NOTES   183

BIBLIOGRAPHY   217

INDEX   241

ACKNOWLEDGMENTS

I AM INDEBTED TO MANY people and institutions who made this book possible. The idea for this book first emerged from conversations at the University of Western Ontario with my PhD supervisor, Nancy L. Rhoden, whose continued generosity, patience, and wisdom have been indispensable. I cannot overstate how grateful I am for her kindness and mentorship throughout all the many iterations of this project.

Over the years of intermittent writing and revising that went into this book, I have been fortunate to receive advice and critiques from many friends and colleagues. In particular, I would like to thank Jane Errington, Nancy Christie, Nina Reid-Maroney, Bryce Traister, and Laurel Shire, who provided feedback and valuable suggestions on an early manuscript draft. I am also grateful to conference organizers, chairs, and panelists over the years who provided opportunities to share my research at different stages of development, including Mary Beth Norton, Carol Berkin, Kacy Dowd Tillman, and Liam Riordan.

I conducted research for this book with financial assistance from the Social Sciences and Humanities Research Council of Canada, the University of Western Ontario, Huron University College, and the United Empire Loyalist Association of Canada. I received warm welcomes and essential help from archivists and librarians, including Linda Hocking and the staff of the Litchfield Historical Society, Tom Lannon at the New York Public Library, Ted O'Reilly and the staff at the New-York Historical Society, Diana McCain at the Connecticut Historical Society, Christine Jack at the Harriet Irving

Library, University of New Brunswick, and Paul Banfield and his staff at Queen's University Archives in Kingston, Ontario.

A particular thanks must go to the membership of the United Empire Loyalists Association of Canada for their financial support and their kind reception at many presentations as I worked through the ideas in this book. I am continually amazed at the passion and knowledge of UELAC members. In particular, I would like to thank Doug Grant, Bonnie Schepers, Fred Heyward, Carl Stymiest, and Barbara Andrews, among many others, including Stephen Davidson, from whom I first learned of James Murray and his wig.

Sincere thanks to Nadine Zimmerli at the University of Virginia Press for her kind support, crucial advice, and keen editorial eye throughout the publishing process, and thanks to Wren Morgan Myers, Laura Reed-Morrisson, and all the editors and staff at the Press. My gratitude to Tom Cutterham, Rebecca Brannon, and the anonymous readers who provided important and challenging critiques of the manuscript.

The history department at Huron University College is a wonderful home in which to work and teach, and my colleagues Thomas Peace, Nina Reid-Maroney, Amy Bell, Jun Fang, and Geoff Read have been incredibly supportive. So many friends and colleagues at Huron, Western, and elsewhere have helped in enormous ways, either through discussing the book with me or just helping me forget about work for a while. My appreciation to John Hope, Andrea King, Nicolas Virtue, Oliver Charbonneau, Jeremy Marks, Robert MacDougall, Robert Wardhaugh, and Marilla McCargar. Special thanks to Paris McCargar-Olivier, Oliver King-Hope, and Augie and Lily Charbonneau for teaching me some of the most important lessons about loyalty. And my deepest gratitude to Courtney Davis, my partner in all things, for her tireless patience and love; thank you.

Finally, I dedicate *Dishonored Americans* to my parents, Keith and Patricia Compeau. The origins of this book can be traced back to family trips along the East Coast of the United States that included visits, at my insistence, to sites of memory of early American history. Thank you for your ever-present support, indulgence, and encouragement.

DISHONORED AMERICANS

Prologue

ACCORDING TO SOUTH CAROLINIAN lore, the first shots of the American Revolution rang out inside a Charleston tavern. On the night of August 15, 1771, the Tory Peter De Lancey and the Patriot Dr. John Haley settled the great political argument of their time with a duel in the private dining room of "a genteel house of entertainment." The best-known account of this affair comes from the nineteenth-century historian Joseph Johnson, who portrayed the encounter as a romantic microcosm of the American Revolution. De Lancey was an "elegant and accomplished royalist," while Haley "warmly espoused the popular cause in opposition to royalty." Though a recent migrant to the colonies, the Irish doctor embodied the true revolutionary spirit against De Lancey's old-money Toryism. When the doctor foiled De Lancey in their argument, the haughty Loyalist intentionally provoked the doctor "by giving him the 'lie.'" Haley responded as men of honor would and challenged the royal official to a duel. The spirited young men agreed to exchange fire right then from either end of a dinner table. With no witnesses and no seconds, they fired at the same moment, and De Lancey fell dead.[1]

According to Johnson, Haley fled to "the Whigs" who "defended [him] and concealed him until his trial came on." The doctor assembled an impressive legal team for his counsel, including "James Parsons, Charles Cotesworth Pinckney, Thomas Hayward and Alexander Harvey, Esquires." Other sources include John Rutledge among the defense.[2] It was clear to Johnson that such eminent men took the case for the cause of liberty. Their chief difficulty, however, was to prove that the "duel" was indeed honorable,

{1}

as it did not follow the accepted forms. Duels were uncommon in America prior to the Revolution, but the general customs were widely known. Gentlemen exchanged fire outside in the light of day, with trusted friends in the role of "seconds," serving as conciliators and witnesses for each participant. A surgeon might also attend. Most importantly, there would have been time allotted, perhaps a week, for the parties to come to an amicable resolution of the dispute.[3] Haley and De Lancey followed none of these conventions.

Despite the irregularities, the defense convinced a jury of Haley's peers that the shooting was indeed a legitimate duel between gentlemen and "that there was not the least Degree of Malice on [Haley's] part." De Lancey consented to the terms, which, between gentlemen, absolved Haley of any underhandedness. Though unconventional, the jury considered this an honorable affair. The court convicted Haley on the lesser charge of manslaughter, and the governor pardoned him—a typical outcome for surviving duelists. According to Johnson, Haley's "acquittal was considered a great triumph by the Whigs and popular party," and to "the royalists a proportionate source of chagrin."[4]

If this was in fact a duel between a Loyalist and a Patriot, it would be the only one recorded in the revolutionary era. The evidence, at first glance, would seem to support the claim. De Lancey's relatives were prominent Loyalists in the American Revolution, so it is fair to assume that he would have shared their sympathies. Dr. Haley served in the Patriot militia during the conflict and gained a swashbuckling reputation. The historian and delegate to the Continental Congress David Ramsay, himself a prominent South Carolina physician, noted in 1776 Haley's "willingness to settle medical controversies with the sword."[5]

Yet an anonymous report published shortly after the affair demonstrates that far from representing warring camps, Haley and De Lancey belonged to the same social circle of young, wealthy gentlemen. According to the article, the duelists spent the day before the shooting among a larger group of friends, and though some of the details confirm the general outline of Johnson's tale, the political controversies of the day played no part. Like many seconds' testimonies, the authors intended to combat "a great number of contradictory and infamous reports" but explained that the "dispute between these gentlemen, was so sudden, and so secret, that not one of the friends of either can pretend to give any certain account of the cause."

The anonymous authors intended to protect the reputations of both the duelists and their wider social network by carefully framing the encounter, and De Lancey's killing, as a legitimate affair of honor. Around seven in the evening, the authors explained, the two men separated from the rest of their friends and went out to a balcony where they "were observed to converse rather gravely, & set their watches, but no high words passed nor was there the least appearance of any difference." Unlike Johnson's impulsive young duelists, these gentlemen were restrained and engaged in sober reflection. They agreed to the time and terms and synchronized their watches. Later that evening, according to the report, De Lancey rented a private dining room at Holliday's Tavern where he acted the busy host, ordering in candles and refreshments. When Haley arrived, the men dismissed the waiter, locked the door, "and presently the report of pistols was heard." As the smoke cleared, Haley displayed the paradoxical ideal of gentlemanly compassion that followed a moment of necessary cold-bloodedness. "[W]ith visible concern in his countenance," Haley "called at several of his friends houses, 'begging a Doctor might be sent to poor De Lancey,' whom he believed he had hurt." This description of the duel, or something like it, persuaded the Charleston jury to acquit Haley.[6]

The tale is complicated even further by a letter from Peter Manigault, another Charleston gentleman, to De Lancey's prominent brother-in-law, Ralph Izard. According to Manigault, the two young men were noted hotheads, and it did "not appear extraordinary . . . that [De Lancey] should be killed in a Duel, & that by Haly [sic]." The two men often quarreled, Manigault explained, though he did not claim to know the cause, only that it "always broke out afresh upon their being heated with Liquor." True to form, the two men had spent the day together drinking heavily with several other young gentlemen before their meeting. At some point in their binge, the pair agreed that it was time to end their feud once and for all.

Manigault himself learned of the "appointment" from a friend who mentioned it nonchalantly while drinking at a different tavern. No one seemed concerned when they spotted Haley walking down the street "staggering drunk." The other gentlemen "took no notice of the Matter," thinking the cockeyed youths had already fired their pistols and were stumbling away to pass out. Only later, when Manigault walked past Holliday's Tavern and witnessed the assembled crowd, did he realize the madcaps had gone through with it and De Lancey was dead. Manigault reported with grim astonishment that the two exchanged fire in a room measuring "15 by 12 feet" and added the gruesome detail that the summer heat, combined with De Lancey's "Liquor & Passion, caused so quick a Putrefaction that it was absolutely necessary to bury him" the next day. And yet, despite all of this, Manigault assured Izard that "no body suspects foul Play."[7] As far as they were concerned, as tragic and as asinine as this affair may have been, it was within Haley and De Lancey's rights as gentlemen. Drunk or not, they had both agreed to the terms. Honor was a pliant concept, and if the gentlemen of Charleston agreed that this killing was honorable, then it was.

Far from being an affair of honor fought between a Loyalist and a Patriot over the great political questions of the day, this was instead the deadly behavior of drunken and reckless young men with too much time and money on their hands. De Lancey's killing only became attached to the aura of the glorious cause in later generations. Yet at the time it was neither considered criminal nor dishonorable by the elite of Charleston, who closed ranks around their own to protect both Dr. Haley and the reputation of their genteel community. To modern eyes this might seem like gross corruption and the disingenuous invocation of self-serving rhetoric, but South Carolina's patricians accepted the utility of the duel. Notions of honor may have provoked the feud, but they also channeled the quarrel into a single clumsy act of ritualized violence instead of drawing the community into a prolonged and bloody vendetta.[8] De Lancey's death was by no means an ideal outcome, but it provided a decisive end to the affair and maintained cohesion among Charleston's white ruling class for a time. Just a few years later this community and scores like it across the colonies were split by civil war.

The conflict that erupted between Loyalist and Patriot gentlemen in the American Revolution was deeply personal, but they fought no duels. The war altered who was worthy of a gentleman's honor in America. A dutiful Loyalist would not accept a challenge from a criminal rebel, nor would an honorable Patriot ever demand satisfaction from a dishonored Tory. They were no longer equals. Hostile encounters between Loyalists and Patriots in the Revolution instead became matters of popular justice and crowd action. The Loyalists examined in this book would never gain honorable satisfaction from their former countrymen. Instead, Loyalist gentlemen had to hope for a British victory in the protracted Revolutionary War. But war, according to the famous military strategist Carl von Clausewitz, "is nothing but a duel on a larger scale."[9]

INTRODUCTION

Political Death

ON THURSDAY, JULY 20, 1775, the Reverend Jonathan Boucher arrived at Saint Barnabas Church in Queen Anne's Parish, Maryland, to find two hundred armed militiamen waiting for him. The Continental Congress had asked all colonists to gather that day for "public humiliation, fasting, and prayer" in support of colonial resistance. Boucher, an outspoken Loyalist, instead planned to admonish his parishioners to "sit still" and take no part in a rebellion against the Crown. The militia leader, "a very great Patriot" named Osborne Sprigg, warned Boucher not to preach, and the Loyalist's few friends begged him not to provoke the crowd. Boucher stubbornly persisted and told his friends "that once to flinch was ever to invite danger." He would preach "with my sermon in one hand and a loaded pistol in the other." Yet Boucher never made it to his pulpit. When the Patriot crowd surged forward and surrounded the clergyman, Boucher grabbed "Sprigg . . . by the collar, and with my cocked pistol in the other hand, assur[ed] him that if any violence was offered to me I would instantly blow his brains out."[1]

Boucher described this encounter as a matter of honor, not just between himself and Sprigg but as part of a wider, asymmetrical battle between representatives of refinement, morality, and civilization and the deluded colonial mob. He could have walked to the pulpit unarmed, in imitation of Christ, but he did not. Masculine honor compelled Boucher to defend his divinely and royally ordained rights with the threat of armed force. Having made his point, and with Sprigg at his supposed mercy, Boucher consented to leave. Far from being impressed by the clergyman,

{7}

8   DISHONORED AMERICANS

the militia jeered Boucher as he exited the church still clutching his pistol (and Sprigg). To add more indignity to the scene, drummers struck up the "Rogue's March," the tune played when disgraced soldiers were expelled from a regiment. As Boucher rode off, all he could do was curse Sprigg as "a complete coward and scoundrel"—but it made no difference.[2] The crowd literally drummed Boucher out of his own church.

Reflecting on his experiences, Boucher likened the storm of harassment and insults he endured to being "pelted to death." The crowd did not tar and feather the Loyalist, nor did they ransack his home, but they dishonored him nonetheless. It was no surprise to Boucher that unscrupulous men like Sprigg could inflame the "bulk of the people," who were "wrong-headed, ignorant, and prone to resist authority," but he was bewildered and grief-stricken when gentlemen he considered his peers abandoned him to his fate. He castigated his "old friend" George Washington: "You cannot say that I deserved to be run down, vilified, and injured . . . merely because I cannot bring myself to think on some political points just as you."[3] But the moment for gentlemanly debate was over. George Washington now commanded the siege of Boston and referred to Loyalists as "execrable Parricides" targeted by "the Fury of justly-enraged People."[4]

For Loyalists like Boucher, the very foundations of society—honor, virtue, respect—all appeared to be crumbling. Yet American revolutionaries believed that they fought in defense of those same principles, and they, too, embraced the language of honor to justify their demands for conformity and resistance to the Crown.[5] Boucher's stubborn loyalism set him apart and dishonored him in the eyes of Patriots, and his elite status served as a lightning rod for popular demonstrations of collective honor. Degrading once-respected gentlemen like Boucher purged revolutionary society of an internal enemy, and it assured Patriots of all ranks that by rejecting loyalism, they would be empowered as honorable men and free from the shame inflicted on Tories. As a contributor to a Vermont newspaper explained shortly after the war, "A Man's *honour* is his political life; and the moment he sacrifices it, he dies a political death—he is no longer a useful member of the community, but is truly a burden to society."[6] Boucher could no longer claim respect and deference from his parishioners, nor was he welcome in the company of his fellow colonial gentlemen, like Washington. Boucher was politically dead.

Patriots described white male Loyalists as "traitors," "absconders," or "absentees," but the phrase "political death," found scattered in legal records and print media of the era, best captures the complex Loyalist ordeal. "Political," in this sense, did not refer only to the high politics of councils and assemblies. Rather, it encompassed the broader public roles of gentlemen as authority figures, householders, and supposed moral examples for the people. Revolutionary crowds, courts, committees, and the press maintained social cohesion and discredited and expelled opposing voices by attacking the public lives and private spaces of influential Crown supporters. Political death was the final stage in the process of popular condemnation, social ostracism, and, as the conflict intensified, the legal attainder or banishment of propertied men who remained loyal to the Crown. Patriots denied politically dead Loyalists the rights and identity of gentlemen, and demonstrated the power of the majority to determine who was worthy of respect and privilege and thus who could wield power in America. A crucial but not fully recognized factor in the Patriot victory, political death definitively connected Loyalists with dishonor.

Across revolutionary America, Patriots employed a variety of rituals and insults to dishonor prominent Loyalists like Boucher and demonstrate the demise of British power in the colonies. Georgia Patriots even held a funeral marking King George III's political death in the summer of 1776. "Forasmuch as George the Third, of Great Britain hath most flagrantly violated his coronation oath, and trampled upon the constitution of our country, and the sacred rights of mankind," went the eulogy, "we therefore commit his political existence to the ground." Patriot writers insisted that the colonists had not committed symbolic regicide; rather, the king, like the Loyalists, had committed political suicide. A year earlier, a contributor to the *New-York Journal* explained: "When the King of Great Britain violates the constitution . . . he unkings himself. . . . The person remains, but the constitutional King of Great Britain no longer exists in him. Nor can he be recovered from that degradation, that moral and political death."[7] Just as George III had "unkinged" himself, in the eyes of Patriots, Loyalists like

Boucher unmanned themselves and killed the nascent citizens within them by remaining royal subjects.

Jonathan Boucher sold his property and left the colonies before the legal consequences of political death caught up with his social ostracism and public shaming, but other Loyalists were not so fortunate. From New Hampshire to Georgia, legislative assemblies passed sweeping laws targeting Loyalists, their property, and their freedom within the revolutionary states. The Connecticut Loyalist Joel Stone wrote that his Patriot enemies considered him "unworthy to live," but revolutionary authorities rarely followed through with their threats to execute Crown supporters.[8] Instead, they focused their energies on containing and neutralizing the spread of loyalism through a concerted legal campaign that targeted Loyalists' rights as citizens and householders. Rather than hang Joel Stone for his loyalism, Connecticut authorities confiscated his property and declared him "politically deceased."[9] As the lawyer and signer of the Declaration of Independence Francis Hopkinson explained, "an individual may have *two* lives, and exist in one, though deprived of the other—that is, an individual may be alive in health in *fact,* and at the same time absolutely dead in *law.*"[10] This concept drew on the English legal concept of attainder, under which the state could charge and convict traitors without trial. In the Revolution, Patriot governments and courts employed this legal procedure to strip Loyalist men of their right to own property, effectively causing the legal death of attained householders and cancelling their posthumous rights as husbands and fathers. Loyalist wives and children could usually inherit nothing from a confiscated estate.[11] Indeed, attainder was such a severe punishment, and so potentially dangerous in the hands of a tyrant, that it was banned in the American Constitution.[12] Yet during the Revolution, confiscated homes stood as monuments to the Loyalists' political death.

Whether enacted informally through insults or shaming rituals, or officially through acts of attainder, property confiscation, or imprisonment, Patriots drew on the power of dishonor to strip Loyalists of their status and manhood. The Pennsylvania Loyalist Joseph Galloway described these experiences as "penalties more severe than death itself," and that was precisely what Patriots intended.[13]

For generations after the Revolution, historians and novelists recalled the Loyalists as an elite minority of cruel patricians who embodied the vanity and corruption of Old World gentility.[14] Historians demolished this myth long ago and continue to reveal the diversity of Crown supporters and the contributions of women, the poor, free and enslaved African Americans, and Indigenous allies in the struggle.[15] Yet white landowning Loyalists dominate the historical record, and their writings have been used to explain loyalism in general. This book seeks to explain middling and elite Loyalists' distinct motivations and mentalities and the unique threat revolutionaries believed such prominent men posed. The intent is not to overshadow the agency of other participants in the American Revolution but to dissect the cultural sources of power and legitimacy shared by Loyalists and Patriots.

Dishonored Americans provides a new reading of the civil war between Loyalists and Patriots by focusing on the central importance of honor culture in their struggle. Political ideology divided Patriots and Loyalists, but they fought their war within a shared system of signs, symbols, and customs charged with deeply moralized, gendered, and racialized meanings determining who was worthy of respect and privilege. Patriots effectively neutralized the Loyalist threat through their intense invocation of the power of dishonor, and Loyalist gentlemen spent the entire conflict, and the rest of their lives, reacting to the experience of collective and personal political death.

This book draws on the experiences of Loyalists from across the Thirteen Colonies, though Crown supporters from New England appear more frequently because of their extensive documentation and vivid accounts of political death, and those from the middle colonies predominate because of their numbers. South Carolina produced thousands of Loyalists, though as will be seen in chapter 5, many reintegrated and put the war behind them in the 1780s. Virginia, by comparison, produced few prominent white Loyalists. Lord Dunmore's proclamation offering freedom to the enslaved attracted thousands of Black Loyalists but drove neutral or Loyalist-leaning whites into the Patriot camp.[16] Despite these regional variations, Loyalists endured ritualized dishonor and insults throughout Revolutionary

America. This is demonstrated in the experiences of men such as William Bayard and Cadwallader Colden Jr. of New York, who were, by colonial standards, fabulously wealthy grandees sitting at the pinnacle of the colonial hierarchy. Other Loyalist gentlemen were like James Moody, a prosperous New Jersey farmer, and Thomas Brown, a newly arrived English gentleman eager to make his fortune on a Georgia plantation. Joel Stone was an ambitious local merchant at a crossroads in northern Connecticut, and John Peters was from a prominent New England family settling a new town on the Vermont frontier. Though separated by vast sums of money, education, regional culture, and political networks, Loyalists like these were connected by the experience of political death and their quest to restore genteel respectability, patriarchy, and the gentleman's notion of honor.

The very term "gentleman" was infused with power, and yet it was a loose and ambiguous title in both colonial America and Britain. For many of the Loyalists and Patriots encountered in this book, their claims to this status were tenuous and aspirational.[17] Gentlemen envisioned an ideal world in which they respected their peers, deferred to their superiors, and treated the common people kindly and fairly but from a distance. Long before the Revolution, the relatively widespread prosperity of the colonies meant that self-styled gentlemen found their pretenses to authority questioned or denied by their fellow colonists. Ideals of deference were perhaps found more in the minds of the elite than in reality.[18] Colonial gentlemen could be quite sensitive when it came to matters of respect, and historians have noted resentment to perceived British insults among the more subtle causes of the American Revolution. Yet gentlemen were conflicted on the use of violence to defend their honor. Reflecting on the tumult at Saint Barnabas Church, Jonathan Boucher wrote, "there is nothing I so much dread and detest" as fighting.[19] To modern eyes, gentlemanly honor culture was filled with paradoxes, but it made sense to those living within it. The defense of family, reputation, or rights was a duty all men of honor had to accept, however unpleasant it might be. Boucher's willingness to prove his mettle in combat was matched by his sensibility to deplore the need to do so.[20]

A gentleman could be identified by his refined manners, education, and fashion sense, hallmarks that were collectively referred to as "gentility" and were thought, at least by those who possessed them, to be outward expressions of inward virtue.[21] Revolutionaries accused Loyalist gentlemen of hoarding offices and claiming privileges that could only be won through unmanly obsequiousness and blind obedience to the British. Thus, Patriot attacks on such Loyalists often targeted their symbols of refinement—clothing, homes, horses, and other possessions. These were not necessarily attacks on the privileges and powers of gentlemen in general but rejections of Loyalist claims to that identity and the power that came with it. To the Patriots, Loyalists were false gentlemen who might look the part but did not possess the most important quality of a gentleman: honor. Only by understanding what it meant to be considered an honorable gentleman in the eighteenth century can the full impact of the Loyalists' political death be appreciated.

In the eighteenth-century world of slavers and the enslaved, of patricians and plebeians, of masters and servants, it is difficult to overstate the importance of honor. All men and women could aspire to a kind of honor, but gentlemen understood their honor as a rare commodity. An honorable reputation provided access to credit and loans, entry to patron-client networks, and a voice in public affairs. In times of war, rank-and-file prisoners rotted in unsanitary cells, while gentlemen officers were lodged in private homes and permitted freedom to move about as they pleased on account of their honor. A deadly fight between two laborers could end in a hanging, whereas a duel between gentlemen might not even be brought to trial. Gentlemanly honor culture dictated that men, though differing in political ideas and even on opposing sides in war, were uniquely worthy of respect.[22] Historian Toby Ditz refers to the hegemonic ideals and practices that privileged men in early America as "the ruses of masculine privilege."[23] The sacralization of elite white manhood in the concept of honor was the most profound of these ruses. A man could access tremendous power and privilege, but only if others accepted his claim to gentlemanly status. Aspiring patricians asserted their claims through any number of daily masculine performances and rituals, through conformity and cooperation with others of their class, through gifts, favors, and obligations, and, when necessary, through violence.

By virtue of their wealth, race, and gender, eighteenth-century gentlemen genuinely believed they were entitled to an elevated right to respect and power over others, a belief most acutely displayed in their relationship to the enslaved. Slavery was a central pillar of honor for colonial gentlemen. Slaveholders regarded themselves as divinely ordained patriarchs who provided the enslaved with the necessities of life and a useful purpose. Masters could therefore feel confident that the honor they derived from people they enslaved was a sign of God's favor, even though respect and obedience were coerced through violence.[24] That such a brutal system could exist concurrently with notions of politeness and civility is another example of the paradoxes inherent to honor culture. As Orlando Patterson so eloquently writes, "Those who most dishonor and constrain others are in the best position to appreciate what joy it is to possess what they deny."[25] American Revolutionaries invoked the language of honor to disrupt the political hierarchy of the British Empire and Loyalists invoked honor to defend it, but neither side was ever radical enough to challenge the racial and gendered foundations on which their power rested.

For all the importance gentlemen placed on their "sacred honor," it was profoundly subjective and pliable, and while British general John Burgoyne could write about the "maxims upon which all men of honor think alike," in practice honor culture was an intricate labyrinth.[26] Gentlemen routinely debated the "punctilios," or finer points of honor, and regional and professional variations abounded in the Atlantic world.[27] Elite Britons and colonists invoked their honor so regularly and in such an array of circumstances that it can be tempting to dismiss it as too ubiquitous to have meaning. Indeed, honor's slippery definition, combined with its pliant nature, has led historians to question whether honor has "any practical utility as a historical category." Yet despite honor's paradoxes and pliancy, elite men and women cherished their honor to the point that some were willing to die (and kill) to defend it. Thus it needs to be taken seriously as a motivating factor. Historian Courtney Erin Thomas argues that the use of the term "honor" in the early modern period was not unlike "invocations of the terms 'freedom' or 'patriotism' in modern American society." Though the words can be understood very differently, "to those articulating them, they are very meaningful." Indeed, honor's pliability was one of the aspects that gave it power.[28] Alexis de Tocqueville noted this on his journey through the United States, writing that "whenever men collect together as a distinct community, the notion of honour instantly grows up amongst them; that is to say, a system of opinions peculiar to themselves as to what is blamable or commendable."[29] Groups decide what is honorable and what is not, and thus who is honorable and who is not.

Samuel Johnson's dictionary provides thirteen definitions of honor, including dignity, rank, reputation, fame, "nobleness of mind," "due veneration," "dignity of mien," and a "public mark of respect," among others, which seems to entangle the term even more. Yet those definitions hint at a way out of the labyrinth. Eighteenth-century elites thought of honor in terms of both social hierarchy and a collection of virtues, such as honesty, refinement, magnanimity, rationality, courage, and competence, that supposedly legitimized rank. Gentlepeople could therefore think of honor as something driven by conscience and as a system or structure of rank built around public acknowledgment of such virtues and signs of respect. These observations support the anthropologist Frank Henderson Stewart's definition of honor as a "right to respect" or a "claim-right" that places a duty on others to treat an individual or group with culturally specific expressions of deference or esteem that recognize their rank and dignity. This is the definition of honor and its function that most informs this book.[30]

For the elite or aspiring elite in colonial America, to successfully claim honor, to have one's right to respect acknowledged by one's community and peers, was to be a gentleman with all the rights and privileges that came with that station. To claim honor, therefore, was to claim social and economic power. The impact of having that power stripped away, losing the esteem of peers and the right to a gentleman's respect—being dishonored—is an understudied aspect of the American Revolution and is the subject of this book.

Historians have demonstrated how American revolutionaries democratized honor and redefined systems of privilege and power with new ideas of republican virtue and merit.[31] These are important insights, but historians have overlooked the significant role Loyalists played in shaping Patriot thought and behavior, as well as the development of Loyalist concepts of honor. As Robert G. Parkinson has demonstrated more broadly about the American Revolution, Patriot writers and leaders "embraced the most powerful weapons in the colonial cultural arsenal: stereotypes, prejudices . . .

and fears about violent Indians and Africans" to unify American colonists.[32] Anti-Loyalist attacks and rhetoric drew on the same arsenal. The Tory archetype helped Patriots define their concept of honorable manhood. When revolutionaries shackled the Loyalist Cadwallader Colden to an enslaved man, or cursed Loyalist rangers as painted "savages," or when the *Connecticut Courant* dismissed the Tories as Jacobites, they were associating Loyalists with notions of servile African Americans, ruthless Indigenous warriors, and ferocious Catholic Highlanders who submitted to an absolutist tyrant. Patriots also drew upon what Toby Ditz calls the "symbolic woman," a set of popular misogynistic tropes, to deride Loyalists as feminine, luxury-loving, pleasure-seeking cowards.[33] Thus, Patriot attacks on white Loyalist gentlemen reveal how the oppression of women and racialized and marginalized groups contributed to the construction of white masculinity. Any divergence from the character of a true gentleman could be read as shamefully feminine, emotionally unhinged, cowardly, or slavish. The American Revolution intensified this rhetoric, and white Loyalists became associated with a kind of gendered and racial degeneracy. The presence of large numbers of Black Loyalists only exacerbated Patriot fears.

Loyalist and revolutionary elites developed different political ideologies, but they lived within the same culture of gendered and racialized tropes; therefore, Loyalists acutely felt the sting of Patriot insults. In response to attacks on their manhood and virtue, Loyalists developed their own honorable identity. Although historians have described a simple Loyalist honor code centered on "submission to established authority,"[34] it was in fact far more complex. Gentlemen refugees shared and compared their experiences in letters, in narratives, and in their official claim submissions, and they struggled to make sense of their collective and personal defeats. They debated the moral and practical demands of their allegiance and the decisions they made in support of their families and their cause. In this process, they constructed some broad traits of the honorable Loyalist gentleman. The Loyalist man had the true best interests of the colonies at heart and was wise and sober enough to understand that the rebellion would lead the colonies to certain ruin. They were also modern gentlemen who believed that their virtues, emotional restraint, and politesse imposed a duty to preserve civilization in the face of colonial savagery and disorder.

They were devoted to the idea of freedom of conscience and independence of thought. Only in the most depraved circumstances, they argued, could these virtues bring about a man's ruin. Political death represented a terrible injustice and a deep moral wound that for some Loyalists demanded vengeance, and for others, healing and reconciliation.

What follows is a cultural history that uncovers not only what Loyalists and Patriots thought but *how* they thought. Dramatic evidence of how honor was performed as much as felt survives in letters, memoirs, diaries, court transcripts, military records, and print media. The methods of cultural history provide ways of reading social interactions and contextualizing physical descriptions of bodies, clothing, rituals, and other symbols for their deeper power and meaning. This is an attempt to uncover the cultural, emotional, and even cosmological justifications of political positions and explain the deeper significance of crowd action and insults. Mentalities were expressed as binary oppositions of the manly and effeminate, the civilized and the savage, and the honorable and dishonorable. Such notions were clearly articulated in the print culture of the period and in personal writings, but they can also be read in the behavior of historical actors and in their use of objects that embodied and expressed these ideas. Wigs, feathers, hats, shackles, swords, rags, and other seemingly mundane objects were symbols employed to express cultural meaning.[35] This is a study of how transatlantic cultural forces, and the pain of political death, were experienced in homes, on the street, in courtrooms, in taverns, on battlefields, in prisons, and on the body.

This approach reveals how notions of dishonor shaped the conflict between Loyalists and Patriots. From the perspective of the twenty-first century, and when compared to the bloody revolutions since the American War of Independence, Patriot action against gentlemen Loyalists might appear restrained. Thomas N. Ingersoll argues that New England policies against Loyalists were in fact "humane" and that most violence was directed "at the trim of [Loyalist] homes: windows, shutters, fences, gates, shrubbery" or involved "mere verbal abuse." In sharp contrast, Holger Hoock argues that across revolutionary America, Patriots employed "acts of violence and the threat of violence . . . to crush [Loyalist] dissent."[36] An understanding of eighteenth-century honor culture reveals how modern historians could come to such seemingly irreconcilable positions. It is true that there was no murderous campaign of mass violence against white Loyalists, yet humiliation and dishonor directed at gentlemen must be understood as a genuine form of violence within the cultural context of the eighteenth century. In *The Theory of Moral Sentiments,* Adam Smith writes that, according to the "laws of honour, to strike with a cane dishonours, to strike with a sword does not, for an obvious reason." That reason is no longer so obvious. "Those slighter punishments," Smith explains, "when inflicted on a gentleman, to whom dishonour is the greatest of evils, come to be regarded among humane and generous people, as the most dreadful of any." And though the state may take the life of a gentleman, it "respects their honour upon almost all." To "scourge a person of quality, or to set him in the pillory, upon account of any crime whatever, is a brutality of which no European government . . . is capable."[37] Among the international fraternity of gentlemen, unless a crime was particularly egregious, physical death might settle accounts for a transgression or personal failure and even restore a man's honor. To shame and dishonor, to bring about a political death, was cruel beyond belief.

This language of honor was not mere rhetoric, nor were Loyalist gentlemen exaggerating their suffering simply to evoke sympathy. Violence was endemic to colonial America, but how and to whom violence was inflicted depended on status, race, and gender. An enslaved person or a disobedient sailor might be flogged, but customs of respect protected a gentleman's body. This was a widely accepted cultural reality. Anti-Loyalist action involved very specific kinds of transgressions that may not appear as violent to historians as they did to Patriots and Loyalists. Even seemingly small trespasses against a genteel body or household could be regarded as revolutionary acts within a society so deeply concerned with honor as eighteenth-century America.

Political death and its dishonor intensified the civil war between Loyalists and Patriots. Revolutionaries regarded Loyalists as traitors and therefore illegitimate combatants, whereas Loyalists saw their enemies as criminal rebels. Insults and abuse provoked reprisals, and the symbolic violence of the early conflict transformed into a war of atrocity and revenge. Dishonor followed the Loyalists throughout the conflict, and by the end of the war revolutionaries had cast Tories as their most ruthless enemies, men whose lust for vengeance transformed them into the very antithesis of white gentlemen. British officers, too, harbored deep suspicions about the motives of wounded Loyalists in their ranks and attempted to restrain exiles' attempts to strike back at their persecutors. Indeed, Loyalist gentlemen recorded as much resentment toward British slights as toward Patriot insults, and the refugees protested bitterly against the negotiated peace that ended the war by sacrificing their fortunes and honor in America.

Yet even with the dishonor, violence, and legal punishments, there were very real limits to political death. This was not the permanent social death of the enslaved described by Orlando Patterson.[38] The race and gender of politically dead white Loyalists still offered protections and granted far more privileges in disgrace than the enslaved ever had. In some instances, Patriots regarded loyalism as a temporary moral disease that could be treated with "severity." While the *Essex Gazette* described the incurable Loyalist William Browne as "politically deceased of a persistent and mortal Disorder," Patriots hoped isolation or ostracism could help other Loyalists see the error of their ways before the infection proved fatal.[39] Social and family networks also supported individual Loyalists regarded as good if misguided men, a fact that aided in the postwar reconciliation and reintegration of many elite Loyalists.[40] Loyalist patriarchy usually remained intact, and Patriots treated women in Loyalist households as extensions of their dishonored husbands or fathers.[41] Many of the Loyalist refugees explored in this book went on to become public figures elsewhere in the British Empire yet maintained personal ties to their former homelands.

The continued social connections between Loyalists' friends and family again demonstrate honor's pliancy and explain why Loyalist persecution was more ritualized or focused on property than it was physically lethal. The internecine nature of the conflict meant that revolutionary authorities had to tread carefully lest their actions create new enemies or harm their cause. Family loyalty was a central plank of eighteenth-century honor, and frustrated revolutionaries noted how kinship ties often overrode political or military considerations.[42] The persecution of a well-liked man for loyalism could threaten to fracture sometimes tentative support for the revolutionary cause. G. Selleck Silliman, a general in the Continental Army, lamented that the people "have every kind of relationship that you can mention among the enemy . . . when they see vigorous measures pursued . . . of taking or slaying a father, a son etc. the tender sensations that they feel . . . run them into modes of behaviour that are altogether inconsistent with the Character of a Patriot." A nineteenth-century Connecticut historian admitted that the execution of a local Loyalist "did not advance the cause of independence" in his town.[43] Thus, political death, however traumatic for those who suffered it, served a very practical purpose for maintaining unity among American revolutionaries. A dishonored man could eventually be redeemed; a dead Tory could not.

The experience of political death also provided the Loyalists with a unifying experience. Brad A. Jones demonstrates that British loyalism in the Atlantic world was a coherent and consistent set of ideals supporting the Crown. Though the details of their message evolved over the course of the war, Loyalist writers throughout the British Empire argued that the rebellion was unjustifiable and unnatural, and at the same time, they embraced Whig concepts of liberty and government by consent. Both the defense of individual rights and the authority of the king were ancient tropes in the English tradition and, in the Loyalist mind, were not at odds. In fact, Loyalists regarded the Crown as a defender of individual rights and property in the face of rebel abuses.[44] While ideological arguments were crucial to Loyalist gentlemen, the personal experience of rebel tyranny and injustice provided all the evidence they needed to defend their cause. Ruma Chopra argues that historians have not adequately explained why Loyalist ideology provoked such a ferocious response from revolutionaries. "Critically," she adds, "the exchange and interaction between the two sides remains untheorized."[45] Incorporating honor culture into the examination of the war between Loyalists and Patriots helps explain the intensity of the conflict. The Loyalists' most potent arguments were cultural and emotional ones built on the ties of honor and duty, family allegiance, and personal freedom. These were weighty moral positions that struck a chord with colonists, and revolutionaries found that an effective way to counter such arguments was to dishonor those who made them.

The Loyalists' political death provides significant new insights for the study of eighteenth-century honor culture. Most importantly, it demonstrates how honor's power derived from its pliancy as both a set of ethical principles and a resource through which to claim respect and privilege. If a gentleman's true power was measured in the number of people who obeyed and respected him, and if that obedience was predicated on his ability to protect and provide, then elite Loyalist manhood would appear to have suffered a fatal wound. Yet the Loyalists reframed their dishonor and the indignities they suffered as voluntary martyrdom not just for the British constitution but for a moral, Christian cause. This was a central element of the Loyalists' honor—they willingly accepted dishonor in their communities as a sacrifice for higher principles and greater rewards from their grateful king. Ancient ideas of stoic forbearance combined with modern notions of sensibility in the Loyalist self-perception. Bereft of income, Loyalist refugees relied on the British in their struggle to maintain their elite identity but refashioned this dependence as a form of sacrifice that placed a debt of honor on the Crown. From the outbreak of the revolutionary crisis to the decades after the Treaty of Paris, Loyalists fought to overcome their political death and reclaim their status as gentlemen.

The political death of white propertied Loyalists was a critical element of the Patriot victory in the American Revolution. This was achieved through the weaponization of honor culture that drew on gendered and racial archetypes in a way that most colonists could understand and articulate on a visceral level. The central role that honor played in the civil war between Loyalists and Patriots is a vital but largely unexplored aspect of the conflict. Patriot writers successfully portrayed Loyalist gentlemen as collaborators and traitors, a source of moral corruption that needed to be constrained or removed from society. The dishonors and legal punishments of political death stripped Loyalists of their claims to gentlemanly honor while conspicuously reinforcing or accentuating the rights of Patriots and the Revolutionary elite. The Tory became a uniquely reviled villain of the Revolution. For their part, the Loyalists explored in this book regarded the American Revolution as a catastrophe that overturned not just a government but the natural order. To them it was a morally unequal contest between a minority of virtuous gentlemen (and their dutiful followers) and a crowd of grasping usurpers. Loyalist gentlemen were defined by their experiences of dishonor. As they struggled to rebuild their households, reestablish their patriarchal authority, and restore their identity as gentlemen, Loyalists were forced to decide whether to abandon their allegiance, joining their countrymen as American citizens, or whether martyrdom for the Crown was the true mark of honor.

1

Dishonor

REVOLUTIONARIES DISHONORED LOYALISTS IN many ways. In 1769, an angry crowd at Faneuil Hall hissed and jeered at the Boston magistrate James Murray after he posted bail for a hated Tory. To show their contempt, someone snatched Murray's wig and exposed "a pate, clean shaved by time and the barber." With the wig atop a pole, the crowd paraded Murray and his few remaining friends to their homes. The *Boston Evening-Post* included a mocking report that the Patriots escorted the Tories safely, without "suffering a hair of their *exposed* pates to be touched."[1] In early 1776, the baronet of the Mohawk Valley, Sir John Johnson, fled his house arrest to join the British army in Canada. In retaliation, Patriots ransacked regal Johnson Hall and arrested Johnson's wife, Mary Watts Johnson. According to the Loyalist Thomas Jones, "to add insult to insult," a "dirty" Patriot cobbler climbed aboard Lady Johnson's carriage in "a suit of Sir John's clothes, and a clean shirt, and pair of stockings stolen at the Hall" and sat with her on the journey to Albany. Cadwallader Colden Jr. wrote that in 1777 his rebel guards chained him "with the other Prisoners" and "just before me was Placed an Indian & behind me a Negro."[2] Colden, an enslaver himself, found he was literally in the ranks of dishonored Americans.

These insults were invested with meaning. Eighteenth-century Anglo-Americans took comfort in the idea that social status and virtue could be read on the body. The same way that rags and scars bore witness to the supposed criminality of the vagrant, or skin color might indicate freedom or slavery, the gentleman's refined appearance revealed his virtues.[3] A

{23}

dishonored gentleman was therefore an unnatural violation of this rule, and Patriots believed they were duty-bound to expose the truth behind the Loyalists' genteel disguises. Wigs and stockings, manor houses and carriages, elegant ladies and enslaved servants were all part of a colonial gentleman's self-presentation. Patriot insults inverted these symbols of gentility and degradation to mark Loyalists' political death. By denying Loyalists gentlemanly honor, Patriots stripped them of the privileges and identity of elite white males.

In the decade leading to the outbreak of armed rebellion, Patriots engaged in a relentless campaign of insults and dishonor. The revolutionary press reviled Loyalists as Judases, parricides, treacherous cowards, and racial degenerates who prostituted their manhood and sold their countrymen's freedom for luxuries and government preferment. A recent study argues that the revolutionary press failed "to generate sustained hatred for the king's supporters" and "fix a durable image to the Loyalists" that lasted beyond the war.[4] Yet by 1775, revolutionaries had created a consistent and coherent dishonorable Tory archetype to graft onto formerly respected men in the heat of the conflict. Ideas of Loyalist dishonor empowered Patriot crowds to intensify traditional rites of popular censure meant to preserve the common good and social order. Rituals like the charivari, or "rough music," became more violent and broke through customary barriers that protected elite households, families, and bodies. Historians have shown that these crowd actions accomplished several related goals. The insults marked the Revolution's internal enemies and served as warnings to others. The power of crowd action therefore prevented the spread of loyalism and in many cases compelled Loyalists to flee revolutionary society. Finally, insults and public scenes like the ones described above provided opportunities for public demonstrations of popular commitment to the revolutionary cause.[5] Publicly dishonoring Loyalists was a vital part of Patriot ascendancy. The symbolic violence against the Loyalists also signaled revolutionary Americans' understanding of the power embedded in the concept of the "gentleman." Stripping this prized status from a Loyalist was a suitable punishment for his betrayal. Just how far revolutionary crowds might take this was a source of deep concern for some Patriot gentlemen.

Every work of Loyalist history refers to the insults royal supporters experienced in the American Revolution, but few examine the deeper implications of those insults within eighteenth-century honor culture. Patriots and Loyalists inhabited a culture steeped in hierarchies expressed through rituals and signs of respect. In the late 1760s and early 1770s, Patriots calibrated their violence against elite Loyalists to violate these norms through insults drawn from folk custom. Tar and feathers might be the most iconic shaming ritual of the American Revolution, but dishonor took many forms when directed at patrician Loyalists. Vernacular culture, personal relationships, family connections, and the varying intensity of the political crisis contributed to an array of deeply personalized experiences. Patriot crowds targeted Loyalist homes, property, and members of their households as extensions of the dishonored men, but the insults themselves were only part of the performance. Everyone involved experienced these insults differently depending on their social position.[6] Onlookers evaluated Loyalist responses for signs of defiance or contrition, newspapers spread reports of Tory dishonor, and Loyalist families endured a terrifying ordeal. Loyalist gentlemen themselves relied on honor's pliancy to transform their indignities into martyrdom for the British cause. Ultimately, if threats and harassment drove Loyalists from their communities, property confiscation by the states made the popular rejection of Loyalist honor a legal reality. Traditional shaming rituals used humiliation to compel atonement, but revolutionaries also employed insults to terrorize stubborn Loyalists and proclaim their political death.

Dishonor always threatened public men in the eighteenth century. Bad luck in business or relationships might sink a gentleman's reputation as much as his own foolishness, idleness, criminality, or drunkenness. In colonial American culture, each of these vices was associated with stereotypes of specific marginalized groups: the enslaved were incompetent and servile; unrestrained youths were led by their passions; Indigenous Americans were dominated by anger and violence; women were easily seduced by lust and luxury.[7] Gossip and rumor followed men who were "unmanned,"

26   DISHONORED AMERICANS

or "henpecked," by a wife's public scolding and disobedience, or worse, cuckolded by her infidelity.[8] Men were equally concerned about charges of cowardice. The British officer Ambrose Serle recorded in his diary that when his pilot sailed their craft too close to rebel artillery, "I made no objection, lest it should be imputed to Cowardice, with which, I thank God, I am not much troubled." Serle chose to risk his life and their vessel rather than wisely suggest a different course. The New York poet Hannah Lawrence Schieffelin wrote that such actions were fueled by "the delicate sense of honour, and fear of reproach that influence the minds of the truly brave."[9] A gentleman's "fear of reproach" and insult was very real, and many would rather risk cannon fire than their "delicate" honor.

Eighteenth-century insults tended to draw on all these tropes, but how gentlemen were expected to respond was not always clear. Gentlemanly honor culture had undergone remarkable changes in the eighteenth-century Atlantic world. Historians have observed that the rise of the "polite gentleman," whose reputation supposedly mattered less than the cultivation of an inner life and Christian morals, challenged masculine honor built on household patriarchy and violent competition. Yet, while there was a notable decline in incidents of public insult and duels in eighteenth-century London, "primal" honor culture remained a source of violence in many parts of the empire, and the seemingly endless imperial conflicts of the eighteenth century encouraged traditional martial virtues. According to Markku Peltonen, the rise of polite culture simply provided new ways to give offense.[10]

Duels are the most well-known rituals for settling insults between gentlemen, but they were comparatively rare in colonial America and only became more common with their adoption by Continental officers in the Revolution.[11] Generally, most insults between gentlemen did not lead to the field of honor. Though there were distinct regional variations in honor culture throughout the Anglo-American Atlantic, genteel society tended to embrace a spirit of "restraint and reconciliation," and there were more peacemakers than duelists. Apologies after sobering up might settle matters, or the friends of the offended parties could iron out honorable compromises to avoid bloodshed.[12] Or men might just brood and nurse their enmities. Gentlemen also had to endure disrespect from men of higher rank or greater influence. The Loyalist merchant John Porteous fumed that the Detroit commandant, Major Henry Bassett, publicly called him a "Mushroom the production of a night . . . [and] a Cat that was always growling but could not mouse." Porteous swallowed his pride and held his tongue rather than risk his partnership's trading interests at the British fort.[13]

Slights and impertinence from the lower orders were equally complicated. The elite liked to believe that the common people owed them deference and that they owed the common people leadership and a moral example to follow. The "Rules of Civility" copied out by the teenaged George Washington provided instructions on the idealized interactions between social ranks. Rule 37 informs the reader that "In Speaking to men of Quality do not lean nor Look them full in the Face, nor approach too near them . . . Keep a full Pace from them." Another advises that "Artificers & Persons of low Degree ought not to use many ceremonies to Lords, or Others of high Degree but Respect and high[ly] Honour them, and those of high Degree ought to treat them with affibility & Courtesie, without Arrogancy."[14] These were basic rules of deference and condescension, but a gentleman was wise to ignore slights and infractions from single plebeians rather than lose his temper in an undignified attempt to enforce convention. When the unpopular Boston Loyalist John Malcolm boiled over with rage and struck a lowly shoemaker for an insult in 1774, his impulsive act provoked the most infamous example of tarring and feathering of the entire conflict. Incensed Bostonians dragged Malcolm from his house, stripped him, tarred and feathered his body, and paraded him through the streets in the dead of winter. Ann Hulton recorded that they whipped him, beat him with clubs, and threatened to hang him if he did not renounce the king and Parliament. Malcolm refused to damn the king until broken in a "Spectacle of horror & sportive cruelty" that went on for five hours.[15]

Such crowd actions drew on existing rituals of public displeasure and demonstrated the power of the common people to decide whether gentlemen had abrogated their responsibilities and lost their elevated right to respect. Prerevolutionary New England crowds would warn the intended victim of an impending visit and give him time to leave. The mob would then enact its ire through vandalism on the absent target's home. The chastened householder could return to pick up the pieces and work to show his contrition.[16] The intensification of these rituals in the Revolution meant that there was little Loyalist men and their families could do except flee or renounce their allegiance.[17] In many situations, Loyalists determined that a prudent escape was the wisest and least dishonorable course when threatened, but it was a difficult choice. A Loyalist who chose to flee also chose political death.

Men who fell afoul of Patriot crowds or committees could apologize and be forgiven if they expressed themselves correctly. Recantations were often formal matters of official record. In December 1775, Stephen Baxter stood before the committee in Stamford, New York, to beg forgiveness for opposing colonial resistance with his "horrid cursing and profane language." The same committee also accepted James Miller's recantation of his "indecent and abusive language" against Congress. Such recantations could be published in newspapers or as handbills, but whether such public atonement served as absolution or as another form of dishonor is an open question. After rebels beat, scalped, tarred and feathered, and even set fire to Thomas Brown of Georgia, they hauled him in front of a crowd in Augusta, where he reportedly "repented of his past conduct" and pledged himself to the Patriot cause. At his first opportunity, Brown fled to British protection. The *Georgia Gazette* declared that he had "publicly forfeited his honor and violated the oath voluntarily taken . . . [and] is therefore not to be considered for the future in the light of a gentleman."[18] In this case, the forced recantation was simply a trap.

James Murray's response to the crowd's insults the night a Bostonian stole his wig perhaps demonstrates the best a gentleman could hope for in such a situation. This event took place in 1769, when cooler heads and calming voices could restrain a crowd from more serious violence. As he entered Faneuil Hall, members of the crowd "hiss'd" at the magistrate like an audience reacting to a villain's first appearance on stage. Murray responded with an ironic bow. "I was hiss'd again, and bowed around a second time" Murray wrote. "A small clap ensued." The Loyalist remained composed and responded with a mock gesture of his own that was witty enough to answer. But when a member of the crowd dared to steal Murray's wig directly from his head, it seemed to unleash the crowd's passions, and all Murray could do was retreat with whatever dignity he had left. Had he lunged and snatched at the wig thief he would have looked even more like an impotent fool. In the meantime, the *Boston Evening-Post* amplified and spread his humiliation. "[O]ur Liberty lads have such a rage for publication," Murray seethed, "that everything must go to the press and be seen through their distorted medium." Murray demanded "honorable satisfaction" from the editor, but his challenge, like all Loyalist challenges, went unanswered.[19] This event set Murray on a path that led to his official banishment nearly a decade later.

As seen in the cases of Brown and Murray, the crowd and the press worked in tandem to dishonor Loyalists. Patriot newspapers, pamphlets, and broadsides were filled with epithets condemning Loyalists as liars and spies, as dependent and effete courtiers, and as traitors to their race, country, and civilized society. The Patriot press portrayed the Loyalists as everything from spineless cowards and lap dogs to subhuman amphibians. An article from the *Connecticut Courant* in 1775 presented the typical Patriot charges of Loyalist betrayal and degeneracy. It reported that the "Judases" who formed the Loyal Fencible Americans in Worcester, Massachusetts, may have contained some "*head Tories*," but the majority were "a few negroes, and some Scotch rebels and convicts."[20] The description of this pathetic band implied racial upheaval, criminality, and Catholic Jacobite surrender to absolutism. Another report of a Loyalist force described them as consisting of "200 (Boys, Negros etc.)" who were poorly armed and awaited the king's fleet to protect them and "make them Masters of our estates." The Tory leaders of this group were described as feeble, dependent cowards whose "reigning Principle is Lying."[21] The reams of printed attacks were intended not only to show the intellectual, political, and moral bankruptcy of the Loyalists and their cause but also to demonstrate their degeneracy and failure as men.[22]

The infamous case of Joshua Loring provided Patriot writers a prime example of depraved Loyalist manhood. Loring had acquired the lucrative position of commissary for American prisoners of war in occupied New York. Patriots attributed his rise to his wife, Elizabeth, who allegedly had an extended sexual relationship with General William Howe.[23] Throughout the Atlantic world, the cuckold was a stock character mocked for his miserable failure at maintaining the most basic element of patriarchy. His impotent weakness and gullibility were to blame as much as his wife's lust.[24] Loring's tale of cuckoldry was made all the worse by the idea that he eagerly traded his wife's honor for government preferment. A satirical poem printed in the *Pennsylvania Evening Post* took a gleeful jab at the debauched arrangement between the Loyalist, his wife, and the British general:

> Sir William he, snug as a flea,
> Lay all this time a snoring;
> Nor dreamt of harm, as he lay warm
> In bed with Mrs. Loring.[25]

The scandalous tale made it to England, where it circulated in an open letter linking the affair to the British army's failure to destroy the ragtag remnants of the American army in late 1776. Instead of pursuing the rebels, William Howe "was at New York in the lap of Ease," it read, "or, rather amusing himself in the lap of a Mrs. L_____, who is the very *Cleopatra* to this *Antony* of ours."[26] Such an arrangement was not unknown in elite British circles, but the indiscretions of a Loyalist cuckold and the commander of British forces were sinking the honor of the empire in America.[27] For Patriots, this case proved that Loyalists would sacrifice their most essential virtues for their British masters.

Patriot writers pointed to Loring's dishonor as just one disgrace among countless others waiting to be revealed. Whig polemicists stoked fears that Tories everywhere secretly plotted against American freedom. The damning leak in 1773 of correspondence between Gov. Thomas Hutchinson and other high-ranking Massachusetts officials, in which they mused about the need for "an abridgement of what are called English liberties" to preserve peace, provided Patriots early proof of a Loyalist conspiracy.[28] A contributor to the *Boston Gazette* warned readers that "against the secret destroyer . . . who hides his dagger under the veil of friendship . . . innocence is no protection—valour is no adequate defence." "The thrust of a duelist may be parried," he argued, "but who can repel the stab of an assassin?"[29] By linking all Tories in a great conspiracy against the liberties of America, Patriots justified actions taken against individual Loyalist gentlemen who were doubtlessly involved. John Peters recorded that the committeemen in Moorestown, New York, "insulted" him and ransacked his home in their search "for Letters of secret correspondence with General Carleton, with whom in fact I never had corresponded." The authorities in Hatfield, Massachusetts, held Israel Williams and his son under house arrest for several years because of popular paranoia that the family was involved in a Tory conspiracy, though no evidence was ever discovered to incriminate them.[30]

Secret Tories were thought to be especially common in the ranks of merchants. Popular distrust of the "Art & Mystery of a Merchant" was common enough in the eighteenth century but was exacerbated in the imperial crisis. As T. H. Breen has shown, British consumer products became charged with political meaning in the years leading to the Revolution, and traders bore the brunt of suspicion from both the revolutionary press and authorities. Colonists engaged in "rituals of non-consumption," in which they demonstrated their homespun virtues and dedication to the collective good. Revolutionary committees carefully judged merchant sincerity and willingness to sacrifice their livelihoods for the cause.[31] Merchants who continued to sell imported British goods undermined the common cause and spread effeminate decadence and dependence. A letter from "Britannicus" published in the *New-York Journal* reminded readers that luxury was "the handmaid to Bribery and Corruption" that would grow into the "secret and certain destroyer of virtue" and become the "engine of despotism."[32] Thomas Paine also attacked merchants who "would sell their Birthright," and asked his readers, "What are salt, sugar, and finery to the inestimable blessings of 'Liberty and Safety'?"[33] It was not just wealthy merchants who fell under suspicion. In 1776, the Committee of Inspection in Simsbury, Connecticut, banned the sale of "indigo, feathers, wooden dishes, teas, and many other goods, and wares of various kinds" by "strolling petit chapmen," for whom there were "great grounds of suspicion" that such men were forming "inimical combinations and correspondence . . . and carrying on with the enemies of the United American States."[34] From wandering peddlers to rich traders, the effeminate, greedy, and luxury-loving Tory merchant remained a stereotype throughout the conflict and long after.

By 1775, or even earlier, the Patriot press set the archetype of the dishonorable Tory. The Loyalists were unmanned by their dependence on royal power, their supposed alliance with African Americans and Catholics, and their secret attempts to enrich themselves by enslaving their countrymen. If all Loyalists were depraved and immoral men, then so too were their political principles. The press presented the conflict as a Manichaean struggle, in which the Loyalist of whatever rank became the antithesis of the Patriot. A Tory gentleman was a corrupt leader who abused his power; a Tory merchant was a selfish cheat; a Tory farmer was a dependent weakling, and so on. The teenaged Alexander Hamilton ridiculed the Loyalists' "defect in vigour" and the "impotence of [their] insidious efforts" to oppose the Patriots' "manly and virtuous struggle."[35] Thomas Paine's stinging indictments of Loyalist manhood are strewn throughout his writings. Tories, he writes, "are in general slaves to fear, and submit to courtly power with the trembling duplicity of a spaniel." Paine's "spaniel" insult would call to mind the lapdog, a "a misogynist trope of female venereal concupiscence" and a symbol of useless luxury. A spaniel was merely a "trifle," fussed over by pampered women, that provided no practical contributions to a household or farm.[36] The denigration of Loyalists does not end with the slave or lapdog analogies. Anyone who believed the Loyalist arguments, Paine insisted, had "forfeited his claim to rationality" and was an "apostate from the order of manhood . . . one who hath not only given up the proper dignity of a man, but sunk himself beneath the rank of animals, and contemptibly crawl through the world like a worm." Paine could not have chosen two more powerful images than the useless spaniel and the crawling, corpse-eating worm. He summarizes his insults by addressing the Tories directly. "[I]f you . . . can still shake hands with the murderers," he writes, "then are ye unworthy [of] the name of husband, father, friend, or lover, and whatever may be your rank or title in life, you have the heart of a coward, and the spirit of a sycophant."[37] Men could only claim morality and honor by supporting the Revolution.

Printed insults and descriptions of Loyalist treachery both reflected the popular mood and provided justifications for anti-Loyalist crowd action. The Revolutionary cause was novel, but the crowds drew on and intensified traditional communal rituals such as the charivari, normally reserved for adulterers, wife-abusers, or mismatched couples. The British-born Boston Loyalist Anne Hulton noticed early in the crisis that "the Mobs here are very different than in O[ld] England where a few lights put into the Windows will pacify, or the interposition of a Magistrate restrain them, but here they act from principle & under Countenance, no person daring or willing to suppress their Outrages."[38] Crowds also drew on traditions within the judicial system of colonial America, which employed public shame as a deterrent and demonstration of public order. Petty criminals could find themselves in the pillory, whipped through the streets, or branded.[39] Patriots redirected these customs to mark Loyalists and purge them from revolutionary society. Crowds targeted Loyalist households, invaded private spaces, and mistreated Loyalist families all to demonstrate the ultimate failure of Tory patriarchs. Loyalists could no longer count on their genteel privilege to protect them. "A Son of Liberty," writing in the *Connecticut Gazette* in 1775, advised the "Committees of Inspection" to give the Loyalists "no Quarter . . . convince, convert, or confound them. However dignified . . . with conceptions of their Importance, cause them to bow before you, and lick the Dust."[40]

Loyalist patricians regarded such violations of traditional norms as evidence of social collapse, and they felt the sting of insult in simply being questioned by lesser ranks. James Allen of Philadelphia lamented that "the most insignificant now lord it with impunity & without discretion over the most respectable characters." Benjamin Marston regarded his interrogation by a Massachusetts committee as both an extended insult and an example of the ingratitude of leading committeemen like "Captain Weston," who "owes his whole existence to the very people he is now insulting." The contempt Marston felt toward his captors is evident in the way he connected their appearance with their lack of virtue. In his journal, he refers to the committeemen as "creatures" and "bodies." One was a "pious-looking whining body"; another, "a Simpering . . . kind of body." Marston's description of his interrogators fits with the wider elite conceptions of the loafing, ham-fisted poor led by their bodily appetites. When Marston observed that "Mr. Drew" wore a "ragged Jackett & I think a leather apron" and that another interrogator in the group "can do dirty work," he was not simply casting aspersions on their fashion sense or their toleration of muck but

34 DISHONORED AMERICANS

making a pointed moral statement. The Loyalist gentleman found it extremely galling to be at the mercy of such men and took their every attempt to restrict his movement as an outrage.[41]

Testimonies submitted to the Loyalist Claims Commission after the war are filled with references to "many insults," "outrageous insults," "shameful and degrading abuse," "incendiary letters," and a variety of other indignities that Loyalists were too discreet to specify but that no doubt expanded on the themes read in the press. The most infamous insults meted out against the Loyalists targeted their bodies. The cultural importance of bodily appearance and clothing for eighteenth-century people is hard to overstate. As Marston demonstrated, the body and clothing announced a person's place in a spectrum of distinction and degradation. The stark contrast between the treatment of plebeian and patrician bodies is evidence of the chasm of rights and respect that separated people in colonial America. The enslaved, vagrants, and the poor could be flogged, branded with hot irons, or otherwise disfigured, whereas propertied white men would never face such physical torments and permanent marking.[42]

Revolutionary insults against genteel bodies were transformative, both for the crowd and for the target. The scars or brands on criminal or enslaved bodies showed the coercive power of the law and the master class. The violent shaming rituals directed at Loyalists displayed the power of the majority to enact popular notions of justice and ritually transform a patrician into an object of scorn—and the crowd into the guardians of true honor. In 1774, Jesse Dunbar violated a boycott and purchased livestock from a despised Tory councillor. In retaliation, a crowd sealed Dunbar inside the hollowed carcass of one of the oxen and carted him through several towns from Plymouth to Duxbury, Massachusetts. By the end of the ordeal, the revolutionary mob allowed Dunbar to walk beside the cart, but they covered him in the animal's entrails and finally dumped the unfortunate man "in front of the counsellor's door."[43] The crowd transmuted Dunbar into a beast of burden, the very object that had led him astray, and then returned him to the Tory councillor who broke the boycott. Dunbar would have been humiliated and exhausted, and no doubt traumatized by the experience, but he was neither whipped nor physically scarred. Even when the conflict degenerated into a bitter civil war, revolutionaries were more likely to imprison Loyalist officers than permanently disfigure them. Dishonor was considered sufficiently devastating for a formerly respected man.

The transformative nature of anti-Loyalist insults also drew heavily on racialized tropes. Of all the crimes attributed to Tories, the most egregious was their willingness to transgress racial boundaries and fight alongside Indigenous warriors or enlist African Americans as soldiers against their white countrymen. Indeed, Patriots argued that Loyalist political choices and behavior were products of their racial corruption. A satirical article in the *Boston Gazette,* for example, imagined a meeting between the head Loyalists of New York in which they debated how best to take revenge on their enemies. Among their inventive reprisals, Joseph Allecock wanted "to Negrofy" his enemies, while a Loyalist named Reylander sought "to make Indians of them." A postscript explained that Reylander's chosen revenge was a reference to his "being of Indian breed."[44] Captain William Woodford ordered a Scottish Loyalist captured fighting alongside Black Loyalists at the Battle of Great Bridge in late 1775 to be "coupled to one of his brother black soldiers, with a pair of handcuffs." The Virginia legislature regarded this punishment as too humiliating even for Loyalists and ordered the captive Tory exchanged.[45]

The case of Peter Guire of Fairfield, Connecticut, demonstrates both the intensification of shaming rituals by the end of the war and the ways in which revolutionary crowds drew on racialized punishments. Guire, a yeoman who farmed around forty acres of land before the war, returned to Connecticut in 1783 to collect his wife and children, who had remained behind when he fled to New York in 1776. A witness testified to the Loyalist Claims Commission in New Brunswick that an incensed mob captured Guire and "branded him with an Hot Iron on the forehead with the Letters G.R." for George Rex. Branding was reserved for marking the bodies of cattle, criminals, or the enslaved with symbols that either announced their crime or their owner. This intensely violent act transformed a white landowning farmer into a man permanently marked as the king's slave. The crowd cursed Guire, like Cain, to spend the rest of his life marked as "a spectacle of horror for all mankind." Indeed, branding was considered such a powerful punishment and deterrent that an early nineteenth-century American opponent of capital punishment argued for branding criminals instead, because it was the mark of "complete political death."[46]

Ritualized attacks on Loyalist bodies, whether patrician or plebeian, varied considerably. A list of reported bodily insults could go on for pages, but they all contained this transformative element. The most iconic was tarring and feathering. Like effigy burning or other folk customs, tarring and feathering had a long history in the English Atlantic. Originally a maritime custom with roots dating back to the medieval period, the ritual of tarring and feathering could be permanently disfiguring, but it was always humiliating. Throughout the early modern period, the punishment was used in England against drunkards, rapists, and thieves. The first recorded instance of it in the colonies was not until the mid-1760s, yet it quickly became familiar to the residents of seaside towns. Revolutionaries employed tar and feathers against customs officials, government agents, and others considered collaborators, such as the New Englander who lured a Boston woman into the clutches of British soldiers in 1769. The *Boston Evening-Post* described how the man was then "carried about the town for two or three Hours, as a Spectacle of Contempt and a Warning to others."[47]

One of the most infamous examples of tar and feathers occurred in the autumn of 1775, after the physician Dr. Abner Beebe rebuked the local committee in East Haddam, Connecticut, for abusing his uncle. In response, the local committee posted advertisements in the *Connecticut Gazette* declaring him "inimical to the liberties of the people of America." This incited a group that "stripped [Beebe] naked & hot Pitch was poured upon him, which blistered his Skin." The Patriot mob then threw him in a pigsty and forced him to eat dung. Rolled in filth and blackened by pitch, he ceased to look like a man at all. Beebe's attackers then turned on his house and destroyed his gristmill. To conclude the shaming ritual, Beebe was "exposed to a Company of Women." In response to these indignities, all Dr. Beebe could do was insert a note in the newspaper pleading his innocence and begging to be either granted a trial or left alone.[48]

Despite this and other widely documented cases of tarring and feathering, comparatively few gentlemen Loyalists found themselves at the end of the tarring mop. It may be that Loyalists were simply adept at eluding the mobs, or they perhaps relied on the intervention of local allies to redirect, pacify, or slow crowd action long enough for them to escape. Because such rituals were considered so extreme, crowds could be satisfied with insulting proxies to gentlemanly bodies. Peter Oliver reported that when a mob failed to seize Timothy Ruggles, they instead "cut his Horses Tail off & painted him all over." A crowd tarred and feathered one of Samuel Seabury's pamphlets, and mobs also smeared the homes and stores of numerous merchants.[49] In the end, it only took a few examples for Patriots to make their point. William Aitchison, a Norfolk merchant, wrote to fellow Loyalist James Parker that "a large tar mop was erected near the Capital [with] a Bag of feathers [tied] to it and a Bar[rel]l of Tar underneath" to intimidate men into signing the Patriot non-importation agreement. In this case it had the desired effect. Aitchison warned his friend to comply with the committee because, he wrote, "there is no contending against such Numbers."[50] Gentlemen across the colonies no doubt chose discretion as the better part of valor.

Revolutionary mobs targeted stately houses more often than patrician bodies. The house was the most visible emblem of a gentleman's status. Henry Glassie argues that the style and location of a home "told you exactly where you stood in the social order" of colonial America. The house projected power and, especially amid the privations of frontier life and the upheavals of the American Revolution, "the house beamed a message of control." Gentlemen went to great expense to design and build their homes, and women, children, servants, and the enslaved were expected to maintain the domestic world. The house was thought to be the expression of a family's soul, and an ordered, genteel home brought honor to a gentleman and his family.[51] As Amanda Vickery writes, the "external perimeter of the house was a frontier in custom and law." The fences and walls of a home protected not only the physical well-being of a man and his family but their privacy as well, which was a key component of respectability and status.[52]

The vandalized home broadcast popular disapproval and helped neutralize the appeal of loyalism. Attacks on Loyalist homes are covered extensively in the historiography, and a few examples will suffice to demonstrate

38 DISHONORED AMERICANS

the revolutionaries' communitarian intent. In the early years of the crisis, a mob tore down the fences surrounding Mathew Robinson's Newport home. This was a clear message to the Loyalist that he no longer had the power to erect boundaries or conceal himself from the surveillance of the townspeople. Edward Stow of Massachusetts discovered the exterior of his house frequently "bedaubed by Excrement and Feathers . . . and repeated again with Blubber Oil and Feathers."[53] Peter Oliver recorded how Patriot mobs vandalized the homes of Jonathan Sewell, Daniel Leonard, and other Loyalist grandees of Massachusetts. Sewell's home, for instance, "was attacked by the Mob, his windows broke & other Damage done."[54] The idea of a "political quarantine" is a fitting metaphor for vandalized Loyalist households that, like markers for smallpox, identified and isolated a moral contagion.[55]

Anti-Loyalist crowd actions also bear many similarities with the folk practices of the charivari or "skimmington," which were common in both England and the colonies. Such rituals were normally intended to ostracize or punish community members for adultery, spousal abuse, or some other transgression not immediately punished by law.[56] Robert Blair St. George notes the long history of house attacks in New England directed at the immorality or unfairness of a householder. Crowds stripped away the "mystifying mask" and exposed "the 'real' person behind the façade to public shame." The Revolution intensified house attacks into attempts "to purge the social body" of the Loyalists' undeserved wealth and influence.[57] The most infamous example of a home invasion occurred during the Stamp Act crisis of 1765, when a Boston crowd ransacked the stately manor of Lieutenant Governor Thomas Hutchinson. The mob destroyed every vestige of domestic gentility, from trees and garden fences to the cupola on the roof. The destruction was so thorough that the mob even tore the wainscoting from the walls.[58]

As the imperial crisis deepened, attacks on the private spaces of gentlemen and their families became more common. The mob that harassed Daniel Leonard's home "fired Bullets into the House & obliged him to fly from it to save his Life." In January 1777, someone alerted the Connecticut Loyalist Joel Stone that the "agents of Congress" were headed to his home. Though he "happily eluded" the crowd, his unmarried sister, Rene, "met the resentment of the mob who from language the most approbrious [sic] proceeded to actual violence breaking open every lock in the house and seizing all the property they could discover."[59] Like many Loyalists, Stone chose to flee and leave his female dependent behind, hoping that local leaders, social convention, or his former neighbors would protect her. Testimonies like his are filled with examples of revolutionaries insulting women as extensions of their Loyalist kin.

The term "insult" could be read very broadly in the eighteenth century and might imply anything from impertinence to physical or sexual assault. Rape was as present in the American Revolution as any conflict, and Patriots accused Hessian and British soldiers of rape to powerful effect in their propaganda. Because a patriarch's authority extended over his dependent women's sexuality, eighteenth-century writers presented rape as an attack on the householder's honor. As Sharon Block explains, Patriot narratives often left out women's agency entirely and instead focused on British rapes as crimes against American patriarchy that would unite men in defense of "American innocence." Few women, Whig or Tory, were willing to publicly testify that they had been raped.[60] Kacy Dowd Tillman explains that to preserve their honor, elite women writers used deliberately vague language in their descriptions of sexual threats and assaults. Rape was an "unspeakable problem."[61] Rebel attacks and invasions of Loyalist homes—breaking through doors, smashing windows, and invading intimate spaces—were charged with transgressive sexual power. Like their attacks on Loyalist men, revolutionaries calibrated their insults to strip women of their genteel status and right to respect. Such affronts were also understood as direct attacks on their absent men. Throughout history rape has served "as means for soldiers to solidify victory by claiming patriarchal rights over women of the vanquished," and men on both sides indulged this impulse during the Revolution.[62]

Loyalist narratives strongly suggest the sexual nature of rebel insults. Thomas Jones's tale of the "dirty" shoemaker who climbed into Mary Johnson's carriage dressed in her husband's clothes demonstrates a clear violation of intimate spaces. Jones's use of the term "dirty" alludes to sexual perversity as much as it does poor hygiene.[63] Likewise, the Boston militiamen guarding the pregnant Sarah Tyne Brinley, wife of the fugitive Loyalist Edward Brinley, were reportedly "always in her room." To add to this constant invasion of privacy, the guard opened the Loyalist's home, "exposing her to the view of the banditti; as a sight 'See a Tory Woman.'"[64] In 1778, a Patriot raiding party plundered and burned the mansion of the absent Loyalist Brigadier General Oliver De Lancey. "Mrs. De Lancey, her two daughters, and two other young ladies" escaped "through the flames in only their bed-dresses; when they were most cruelly insulted, beat, and abused."[65] Loyalists recorded these incidents to demonstrate the depth of rebel depravity, but such stories also reveal how notions of Loyalist dishonor emboldened Patriots to cross not only the household threshold but the barriers that traditionally protected elite women.

Ultimately, Patriot authorities regarded such incidents as collateral damage brought on by the wickedness of their Tory husbands and fathers. Just as a dependent's behavior reflected the honor of the patriarch, so too could the actions of Loyalist patriarchs dictate and justify how Patriots treated their abandoned families.[66] When Mary Johnson complained bitterly of her treatment under arrest in Albany, Continental General Philip Schuyler blamed her circumstances on "the Pain Sir John's Conduct has occasioned me, and how I have been distressed at the sad necessity which obliges me to secure his Person." In his polite but cold letter, he reminds Lady Johnson that by breaking parole, her husband "has forgot the obligations he lays under to me," and as long as Mrs. Johnson remained in the general's power, she should "make [herself] perfectly easy" with her situation unless she wished to make the long overland journey to Canada on her own.[67]

General Schuyler may not have cared much for Lady Johnson, who even wrote directly to George Washington with her complaints, but he held her prisoner out of practical necessity because Sir John Johnson had violated their personal agreement. A parole was a word of honor, and to Schuyler, Johnson's escape was a dirty trick that suggested the revolutionary was unworthy of a gentleman's pledge. This insult placed the embarrassed Schuyler under the "sad necessity" of holding women and children hostage. The aggrieved general no doubt took some satisfaction from the insult to Johnson's patriarchy, but he was adamant that Lady Johnson and the children suffered because of Sir John Johnson's perfidy, not Patriot malice. From the Patriot perspective, Loyalists like Johnson betrayed and abandoned their families just as they had their country.

Loyalist families that remained behind presented a complex problem for revolutionary authorities: were Loyalist wives guilty of treason, or were they blameless victims? Women might be objects of sympathy and regarded as victims of their traitor husbands, or they could be harassed, imprisoned, or evicted and sent across British lines.[68] Under the English law of coverture, a married woman's legal identity was subordinate and inseparable from that of her husband, and her property and legal relationship to the state normally transferred to the husband upon marriage. In matters of political allegiance, women were expected to abide by the decisions of husbands. "The fictive volition of the pair," as Linda Kerber describes it, "was always taken to be the same as the real will of the husband." Even though women could be guilty of treason against the state, wives who crossed enemy lines to be with their husbands were not considered traitors. Both British and Continental authorities were pleased to allow women to join their men, since their departure freed up resources and left property abandoned that could be confiscated and used. Loyalist wives who stayed behind could pose serious obstacles to this plan. In most states, a woman could claim dower rights to a third of her husband's property at death, but how this applied to political death was not at all clear. The Massachusetts confiscation laws passed in 1777 specifically held out the option for wives to effectively separate from their Loyalist husbands and retain their dower rights as if their husbands had physically died.[69] This may have marked a brief recognition of women's political agency, but it also functioned as an attack on Loyalist patriarchy. In Virginia, a state that produced comparatively few Tories, the exiled planter Jacob Ellegood testified that some Loyalist property went "immediately to the Wife & Children . . . upon the Spot & was vested in them one third to the Wife &c as if the father was dead."[70] This was a rare exception, and normally Loyalist women who remained behind were eventually evicted when the state confiscated their homes.

Property confiscation was the most profound element of Loyalists' political death. It scattered families and carved holes in social and economic networks. Property ownership was essential to a gentleman's status and fundamental to the eighteenth-century concept of citizenship. In 1777, the Continental Congress advised all states to confiscate the property of Loyalists who fled to the British or had otherwise assisted the enemy, but many states had already enacted such measures.[71] Patriots felt fully justified in the various confiscation acts. According to a Virginia publication of 1782, the laws were not only "founded upon legal principles" but displayed the "common justice" of not allowing "vicious citizens" to partake in the victories earned by "virtuous citizens."[72] These thoughts were shared by New Jersey governor Robert Livingston, who explained to Benjamin Franklin that there could "be little doubt, that every society may rightfully banish . . . those, who aim at subversion, and forfeit the property, which they can only be entitled to by the laws, and under the protection of the society, which they attempt to destroy."[73] Loyalists, of course, saw confiscation as nothing more than a rebel scheme to steal from their betters. Incensed at the confiscation of his friends' estates, James Allen noted bitterly that "men who could scarcely maintain their families, now live in splendor." Allen feared that confiscation was leading to the collapse of society. "This convulsion," he wrote, "has indeed brought all the dregs to the top."[74]

The justice and necessity of confiscation seemed obvious to most revolutionary leaders, but the laws differed from state to state. In general, states that held more active and numerous Loyalists tended to have harsher laws against them. The legal persecution of Loyalists stemmed from the practical concerns of state authorities who feared being undermined by their Tories, but it may also have reflected embarrassment at the presence of so many Crown supporters in their midst. They had to act swiftly and harshly, or the state's honor might have been impugned within the confederation. Georgia's and New Hampshire's few Loyalists, for example, were given time to sell off their property and depart. New York, which saw the most Loyalist activity of the war, eagerly confiscated Loyalist estates. According to a nineteenth-century estimate, the seized property of the New York Loyalists amounted to $3.6 million, an incredible sum even factoring in wartime inflation.[75]

The confiscation and sale of a traitor's property had been part of English common law since at least 1352. Attainder stripped a traitor of all property rights and included a unique provision known as the "corruption of blood," which prevented transgressors from passing on any property to their heirs. According to the historian J. R. Lander, attainder was "the legal death of the family."[76] The New Jersey legislature, which enacted some of the most virulent anti-Tory laws, including execution "without benefit of clergy," specifically stated that acts of attainder would not include the corruption of blood, perhaps feeling that an attack on innocent members of the family was not in keeping with the ideals of the Revolution.[77] Yet Loyalists believed confiscation had the same effect. The New York Loyalist Peter Van Schaak argued that banishment should be enough to satisfy the Patriots. "By removing the man," he wrote, "the measure of public justice is full; by adding to that punishment [confiscation], it runs over." Confiscation was not a necessary punishment but an act of "vindictive justice." Van Schaak asked whether there could be "a more melancholy spectacle . . . than a whole family overwhelmed with misery from the crime of their chief." The true intention of the law, according to Van Schaak, was to perpetuate the Loyalists' "punishment down to innocent posterity" so that the family "may forever be accompanied by the infamy of their father."[78]

Revolutionary authorities broadcast this infamy through public auctions of confiscated estates. In Massachusetts, advertisements for the sales included the names of dishonored Loyalists, or "absentees," and the genteel properties they left behind. Public auctions were normally held on site and marked a man's political death just as a funeral might his natural death. The community gathering at the former estates acknowledged that their countryman was no longer a householder nor a part of their society. Members of the public could purchase and take over the public and private spaces of former grandees, or just get a bargain on some tools from their former neighbor's barn. The Massachusetts committee advertised the sale of the former lieutenant governor Thomas Oliver's "very elegant" and "beautifully situated" former home as well as his reserved church pew. Auctioneers in Pennsylvania sold Jacob Duché's "bedsteads, tables, chairs, looking glasses." The Connecticut probate court itemized the sale of Joel Stone's estate down to some buttons found in a drawer.[79] The auctioneers penetrated the Loyalists' former intimate spaces and dismembered their lives piece by piece.

Legal property confiscation underscored the fact that men whom the Loyalists once considered their peers not only failed to intercede on their behalf but even participated in their ostracism and political death. To be

44   DISHONORED AMERICANS

mocked by a crowd was galling enough, but as the Connecticut Loyalist Ashbel Humphrey explained, being rejected by fellow gentlemen "almost brought him to the borders of despair." A shocked contributor to the Loyalist *Boston Weekly News-Letter* noted that the mob that harassed Thomas Oliver in 1774 "was not mixed with tag, rag & Bobtail only. Persons of Distinction in the Country were in the Mass."[80] George Watson certainly felt the loneliness brought on by his loyalism. When he attended church one day in Plymouth, Massachusetts, "a great number of the principal inhabitants left" as he entered. This type of social ostracism or peer pressure was effective in stifling Loyalists. The Loyalist Nathaniel Whitworth Jr. explained to his father in December 1775 that he declined some prominent government positions to avoid being "stigmatized with the names of Ministerial Friends, Enemies to their Country . . . tho they are Titles which no honest man will regard[,] yet they are such as every prudent one would wish to avoid."[81] Imperial preferment offered rewards, but the pull of local connections was often stronger.

Patriot gentlemen were conflicted on how to treat their Loyalist counterparts. Historians have shown how uneasy the revolutionary elite was with popular demonstrations targeting symbols of gentility. Delegates to the Continental Congress relied just as heavily on their status as gentlemen to legitimate their authority, and they worried the rank and file might turn on them.[82] Congressional leaders were reticent to openly support mob behavior, and the Congress even attempted to restrain crowd action in 1775, but these orders were short-lived and ineffective due to the localized nature of anti-Loyalist attacks. John Adams, a strong proponent of public order, admitted in 1777 that crowd action was an effective tool to spread "the utmost terror and dismay to every lurking tory."[83]

On a personal level, past relationships as well as notions of honor and civility still guided individual encounters between Loyalist and Patriot gentlemen. The wealthy Patriot Robert R. Livingston interceded on behalf of Cadwallader Colden Jr. when his rebel guards publicly shackled him between an African American and an Indigenous American. Colden wrote that Livingston witnessed "the indignity with which I was used" and "said he was Intirely [sic] Ignorant of it [and] that he was Sorry to see it." Livingston ordered Colden set free and allowed the Loyalist to leave unguarded.[84]

Livingston could not let such an indignity to a fellow gentleman stand, even if that gentleman was a suspected enemy. Likewise, Jacob Schieffelin carried a letter from his Patriot friend William Roberts in case he was captured. Roberts addressed this letter to the influential Philadelphia Patriot Thomas Mifflin and explained that "the Affection you have always professed for me, cannot in any manner be better applied than by assisting [Schieffelin] as much as is in Your Power."[85] Patriots who came to the assistance of their Loyalist friends made a careful distinction between their personal and political obligations. A "Rev. Mr. Rysdorp" testified to the New York Committee for Detecting and Defeating Conspiracies in December 1776 that its prisoner, Ralph Phillips, "was a Person of good Moral Character and very useful to the Community," although "with Respect to his Political Character he does not pretend to Determine."[86] Gentlemen revolutionaries saw no contradictions and felt no shame in helping friends who were also their political enemies. The obligations of civility and demands of personal honor continued to hold power in the minds of gentlemen.

The insults Loyalists endured became essential for crafting their identity and self-presentation. As will be seen in chapter 4, the exiles' near-universal references to insults and dishonors in testimonials and records recast abuse as evidence of Patriot savagery and Loyalist martyrdom. Some Loyalists even pointed to shaming rituals as badges of honor. James Rivington printed a woodcut of his own hanged effigy in his newspaper. John Malcolm showed off scraps of his dried tar and feathers while in England and asked to be made the first "Knight of the Tarr."[87] These were both expressions of defiance against the rebels and statements of their certainty in the Loyalist cause. A. D. Spalding wrote that though Patriot insults and threats drove him from his home and family, he was consoled by "sensations of a Good Conscience."[88] This was a common sentiment. Above all else, the Loyalist experience was a test of character.

Rev. Mather Byles Jr. tried to show his indifference to rebel abuse by dismissing his dishonors as "nothing more than insults in the Street," but other Loyalists went to great lengths to avoid public insult.[89] William Bayard, the prominent New York Loyalist, fled the city in 1775 "to avoid being insulted" and hid for nearly four months amid "unspeakable hardships in a dubious concealment . . . often in Barns, Lofts, Hovels, Swamps and Forests." For a gentleman of Bayard's rank, the ignominy of hiding in filth and skulking through the wilderness was dishonorable enough, but the nadir of Bayard's humiliation occurred when he slipped back into British-occupied New York "in the Disguise and Habbit [sic] of one of my own Slaves."[90] The transformation from honored to dishonored was as stark as it could be. Crossing the frontier in disguise was a necessity, but the metamorphosis from gentleman to slave could be read as a powerful symbol of just how far the Loyalist had fallen. Yet Bayard made no secret of this event and retold the story in private correspondence and in his official claim to the British government after the war. Bayard's disguise became a symbol of his resourcefulness, his willingness to suffer for the cause, and was thus a badge of martyrdom.

Loyalist rhetoric could rewrite Patriot insults as marks of honor, but gentlemen could not escape the practical consequences of being stripped of their money, power, and property. Though they argued it was unfair and unjust, Loyalist gentlemen were unable to meet their obligations to wives, children, and any number of dependents in their social networks. For example, William Bayard served as both executor for the estate of his deceased business partner Barnaby Byrne, who died in 1771, and as guarantor of a yearly stipend of £70 for his widow, Jane Byrne. Confiscation and Bayard's exile ended these payments. In a bitter letter, the widow castigated Bayard as "the sole cause of my Distress and suffering." His political choices had caused her poverty, and the state of New York refused to provide her with anything from the confiscated estate.[91] Bayard and Loyalists like him could point to the cruelty of the revolutionaries, but there was no escaping his failure as a patriarch. Loyalists could claim that they felt no shame at their predicament, but as will be seen in chapter 3, many Loyalists felt honor-bound to seek revenge on their persecutors.

Rather than shame or anger, expressions of deep sadness characterize most Loyalist writings. The exiled Jacob Bailey wrote how he could not contain his "bitter emotions of grief." Joel Stone wrote that he "could not help considering my fate a peculiarly hard one thus being hunted as a common criminal and proscribed without cause."[92] The wealthy New York Loyalist

Sylvester Gardiner wrote to a friend from his refuge in Halifax, Nova Scotia, that he had been driven to a "miserable place . . . from a state of Affluence . . . God knows what I will do."[93] Some Loyalist gentlemen could not cope with their political death and the traumatic loss of status and lifestyle. A prominent Connecticut Loyalist, Fyler Dibblee, recorded that his brother-in-law, despairing at his ruined life, "took a Razor from the Closet, threw himself on the bed, drew the Curtains, and cut his own throat." Another Loyalist, Millington Lockwood, reportedly drowned himself rather than continue in his state of indigence and exile.[94] These Loyalist suicides are striking, but they were rare. Christian gentlemen were expected to embrace a sensitive, yet stoic, perspective on loss. The Reverend Samuel Peters no doubt became proficient at consoling his fellow Loyalist exiles. Drawing on a parable from the Gospel of Luke, he reminded Amos Botsford that "those Men on Whom the tower of Siloam fell were not sinners above all Men"; rather, misfortune struck randomly. The calamities they suffered did not "prove them less righteous for their Loyalty, than [Connecticut Governor] Trumbull for his Rebellion, tho' he died in Bed" at home. "The Wiseman & fool die alike & turn to the Worms."[95] In 1783, William Bayard wrote to his daughter from exile in England that he was ill, alone, and "Gloomy Indeed." But his "Greatest Affliction . . . will be these thoughts of being Separated from you." Nevertheless, Bayard obeyed the genteel strictures of stoic forbearance: "However bitter as the cup may be I must swallow." Nicole Eustace describes the complex culture of genteel grief over the death of loved ones in the eighteenth century and the process elites undertook to "reweave the rent social web" caused by death.[96] As will be seen in chapter 5, it sometimes took Loyalist families generations to reweave those social webs.

By 1775, revolutionary Americans believed they knew their internal enemy. The Tory was a liar, a weakling, a coward, a luxury-loving slave, and a willing cuckold. The Tory acted in secret, and though his appearance was indistinguishable from a true gentleman, he embodied racial and gendered degeneracy. Whereas the fine clothes and houses belonging to men like George Washington or Robert Livingston displayed their inner virtues, the same symbols of gentility concealed a Loyalist's dishonor. Revolutionary insults targeted the Loyalist's reputation, clothes, body, and private spaces. Mobs attacked the symbols of the Loyalists' patriarchy, and their wives and daughters were vulnerable targets for vengeful committees and mobs. Even Timothy Ruggles's unfortunate horse was shamed for his rider's political position. These insults stripped Loyalists of their status and power and marked their transformation from gentlemen to dishonored Tories. State confiscations and banishment canceled the legal foundations of the Loyalists' public existence and announced their official failure as householders and citizens. A Loyalist's journey to political death began with insults and ended with legal proscription.

As will be seen in the following chapters, the Patriot idea of Loyalist dishonor and the reality of political death created a deeply uncertain set of conditions for Loyalists at war. Because Patriots no longer considered them gentlemen, they were no longer immediately offered the customary protections. Yet the cultural potency of dishonor meant that once esteemed and powerful men were rarely executed or physically injured further, although this did occur. Instead—even as states passed laws that called for the execution of Tories—for gentlemen to lose their status and identity, to suffer political death, served as a suitable form of punishment for their treason. Even as they fought against the idea of monarchy and inherited power, the revolutionaries still thought with the symbols of hierarchy and power. The concerted attacks on Loyalist households indicates the importance revolutionaries placed on notions of honor, manhood, and patriarchy within their concept of the common good. Only Patriots were worthy of such privileges.

Loyalists denounced the mistreatment of their families as acts of cruelty that revealed the true depravity of the rebels, but they were usually powerless to defend their households. To have their homes and families subject to seizure and abuse without any recourse was intended as an intolerable shame but was recast by Loyalists as martyrdom. Insults and suffering provided Loyalists with a powerful new set of symbols. They pointed to their lost homes and suffering families as proof that they would undergo any hardship or disgrace for the sake of their principles and their duty to the Crown.

2

Captivity

IN THE EARLY HOURS of June 22, 1776, Continental soldiers arrested David Mathews, mayor of New York, as the architect of the so-called Hickey Plot to assassinate George Washington. Mathews denied any involvement, but the Committee for Detecting and Defeating Conspiracies was certain he was a very dangerous man. Revolutionary authorities transferred the disgraced patrician to Hartford, Connecticut, a destination considered secure enough to hold high-profile captives. The Continentals did not offer Mathews a parole of honor, unlike other gentlemen prisoners. Wary of Mathew's charm, access to wealth, and propensity for intrigue, Connecticut governor Jonathan Trumbull personally instructed the deputy commissary general, Ezekiel Williams, to lock the mayor in the Hartford jail. Under normal circumstances, gentlemen prisoners would be housed in private homes based on their word not to escape or participate in the war in any way until officially released. A gentleman prisoner could entertain guests, attend dinners, talk with whomever he pleased, and send letters. Captured officers might even go home to await their exchange or personally negotiate with their own army on behalf of their captors. Because of such generous advantages, officers were keen to maintain this system by keeping their word and following the rules. But Mathews, like so many other wealthy Loyalists, had forfeited his right to respect in the eyes of his enemies. Trumbull further instructed Williams that the mayor's guards "should be frequently changed and that no person should be long about him," lest common soldiers fall under the spell of Tory lies.[1]

{49}

50 DISHONORED AMERICANS

The imprisoned mayor deeply resented his treatment and complained to Gouverneur Morris of the "cruel aspersions that have been cast" on his honor, asking to be permitted to "clear up my character from such infamous reports as have been propagated against me." His requests had the desired effect. By August, Connecticut authorities granted Mathews a parole to Litchfield, Connecticut, where Captain Moses Seymour hosted him. It seems the mayor had convinced the right people that the allegations were either lies or nothing more than a misunderstanding. Mathews ingratiated himself with the elite members of the community and even imported a fine carriage to thank Mrs. Seymour for her hospitality.[2]

Trumbull had been wise to deny Mathews a parole. With his captors put at ease, and with the help of local Loyalists, Mathews slipped away one night in late November 1776. Incensed at being duped by a master of genteel disguise, Seymour posted an advertisement in the *Connecticut Journal* offering a fifty-dollar reward for the recapture of the mayor, who had "most basely and perfidiously deserted" his parole. As in any advertisement for a fugitive or a runaway, Seymour included a physical description of Mathews, but he added the cutting warning that the mayor "has a very plausible way of deceiving people." After the war, Mathews proudly told the commissioners in London that he had indeed "formed a plan for the taking of Mr. Washington & his Guard prisoners" but was thwarted by "an unfortunate Discovery."[3] All the allegations were true. To modern observers, lying to the enemy might seem logical, if not wise. Eighteenth-century officers could employ deception on the battlefield to confound their enemies. Lying to another gentleman's face in his own home to violate parole, however, was not only contemptible but also risked the entire system of privileges that elite prisoners enjoyed. To revolutionaries, this was yet more proof of Tory dishonor.

This example, and many others like it, demonstrates the pliancy and fluidity of honor in the American Revolution. Mathews returned to New York and resumed his duties as mayor, and though the revolutionary press referred to him as the "infamous David Mathews," neither he nor the British authorities seemed troubled by his actions. In general, Loyalists chafed at the idea that rebels could extend or expect such civilities, considering how routinely they insulted and abused Crown supporters. Within the punctilious calculations of eighteenth-century honor culture, Mathews could point to the insults he received prior to his parole for all the excuse he needed to justify his escape. But to revolutionaries, Mathews was a traitor who exploited the Patriots' humanity. Since both sides in this civil war viewed the other as criminally dishonored, the customs of genteel captivity that regulated European wars were thrown into disarray. Neither side trusted the other, but they could not completely abandon the rules of war.

Patriot treatment of Loyalist prisoners was therefore deeply inconsistent.[4] Revolutionaries did not always extend the honors of war to captured Loyalists, but they did not universally mistreat Crown supporters. By 1776, most states had enacted treason laws, and regardless of the uniforms Loyalists wore or the British commissions they carried, captured Tories could be sent back to their provincial homelands to face local justice or revenge, confined in cells, or granted paroles and exchanged for American prisoners.[5] Continental, state, and local authorities evaluated and judged the personal honor or dishonor of Loyalist prisoners on a case-by-case basis to determine the appropriate treatment. Even with examples like Mathews (and the wider Patriot consensus that all Tories were dishonorable traitors), some Loyalists received generous paroles. Others were thrown into common jails and even shackled to floors. Judicial executions of Loyalist prisoners were very rare. If revolutionaries considered an offense severe enough, they stripped captives of their genteel privileges. To be shut away in a cell and denied communication with the outside world separated a gentleman from all the things that provided his distinction and identity. Like other attacks on genteel bodies, any physical restraint recalled the criminal or the enslaved and was a painful reminder of the Loyalists' fall from grace. As the captive Loyalist John Ferdinand Smyth wrote bluntly, "Confinement is death and torture to me." The eighteenth-century Irish politician Charles Lucas would have agreed, writing, "As *Liberty* may be called *political Life;* so *Confinement,* or *Imprisonment* may be looked on, as *political Death.*"[6]

Captivity represented the most sustained contact between Loyalist and Patriot gentlemen during the conflict. Unlike crowd action or combat, the experiences of elite prisoners like Cadwallader Colden Jr., William Franklin,

52   DISHONORED AMERICANS

James Moody, and others provide fascinating insights into how men employed honor as a resource that could provide concrete privileges. Like all social interactions between elites, captivity was a kind a performance. Both sides evaluated their adversary's moral character, but they also weighed whether their opponent's behavior acknowledged a reciprocal right to respect. Captives and captors alike watched for any breach of punctilio that could be construed as disrespect, deceit, or bad faith, thus freeing them from the duty to abide by their agreements. Yet they also acknowledged acts of generosity and faithfulness that cemented obligations between captor and captive. Because of their uncertain legal status and popular infamy, Loyalist gentlemen had to choose their words carefully when they petitioned revolutionary leaders or spoke before committees that had the power to extend privileges or humiliate them further. As witnessed in the case of David Mathews, Loyalist gentlemen might show respect to their captors through genteel and obliging behavior in order to lighten their restrictions, even while they planned their escape. Honor's pliancy allowed Mathews and others to behave this way and not feel overly burdened by guilt. Their cause was just, and rebellion against the king was a crime, but this was not a case of the ends justifying the means. Patriots offered no apology or satisfaction to Loyalists for insults and abuses. To Loyalists, then, the revolutionaries were the first to break faith between gentlemen. Loyalists began their captivity under no obligations to dishonorable rebels.

For their part, Patriot gentlemen sitting on committees or in councils were reticent to inflict too much discomfort on fellow gentlemen without sufficient provocation. They were, however, willing to retaliate against Loyalist prisoners who violated paroles, and, as will be seen, revolutionaries were especially keen to make examples of gentlemen who dishonored themselves through blatant deception or who crossed the racial line to fight alongside Indigenous warriors in the brutal war on the frontier. Official records, personal diaries, Loyalist captivity narratives, and printed media are filled with discussions and appraisals of the honor and dishonor of individual captives and captors. These were not abstract or academic debates. Evaluations of honor could be literal matters of freedom and captivity, or even life and death.

CAPTIVITY   53

Until recently, the Patriot experience dominated the history of prisoners of war in the American Revolution. This is understandable, considering that between 8,500 and 11,000 rebel prisoners died in British custody. Patriot leadership and propagandists decried these deaths as intentional war crimes and seized on the alarming mortality rates in British prisons as evidence of the Crown's inhumanity.[7] First written down and spread by the Whig press during the conflict, scores of publications and newspaper accounts detailed the misery of American prisoners floating in prison ships or confined in warehouses in New York City and in England. Ethan Allen's captivity narrative and Philip Freneau's 1781 poem *The British Prison-Ship* are two of the most famous publications describing the horrors Patriots experienced. Allen pronounced his guards in New York "slavish Hessians" and "merciless Britons," yet even their cruelty was "less malignant than the tories." Indeed, of all the characters Allen met, none were quite as gloating and sadistic as the Loyalists, who "exult[ed] over the dead [Patriot prisoners], saying there goes another load of damned rebels." Allen's narrative recounts sacred churches transformed into hideous prisons where captives writhed "in the agonies of death," afflicted with hunger, disease, and cold. He graphically sketches floors "covered with excrement" "in consequence of the fluxe [*sic*]" while the suffering Patriots bravely resisted British temptations to renounce the cause and be released from their torments.[8] The most feared prisons were the rotting hulks in Wallabout Bay off Brooklyn. Philip Freneau's poem describes the "damps, disease and varied shapes of woe" suffered on these decommissioned and dilapidated ships. Every day men died, and their bodies were dragged from below deck for a shallow burial on shore or simply tossed overboard. Modern historians have concluded that British authorities did not deliberately set out to kill their captives. Rather, according to Edwin G. Burrows, the deaths resulted from "a lethal convergence . . . of obstinacy, condescension, corruption, mendacity, and indifference."[9]

Loyalist prisoners scoffed at the reams of Patriot propaganda. "Were the loyalists to take the pains . . . to collect and publish relations of this nature," wrote William Franklin after his own captivity experience in Connecticut, "I am very certain that they would be able to furnish well-attested accounts

of far more barbarities actually practised by the rebels against their prisoners than is even contained in all their exaggerated charges against the
Britons."[10] Many histories of British prisoners tend to focus on the Convention Army captured at Saratoga, which mainly comprised British regulars
and Hessians.[11] The treatment of Loyalist prisoners was largely ignored by
American scholars, who, according to T. Cole Jones, "accepted a carefully
crafted myth of American moderation, humanity, and generosity." There
is ample evidence to support John Ferling's contention that the deliberate abuse of rank-and-file Loyalist prisoners was a "black stain on America's record."[12]

Loyalists, even officers, were aware of the threat they faced if captured
on the battlefield. Ambrose Serle, General Howe's secretary, recorded rumors that "those [Loyalists] who fall into [rebel] Hands are either killed
upon the Spot, or dragged to their Copper Mines . . . surrounded with Terrors equal to Death itself."[13] Newgate Prison, a converted copper mine in
Simsbury, Connecticut, is the most cited example of Patriot mistreatment
of Loyalist prisoners. A nineteenth-century historian called it the "Black
Hole of Connecticut." State authorities claimed that they used the prison
specifically for "the purpose of retaliation," yet the first Loyalist prisoners
were sentenced to its depths long before the British captured any rebels.[14]
The prison loomed as large as any threat in the Loyalist imagination. In
1781, the *Royal Gazette* printed the narrative of two Loyalist privateers who
had escaped from Newgate. They described their descent through a trap
door that "opened the jaws and mouth of what they call Hell," a damp chamber seventy feet below ground. The men remained captive for twenty days,
until they and the rest of the prisoners overpowered their guards and escaped.[15] The Loyalist press celebrated their liberation, but stories like these
served to both demoralize refugees and inflame their calls for vengeance.

The Simsbury mine also reflects the abiding power that rank provided
even to politically dead elite Loyalists. Revolutionaries reserved the prison
for men Washington described as "atrocious villains," such as spies, raiders, and those caught fighting alongside Indigenous warriors. Few, if any,
high-ranking Loyalists ever found themselves at the bottom of the mine
shaft.[16] Such action would certainly have risked British reprisals against
American officers, but there was perhaps a more important consideration.

Continental Army officers desperately wanted to be judged by and included in the conventions of European warfare, and this meant respecting gentlemen prisoners, even Loyalists, unless there were compelling reasons not to.

Undisciplined militias or committees were less interested in these aspirations. In many well-documented cases, local authorities punished homegrown Tories or took vengeance for personal vendettas in blatant contravention of custom or even the British commissions Loyalists carried.[17] Two examples highlight the uncertain fate of Loyalist officers captured by rebel militias. At the Battle of Bennington, during the Saratoga Campaign of 1777, members of the Queen's Loyal Rangers attempted to surrender but were "refused quarter" by New Hampshire militiamen, who also badly abused what Loyalist prisoners they took. When the Saratoga Campaign reached its disastrous end, this example prompted the Rangers' commanding officer, Colonel John Peters, to request written permission from British commanders "to Escape through the Woods to Canada" rather than join the rest of Burgoyne's army as prisoners. This was a controversial move, and Burgoyne later accused the Loyalists of deserting their posts, but Peters knew "how impossible it was that any Capitulation could provide for my Security." Peters's fears had merit. In 1780, a rebel militia convened an impromptu court-martial for Loyalist officers captured at the Battle of King's Mountain in South Carolina. Lieutenant Anthony Allaire of the Loyalist provincial light infantry recorded that Lieutenant Colonel Ambrose Mills, two captains, "and six others . . . fell a sacrifice to their infamous mock trial."[18]

The killings at both Bennington and King's Mountain sparked outrage among British officers. After Bennington, Burgoyne chastised Horatio Gates and reminded him of the "horrors of retaliation" if the Continental forces did not adhere to "those maxims upon which all men of honor think alike." Cornwallis harangued his rebel counterparts for executing "a fair and open enemy to your Cause" at King's Mountain and threatened retaliation "in justice to the suffering Loyalists." Yet despite such threats, Loyalists could not rely on British protection. After the trial and execution of five Loyalists captured at the Battle of Kettle Creek in 1779, Sir Henry Clinton ordered that no reprisals be taken against Whig prisoners in case it placed captive British officers in jeopardy. British commanders even refused

56 DISHONORED AMERICANS

Patriot offers to exchange Loyalist prisoners if there were regular army offi-cers available.[19] As will be explored in more detail in the next chapter, such insults compelled armed Loyalists to seek revenge on their own terms.

Loyalist prisoners taken by the regular Continental Army or held under state or congressional authority could also be treated badly, but conditions were mitigated by Continental officers who were eager to prove themselves professional and honorable soldiers. British forces initially denied Conti-nental Army officers their status as gentlemen—both because they were rebels and because American officers often did not cut the figure demanded in European militaries. Upon first meeting American officers in 1776, a surprised Hessian observer wrote that Continental officers were "nothing but mechanics, tailors, shoemakers, wigmakers, barbers etc. Some of them were soundly beaten by our people, who would by no means let such per-sons pass for officers." Americans smarted at such dismissive insults, and according to Judith Van Buskirk, often attempted to "out-gentleman" the British with their manners and strict adherence to customs.[20]

As more British officers fell into rebel hands, necessity demanded that the British extend the system of mutual respect, but this did not include official Crown recognition of the Continental Army as a legitimate entity. George Germaine instructed General Howe that while exchanges were needed "to procure the release of such of His Majesty's officers and loyal sub-jects as are in the disgraceful situation of being prisoners to Rebels," there should be no "regular cartel," a contractual system of prisoner exchange between equals. Official or not, Continental officers, especially those who could afford to maintain their own privileged captivity, were treated as of-ficers even though this gave "great disgust to all the Loyalists." The Crown finally recognized American captives as bona fide prisoners of war in the spring of 1782, after which British and Congressional representatives nego-tiated a general and equal exchange of prisoners on the European model.[21]

This was the outcome Washington and his officers worked through-out the war to achieve. The general took it upon himself to educate his men and enforce strict adherence to the European standards of profession-alism. When several of his officers broke their paroles and escaped from Long Island in 1777, Washington sent them back. The officers claimed that they were short of money and supplies, and though Washington did not

CAPTIVITY 57

doubt their suffering, the honor of the army was more important.[22] This same concern can be seen in Washington's rejection of a plan to mount a rescue operation to liberate Continental officers. Washington pointed out that those officers left behind would face reprisals, and he added, "No future prisoners, in the hands of the Enemy, would receive the same favourable indulgence." Worse still, Washington stressed that a rescue attempt would be considered "a breach of Honor [and] would certainly be objected against by the Officers released; for it would be said, right or wrong, they, at least, had consented to the measure, if not planned it."[23] Even clerical mix-ups did not excuse officers from their parole. A Continental officer, Isaac Grant, who had been paroled home and then exchanged and restored to active duty, discovered that his exchange had been a bureaucratic error. Rather than risk any sort of dishonor, he quickly resumed his parole.[24] Through these careful observances, Continental officers attempted to show their honorable character so that they would receive the generous paroles that acknowledged their right to respect.

Just as the British army had to accept the practical necessity of extending privileges to rebel officers, Patriot authorities were compelled to at least attempt to treat their elite Loyalist prisoners with leniency and entrust them with paroles. When the Continental Congress transferred Lieutenant Governor Philip Skene to Hartford as a prisoner, Major General David Wooster pointedly instructed Ezekiel Williams to "take care that he is treated with that politeness & civility which is due a Gentleman of his Rank." If possible, the Continental leadership wanted high-ranking British and Loyalist prisoners to return with stories of respectful treatment that might help ensure Patriot prisoners received the same generous terms. John Hancock advised Williams that Skene was to be held on a "Parole within such Limits as your Honor shall point out to them." In other words, because of Skene's rank, Williams could offer more generous terms than the standard parole agreement printed by the Continental Congress.[25]

A Loyalist's rank and perceived honor complicated his status as a politically dead traitor. George Washington's correspondence demonstrates that revolutionaries determined how to treat gentlemen Loyalists on a

58   DISHONORED AMERICANS

case-by-case basis. When Washington transferred some Loyalist prisoners from Long Island to Connecticut, he asked Governor Jonathan Trumbull to extend "every accommodation and Indulgence, having a respect for their rank and Education which may be deemed Consistent with Safety."[26] Washington was anxious to extend courtesies to fellow gentlemen, but his attitude toward rank-and-file Loyalists could be severe. He referred to them as "abominable pests of Society" and later advised summary executions for "some of the most notorious offenders whenever they can be found in flagrante delicto" to terrify other Loyalists.[27] Yet Washington was not always certain where his Loyalist prisoners stood on a spectrum of guilt. He was seemingly stuck in indecision about the status of Captain Albert Cole, a Loyalist captured in 1779. Washington mused to Major General William Heath that he did "not yet know in what light Captain Cole will be considered, whether as a Prisoner of War, or a Citizen."[28] This was a legal and moral distinction that could mean the difference between a generous parole and imprisonment or worse. While Washington may have suggested shooting Tory bandits on sight, he was much more reluctant to mistreat captured Loyalist gentlemen.

Continental authorities were therefore deeply insulted, though perhaps not surprised, when captured British and Loyalist officers refused to abide by the same honor code that the Patriots were so diligently cultivating and extending. General Philip Schuyler wrote to Jonathan Trumbull in December 1775 that he was sending some valuable prisoners to Connecticut for safekeeping after an insulting pattern of parole breaking emerged among British and Loyalist officers. "I fear," wrote Schuyler, "they do not consider their parole of honour as binding."[29] The historical record supports Schuyler's conclusion. Washington even complained directly to representatives of General Howe that British officers "refused to give any parole, and others having broke it when given, by escaping or endeavouring to do so." An assistant to General Howe, Colonel Patterson, met with Washington and agreed that "such was considered as a dishonour to the British army."[30] When the New York Committee of Correspondence arrested Cadwallader Colden Jr. in the summer of 1777, it initially denied him a parole, citing the "Many Instances of gent[n] of [Colden's] Disposition who had Broke their Promise and Paroles." Colden recorded in his diary that his captors were convinced that Loyalist and British officers believed "No faith or Promise was to be kept with Rebels."[31]

Records confirm that many British and Loyalist prisoners did not believe their rebel captors deserved the respect a parole implied. Not only were they rebels but they were also rustic provincials, with no real sense of honor or understanding of their obligations in a parole. British and Loyalists alike were certain that the revolutionary authorities either deliberately whipped up the people to terrorize prisoners on parole or allowed it to happen. The Quaker and suspected Loyalist Thomas Gilpin recorded that country people insulted him and his fellow Friends all through their journey from Philadelphia to their imprisonment in Winchester, Virginia. He believed they "had been encouraged by some Violent people to do so." Gilpin also fumed at the vulgar officer of the guard who intimidated the peaceful Quakers with threats of hanging and bragged with "familiar centiments [sic] & expressions ab[ou]t thumming people's eyes, biting, pinching their Privates."[32] Major Christopher French, one of several officers on parole in Hartford, Connecticut, recorded that the locals were "threatening to insult us daily & even threatened some of our lives." Supreme Court Justice Thomas Jones wrote that he "had his house broken open, completely plundered, and himself carried into Connecticut, *though at the very time a prisoner upon parole.*"[33] Simply put, since rebel paroles could not be counted on for protection, Loyalists and British officers abided by their limits only so long as it suited them.

This cagey attitude can be seen in the case of Captain Samuel McKay, a British commander of Loyalist volunteers taken prisoner at the siege of Fort St. John in November 1775. In April 1776, McKay wrote to George Washington from his captivity in Hartford to ask for an exchange or a new parole to Montreal to tend to his "Wife & a large Family." Washington replied politely, but he refused McKay's request and encouraged the officer to compare his situation with the mistreatment of Ethan Allen "sent to England in Irons." A few weeks after Washington's refusal, McKay fled his parole, which, according to his fellow parolee Major Christopher French, ignited "the Fury of the populace." French recorded that a few days later some "Country fellows" captured McKay, "tied him, knock'd him down, & beat & abus'd him in the grossest manner." The *Connecticut Journal* reported

60 DISHONORED AMERICANS

the capture of "the infamous Capt. McKay, who is so lost to every principle of honor as to violate his parole." Yet rebel abuse of McKay seemed like a far worse crime to his fellow gentlemen prisoners than his breach of parole. Following this affair, the Connecticut government tightened its restrictions on the parolees. The day after McKay was recaptured, Governor Trumbull ordered Philip Skene confined in the common jail for refusing to sign a new parole, which only served to exacerbate British and Loyalist intransigence toward the local committee and set the stage for even more dysfunction.[34]

Despite these repeated violations, Continental authorities continued to offer paroles and even provided recalcitrant prisoners opportunities to redeem themselves. In late 1777, "a Captain Longstreet . . . to his great Dishonour broke his parole" and slipped away into the countryside. A few days later he voluntarily rejoined his captors and proceeded with them to Connecticut. Perhaps relieved that the prisoner had returned on his own volition, Elias Boudinot instructed Ezekiel Williams to "Confine the Captain in Gaol . . . unless by his late Behaviour he has wiped away the stain" of his dishonor.[35] How prisoners could "wipe away the stain" of past misbehavior was a matter left to the personal judgment of jailers and committees.

The captivity of Cadwallader Colden Jr. is an instructive example of how gentlemanly performance and appeals to honor culture could preserve the freedom and dignity of elite Loyalists. Colden, the son of the former lieutenant governor of New York, was well-versed in gentlemanly culture and relied on it to navigate his two-year captivity. Throughout his ordeal he refused to take an oath of allegiance to the State of New York as a point of honor, but he also consistently prevaricated about his Loyalist activities. He presented himself to the New York Committee for Detecting and Defeating Conspiracies as a hapless victim caught in an impossible moral quandary between his previous oaths to the Crown and the demands of the Revolution. All he wanted was to retire to his estate and live in peace. And yet, while under parole, his estate served as a safe house for British and Loyalist fugitives, and he funded a small network of New York Tories.[36] Because of his influence and past friendships with revolutionary gentlemen, however, he maintained his genteel disguise for nearly two years.

CAPTIVITY   61

Colden first came to the committee's attention in November 1776. Authorities seized numerous incriminating letters between Colden and prominent New York Loyalists that left little doubt as to the gentleman's allegiance and the extent of his contacts. Described as "notoriously disaffected" and "too dangerous to be permitted" to remain even under house arrest, he was held in jail for several weeks until the committee gave him ten days to put his affairs in order before being sent to Boston under parole. Colden, however, intended to make things as awkward as possible for prominent committeemen like John Jay, William Duer, and Gouverneur Morris, who were old acquaintances and belonged to the same elite circles. He petitioned his former colleagues to "soften their sentence" and appealed to the "Rights of Private judgement," arguing that his political principles were based in the "freedom of Disquisition and Debate on Topics which affected the Public Weal . . . [which were] the Birth Right of English Men."[37] The committee permitted Colden to appear before them to make his case.

Addressing the committee in person, he reminded his colleagues of the "most unparalleled hard treatment" he had received. He had been locked in the "Common jail" with a murderer and all the "Common Nastyness" for more than a month for no apparent crime other than his refusal to break his oaths to the king as a royal official and lawyer. "How gent[lemen] am I to get over this matter of Conscience?" he asked. Though he was terrified that his unprotected family might be subject to "the Insults & Raviges [sic] of a Soldiery," this could not "Induce me to take an Oath against my Conscience." He admitted candidly that a forced oath would have little weight with him, since "I should undoubtedly conclude that the Sin was in [the] takeing [sic] of the Oath & not in [the] Breaking of it." He concluded his gentlemanly address by thanking the committee and apologizing for having "discover'd so Much weakness in Delivering my Deffence [sic] (for I had let fall a few Tears) But if there was any more punishments in Store for me they would find I had Resolution to bare [sic] them."[38]

Colden was neither naïve nor desperate enough to imagine that the revolutionaries would accept his claim to neutrality, but he openly and honestly admitted that his oath to the Crown superseded all others. His respectful and elegant theatrics combined fortitude with sensibility in order to elicit sympathy from his fellow gentlemen and keep him in his home. Colden

62   DISHONORED AMERICANS

displayed all the ideal qualities of a gentleman: he made a principled point grounded in the language of personal honor, he appeared honest, and he showed deep feeling but also stoicism. His appeal worked, and the committee canceled his transfer to Boston. Yet the revolutionaries were at odds over Colden's fate. Elite members were sympathetic to their colleague, while committeemen from more modest backgrounds were deeply annoyed at the indulgence shown to this wealthy Tory. As a result, the committee relegated Colden's fate to a bureaucratic morass while their prisoner lived comfortably in a private home in Fishkill, New York, for several weeks. Indeed, as the days passed, individual members of the council, such as Colden's former lawyer Robert R. Livingston, openly sympathized with Colden but threw up their hands at the complexity and delay of it all.[39] Colden remained in a kind of limbo, neither held in jail nor on parole.

In January 1777, Colden tired of waiting for the authorities to decide his fate, so he just went home. He wrote to James Livingston that he would return when summoned.[40] Colden's simple yet audacious move worked, and he lived quietly at his Ulster estate much as he had always done. When armed men arrived to take him back to Fishkill in March, Colden was hosting New York state representative William Denning as a guest, "or," he wrote, "I might have Expected to have been Insulted and very Ruffly handled." The committee paroled Colden, but little changed for the gentleman who spent his evenings "in a Sociable manner with the Commissioners without Entering on Politics."[41] That a suspected Tory would have such cordial relations with high-ranking Patriots was unremarkable to Colden and consistent with genteel customs, but it must have been a source of consternation for the humbler sort.

These friendly relations did not prevent Colden from being thrown into the common jail in Kingston, New York, in May 1777 for allegedly aiding or harboring members of a Tory raiding party. Colden vociferously denied the allegations, and Patriot authorities had little evidence to back up their claims. Judging by his later testimony to Sir Henry Clinton, if Colden had not helped this group, he did provide a safe house for other Loyalists. After the local authorities executed the leader of the raiding party, Jacobus Rose, Colden learned he was to be transferred to the state's own prison ships in reprisal for the British practice. In a display of wealth and influence, Colden and a few other imprisoned gentlemen petitioned to purchase their own ship rather than be held with common prisoners. What began as Patriot retaliation for British mistreatment of Continental prisoners ended with Colden and his friends living through the early summer of 1777 "very Comfortably & very merry" on their own private sloop without a guard. He was even permitted to bring a "servant," most likely an enslaved man, on board with him, and at one point was granted a five-day holiday to visit his family.[42]

This indulgence provided some of Colden's fellow genteel prisoners the opportunity to escape. Colden recorded that he attempted to persuade the men not to run off. "Tho' we were under no kind of Parole," he wrote, "by there being no guard put on bord [sic] our vessel it imply'd a confidence put in us by the Captn of the gard [sic] ship which for my part I had a kind of Reluctance in forfeiting." His fellow gentlemen respectfully disagreed and planned their escape, though Colden asked that they conceal any further plans from him so he would not be complicit. When Colden finally discovered that his friends had escaped, he waited until daybreak before informing the captain of the guard, thus giving his friends a chance to gain some distance while appearing to be a model prisoner.[43] Once again, Colden calculated the best outcome for himself within the bounds of honor.

Perhaps because of Colden's refusal to escape, he was granted a parole on land and lived the next year in comfort, though under a constant cloud of committee indecision. This finally ended in June 1778, when the New York Assembly passed "An Act More Effectively to Prevent the Mischiefs ariseing [sic] from the influence and Example of Persons of Equivocal and Suspected Character." This new law criminalized neutrality, and no amount of evasion or delay could keep Colden from either taking or refusing his oath. The act was particularly harsh against men who ostensibly attempted to stay out of the conflict but in fact concealed information and beliefs "Contrary to their faith Pledged by their Paroles . . . and perfidiously from time to time, by active misrepresentations." Neutrals were at best greedy sneaks who might play both sides, or, at worst, crypto-Loyalists who were actively undermining the war effort. After he was presented with the ultimatum,

Colden deliberated overnight but still could not bring himself to take an oath abjuring the king. The committee therefore sent him across the lines into British New York as a bona fide Tory.[44]

In a revealing epilogue to Colden's journal, the newly exiled and penniless Loyalist wrote to General Henry Clinton that "in April 1777 an Officer or Messenger Charged with dispatches from the Commander in Chief at Canada to Sir William How [sic]" was "being pursued, [and] fled to the house of Your Memorialist for protection, which he not only Rec'd but your Memorialist hired guides who conducted him" back to New York.[45] Colden told the New York committee that he had not assisted the British in any way, but he did not seem to have been overly troubled by his apparent dissembling. In fact, it is likely that because the revolutionaries did not specifically ask about this incident, he did not feel he had lied at all. Cadwallader Colden's scrupulous sense of honor allowed him to weave a casuistic web of fine points that, to modern eyes, might seem like dishonesty but to him were the principled actions of a gentleman just trying to survive.

Whereas Colden used genteel performance and hair-splitting punctilio, New Jersey governor William Franklin, the Loyalist son of Benjamin Franklin, simply rejected the parole offered by the revolutionaries who arrested him in June 1776. Revolutionary authorities took Franklin's refusal as a significant insult that denied their legitimacy, but they also regarded it as a serious security threat. Because Franklin was not honor-bound to abide by a parole, they placed him under house arrest in Middletown, Connecticut. An intercepted letter to his wife seemed to indicate that Franklin intended to take advantage of that situation. Writing to the Committee of Safety in Essex, New Jersey, George Washington reported that Franklin told his wife he feared "something may turn up to make his removal improper" (i.e., a parole), which Washington interpreted as "full evidence, that he means to escape if possible."[46] To prevent this, Continental authorities gave Franklin a stark ultimatum: sign a parole or be thrown in jail with common criminals. The risk of humiliation and violence compelled Franklin to sign a parole, but it is likely neither side believed it could hold.[47]

Connecticut authorities closely monitored their valuable prisoner. In April 1777, the Continental Congress learned that Franklin had committed serious parole violations by corresponding with the British and handing out "protections" to the locals in the name of General Howe. In response, he was sent to Litchfield, Connecticut, and confined in a cell above a tavern. Though the former governor denied the charges and demanded a hearing or trial, his requests were rebuffed. "I was closely confined for about eight months," Franklin wrote to Lord Germaine after his release in 1778. "Over-run and molested with many kinds of vermin, debarred pen, ink, and paper and all conversation with every person." Franklin described his experience as being "buried alive."[48] The former governor claimed that he was poorly fed, that his clothes were filthy, and that he was covered with lice. The great man had taken on the appearance of a condemned criminal.

For months Franklin waited to be exchanged, but Continental authorities continued to consider him far too dangerous to release. While other prisoners were sometimes allowed to return to New York to tend to ill and distressed relatives, Franklin was not. When the former governor's wife was on the verge of death, and even with George Washington's humane intercession on his behalf, the Continental Congress reasoned that Franklin could not be allowed any freedoms after a "violation of so sacred a tie as that of honor."[49] Franklin's treatment became a matter of public deliberation. One letter to the *Connecticut Gazette* demanded to know "the true reason of Mr. William Franklin . . . being confined to a loathsome gaol" and wondered why the "Son of the Great Doctor Franklin is treated . . . like a thief or murderer." The anonymous writer declared that if Franklin "broke his parole of Honor, publish it in all the News Papers on the Continent, and (if he's not lost to all the finest feelings of the mind) to be exposed will be worse than death." Just as William Franklin had requested, the writer demanded a trial for Franklin lest "the vile Tories . . . boast that the patriotic Doctor Franklin's son is used with a Rigour, seldom known but in a Portuguese Inquisition."[50] After nearly two years as a prisoner, Franklin was finally exchanged in October 1778.

Despite Franklin's protestations of innocence, Patriot authorities treated their parole violator according to the accepted customs of the time. Franklin was guilty of the illicit communications charged against him, and the Patriots were within their rights to confine him. His actions were both a breach of security and an insult that the Patriots were honor-bound to answer. Yet Franklin felt no dishonor in breaching a rebel parole he was forced to sign, and he no doubt believed the entire debacle was simply orchestrated to embarrass him.[51] Patriots offered Franklin a parole in the first place as a method to prevent his escape; it was simultaneously an expression of respect and a trap. This demonstrates the central paradox of honor's importance in the elite prisoner experience. Honor was not considered an abstract concept but was regarded as a concrete force that could provide security to both captor and captive. And yet honor was also deeply subjective, especially if the parties did not fully accept one another's right to respect.

This subjectivity played a central role in the captivity of Major Christopher French of the Twenty-Second Regiment of Foot, one of the first British officers captured in the war. Whereas Colden and Franklin shared the same background and upbringing as their Patriot counterparts, French's detailed journal of his prisoner experience in Hartford, Connecticut, reveals the sharp clash between the British officer's sometimes cosmopolitan, often pugnacious, Anglo-Irish gentry culture and that of the more austere and restrained New Englanders. Though not an American Loyalist, French found common cause with his fellow prisoners and referred to himself as a Loyalist in his journal. He begrudgingly signed a parole but had difficulty accepting the legitimacy of his captivity. The major especially bristled at the disrespect he encountered from the people of Hartford, which he did his best to repay in kind.[52] French described the locals and the committeemen as little more than country bumpkins bereft of any sense of proper deference to men of learning and rank. This was to be expected, he wrote, because the people were "accustom'd to a Life of equality, where Birth, Riches, nay merit are mostly undistinguish'd," and therefore the New Englanders could "scarcely be found fault with for this method of acting, which arises from Simplicity and Ignorance."[53] Nevertheless, the major seemed to delight in talking down to his jailers, especially the college-educated committeeman Jesse Root, for their failings as gentlemen and their ignorance of the finer points of honor.

French and his fellow officers were continually at odds with their captors, and as Tory activity in western Connecticut increased, so did tensions between the prisoners and the local population. Matters were not improved when the local Black population elected Philip Skene's enslaved servant as their governor "according to annual custom," which added the terrifying prospect of insurrection to the growing fears of a Tory fifth column.[54] After French's fellow prisoner Captain Samuel McKay broke his parole and escaped, the committee tightened restrictions on the other parolees and attempted to rein in the routine disrespect the captive British and Loyalist officers displayed. When the committee brought French in to answer whether he had ever spoken disrespectfully of the committee or Congress, the major replied that he had and that he would call the committee, Washington, and the whole Congress in session "rascals" even if "I had a rope round my neck to be pull'd upon my saying it." French scolded the committee for overreaching and declared that he would burn his parole if they tried to prevent him from "paying the proper Attention to the support of his Majesty's Honor."[55]

Whatever respect remained between the committee and the major evaporated when French issued an order forbidding British prisoners in Hartford from attending Congregationalist services, since the clergy "abuse and revile [His Majesty] by the epithets of Bloody Tyrant etc. . . . and call his Navies and Armies murderers Pirates & Butchers." When French refused to rescind the order, he and his officers were locked in the common jail with "no distinction made between us & Felons." He later wrote that this violated "all laws, Civil or Military, of all nations."[56] The committee saw a clear link between disrespect and a potential security threat. If the prisoners did not respect their captors, they would not respect their paroles and could not be trusted. For French, the rebels had shown their true colors and relieved him of his obligations. Now it was his business to torment his jailers and plot his own escape.

French bombarded the committee and his jailers with constant complaints, insults, and challenges. His mockery was at times imperious and at others juvenile and petty. At one point, French composed an insulting song set to the tune of "Yankee Doodle" for the new bride of one of his guards,

68   DISHONORED AMERICANS

advising her not to marry him because, among other things, "His Parts are small." The Hartford committee, led by Root, kept its cool but also returned fire where it could. French fumed when Root admitted local farmers into the jail to gawk at the prisoners. Among French's neighbors were arsonists, counterfeiters, and a "raving lunatic" whose shrieks and cries kept French up all night. When French demanded that his right to exercise in the yard be acknowledged, Root offered him the use of the yard as a personal favor, which French flatly refused, as he "never accept[ed] favors from any but those I think upon as friends."[57] The feud between French and Root often veered toward the absurd, but it was both a test of wills and a reflection of the larger debate over conflicting ideas of honor in the American Revolution.

The dispute, which went on for months, compelled Jesse Root to submit a meditation on the dangers of "False Honor" to the *Connecticut Courant* in November 1776. Though he does not mention French by name, the major was certain the piece referred to him. Root described the bearers of false honor as "impertinent, saucy, [and] vain," individuals whose ideals were "a war [upon] . . . conscience, upon heaven." False honor "substitutes brutal ferocity [for] fortitude, and breaks through all restraints." All the troubles that led to the Revolution could be blamed on the "cursed principle of false honor" that was used by "British troops" to justify all their violence and oppression. Men of false honor were like vectors that "give the country the plague" and "ought to be cooped in the caverns of the earth." This last line was intended as a thinly veiled threat to French that unless he behaved, he might find himself in the Simsbury copper mine.[58]

In response to what French saw as "an Attack upon me," he penned his own reflection on honor titled "True Honor" under the name "Cosmopolitus," though it was never published. French describes true honor as "mild and gentle in Prosperity, yet bold & manly in Adversity." Using Root's own words against him, French writes that his honor is "Not Vain, not saucy, nor impertinent, but steady and unshaken & fears not tho' many threaten." "In short," he writes, "true honor is as a precious Gem which (tho' buried in the . . . Caverns of the Earth . . .) . . . will shine forth, to the terror of False Honor."[59] The dispute demonstrates honor's importance and its pliancy. Neither man really defined honor in his explanations, yet both captor and captive relied on the concept to justify his actions and affirm his identity as the aggrieved party against his deluded opponent. Unlike Colden or Franklin, there was no major violation that nullified French's parole. Rather, the pattern of disrespect demonstrated that neither side viewed the other as honorable, and thus there was no foundation for a parole. This small episode was part of the wider cultural conflict about the ethics of revolution and loyalty raging in the Atlantic world.

The Hartford committee's irritation at its bothersome prisoner finally exploded into rage when a local girl eloped with a soldier under the major's command. French feared a local mob would soon come for him or that he might be sent to toil in the mine. Just as he had chipped away at the patience of his captors, however, he had also been chipping away at the walls of his cell. On the night of November 15, 1776, he and four other prisoners made their escape through the hole they had dug clandestinely over the course of months. For five days the group of fugitives attempted to make their way to British lines. French even disguised himself as "a Woman with Cloak & Bonnett," but Connecticut authorities recaptured the fugitives and returned them to their patched-up jail. Undaunted, they escaped again on December 27 and successfully made their way to New York.[60]

Since the exasperated committee could not recapture Christopher French, it did its best to blacken the major's name. About two months after he escaped, the *Connecticut Gazette* devoted an entire column to scathing rebukes of Major French and his behavior. An anonymous writer explained that French had initially been "used with the greatest Lenity . . . till he violated (like a Scoundrel) his Parole." The overwrought article describes him as a "peevish, ill-natured, churlish, bigotted [*sic*]" man with a "bloodthirsty Disposition." The writer accused the "descendant of Draco" of responding to kindness with "fresh insults and Instances of uncommon Insolence and Scurrility." French was a "feeble wretch" and a "Baboon" who burned with vengeance "like Nebuchadnezzar's fiery furnace." An acrostic poem followed, which referred to French as a "Monkey in a Cage" and a "Popish Priest." The last letters of his name provided a C for "Crimes black as Hell the Ingrate would applaud" and "H is [for] Honor to maintain in spite of Man and God." The column concludes by attacking French's manhood, calling him a "Hermaphrodite" and an "Ingrate and Churl."[61] French had succeeded in getting under the committee's skin.

The cases of Colden, Franklin, and French demonstrate the intricate debate over how best to treat and secure valuable yet uncooperative and potentially dangerous prisoners. Even with the repeated examples of Loyalists and British officers absconding after agreeing to their paroles, Continental authorities continued to offer paroles to elite prisoners. Revolutionaries had their limits, however, and Loyalists captured operating behind Continental lines or fighting alongside Indigenous warriors could face harsh treatment. In eighteenth-century custom, if one side violated the honorable rules of war, then the other was absolved from the same obligations. In 1775, George Washington, always a fastidious observer of honor's fine points, complained to General Thomas Gage about British abuse of American prisoners. Washington reminded his counterpart that the "Obligation arising from the Rights of Humanity, and claims of Rank are universally binding, and extensive," but added the warning "except in case of Retaliation."[62] As Washington came to learn, the rules of war were rarely clear and, like so many points of honor, the justice of retaliation was a matter of perspective.

The captivity experience of Lieutenant James Moody of the New Jersey Volunteers demonstrates the ways in which Continental authorities could overrule military conventions to retaliate against their internal enemy.[63] Moody achieved a degree of fame (or infamy) during the war for his daring exploits freeing Loyalist prisoners and capturing rebel dispatches. He was even immortalized in 1785 by the British engraver Robert Pollard, who depicted Moody's rescue of a shackled British officer from a Gothic dungeon.[64] Revolutionaries captured Moody in July 1780 and held him at West Point, where the commandant, Robert Howe, granted him a gentleman's parole with a three-mile limit around the fortress. The Patriot press jubilantly announced Moody's capture and printed the orders he carried directing him to capture New Jersey governor William Livingston. Even though these documents were intended "to prevent his being treated as a spy," the newspaper informed readers that because he traveled with a very small party of men behind enemy lines "with weapons concealed," his actions were "characteristic of a spy" according to the rules "of all the nations of Europe."[65] This argument was a stretch, considering that Moody and his men were in uniform when they were captured, but the writer was attempting to build a case against the infamous Loyalist. According to eighteenth-century custom, gentlemen did not skulk in the shadows but fought bravely and openly. Spies were therefore not considered gentlemen and were not normally protected by the genteel conventions of war, as seen in the executions of Nathan Hale, John André, and others.[66] Moved by these arguments, George Washington interceded in Moody's case and voided the Loyalist's parole, ordering him confined under close guard.[67]

Benedict Arnold assumed command of West Point in early August 1780 and took no chances with the wily prisoner he inherited. He ordered Moody shackled, which, the Loyalist later recalled, "caused his wrists to be much cut and scarified." Moody recorded that Arnold confined him in a roofless pit, dug out of natural rock, which often filled with ankle-deep water. Even with this treatment, Moody believed his life would be spared since he was more valuable for prisoner exchange than for Patriot vengeance. The Continental authorities dashed his expectations when they informed him that he was to be tried for the "assassination" of a pair of officers killed fighting Moody and his men. In protest, the Loyalist officer argued that his unit killed the officers fairly in battle. Undeterred, a Continental officer candidly explained that Moody was "so obnoxious," and was "likely to be . . . so mischievous" if exchanged, that the revolutionary authorities planned to use whatever excuse they could to justify his execution. Even if the assassination charge failed, "you have enlisted men . . . for the King's service, and this, by our laws, is *death*."[68] Before the sentence could take place, Moody escaped.

Unlike French or Franklin, Moody had not violated his parole or disrespected his captors; rather, Washington revoked his parole because he did not recognize the Loyalist's status as a lawful combatant. Moody presented his treatment as exceedingly harsh and unjust, especially considering that he carried a British commission, but his experiences were consistent with other captured partisans and raiders. The shackles, however, evoked slavery and criminality and were an insult spared most white captives in the American Revolution. News of starvation and disease aboard the prison ships incensed the revolutionary leadership, but rumors that the British shackled Continental officers provoked an immediate response. In 1779, Governor Livingston retaliated directly by placing Colonel Christopher Billop, a Loyalist, in irons. Elias Boudinot apologized to Billop in writing but lamented

72   DISHONORED AMERICANS

that such harsh treatment was the only way "to teach Britons to act like men of humanity."[69] For Boudinot and Washington, when enemies refused to act like gentlemen, retaliation was the only effective way to prevent further cruelties.

To revolutionaries, no crime demanded retaliation more than the British alliance with the Indigenous nations on the frontier. The American Revolution inflamed generations of racial hatred and atrocities. Patriots blamed men like the lieutenant governor of Detroit, Henry Hamilton, for his central role in setting the frontier on fire, and Whig frontiersmen derisively labeled Hamilton the "Hair Buyer" for allegedly paying for Patriot scalps. He and his officers were thus among the most valuable prizes on the frontier. Hamilton was the epitome of false honor: an accomplished gentleman born to privilege and influence, yet willing to align himself with the very antithesis of civilization.[70]

In February 1779, Colonel George Rogers Clark surprised Hamilton's garrison at Fort Vincennes and demanded its surrender. Patriot Major Joseph Bowman recorded that while Clark and Hamilton negotiated, revolutionaries captured six fighters, including four Odawa or Shawnee warriors, and brought them into the village. After separating the white men from the party, Clark's soldiers "brought the Indians to the main street before the Fort gate," and in an apparent attempt to terrify the besieged garrison into surrendering, "there tomahawked them, and threw them into the river." Bowman's matter-of-fact description highlights the routine nature of such killings and assumes the reader would understand their necessity.[71] Loyalist Lieutenant Jacob Schieffelin claimed to be an eyewitness and provided a more graphic description for the *Royal Gazette*. "Colonel Clark," explained Schieffelin, "took a tomahawk, and in cool blood knocked their brains out, dipping his hands in their blood, rubbing it several times on his cheeks, yelping as a savage."[72] The killings at least demonstrated rebel resolve to take the fort, and Hamilton surrendered his British and Loyalist garrison, which was then marched to Virginia. The murder of the four Indigenous men was not reported in the Patriot press, though news of the capture of Henry Hamilton and his officers was widely celebrated.[73]

CAPTIVITY 73

George Washington supported retaliating against Hamilton and his fellow prisoners. In a letter to Governor Thomas Jefferson of Virginia, Washington explained that "their cruelties to our unhappy people who have fallen into their hands and the measures they have pursued to excite the savages . . . discriminate them from common prisoners."[74] According to Jacob Schieffelin, the rebels paraded Henry Hamilton, Loyalist Justice of the Peace Philip Dejean, and Captain William Lamothe through the streets of Williamsburg "with great pomp" in the rain, before the prisoners were "committed to the dungeon with felons, murderers, and condemned criminals, not so much as a blanket allowed them . . . and heavy chains put on their legs before great numbers of people." Like so many other shaming rituals, the public shackling of once-proud Tories and their infamous British commander demonstrated the triumph of the Revolution and the political death of its enemies. Schieffelin recorded that he and his fellow Loyalist officers "shed tears of indignation that their worthy Chief should be so treated" based on such "infamous falsehoods."[75]

The Virginia legislature published an account of Hamilton's cruelty to justify its reprisals against him and his men. The broadside detailed the "Indian raids" supposedly ordered by Hamilton and the governor's own inhumane treatment of prisoners. Several paragraphs were devoted to the sufferings of the unfortunate John Dodge, a rebel prisoner shackled in a stone cell without blankets, fire, or proper food in the dead of winter. Patriots alleged that Hamilton ordered the half-dead Dodge brought out of the cold until "somewhat mended, and then again, before he had recovered the abilities to walk . . . returned [him] to the dungeon." Other prisoners were said to be placed "into the hands of savages" to be killed or carried off into the wilderness. The last few paragraphs of the broadside contrasted the loathsome conditions suffered by Patriot prisoners with the indulgent treatment accorded British captives. The pamphlet declared that though "we had long and vainly endeavoured to introduce an emulation in kindness [in the enemy]," Hamilton and his fellow prisoners "are free subjects to begin on the work of retaliation." As such, Hamilton, Dejean, and Lamothe were "put in irons, confined in the dungeon of the public jail, debarred the use of pen, ink, and paper, and excluded all converse except with the keeper."[76] To Patriots, the alliance with Indigenous warriors and their alleged

74 DISHONORED AMERICANS

inhumanity against Patriot prisoners stripped the royal officers of any right to respect.

When reports reached British general William Phillips, he wrote to Washington to remind the general that since Hamilton had surrendered based on a negotiated settlement, retaliation was a violation of the agreement and a breach of honor. This troubled Washington's sense of fair play, but it also had larger military ramifications. If British garrisons felt they could not trust Patriot surrender terms, they might choose to prolong sieges and force bloody assaults that would work to no one's advantage. Washington conceded the point to Jefferson, writing that "on more mature consideration, [the issue of retaliation] appears to be involved in greater difficulty than I apprehended." Washington admitted that Hamilton deserved to be punished and that his crimes should be widely published "that the World . . . may feel and approve the justice of his fate." Nonetheless, the offender could not "be subjected to any uncommon severity," since his "capitulation placed him upon a different footing from a mere prisoner at discretion," and they could "not justify the measures that have been taken against him." In the end, Hamilton's fellow prisoners were either paroled or, in the case of Schieffelin, escaped, but Hamilton was not exchanged until November 1780. Despite the intense public rancor against Hamilton and his Loyalist officers, the honors of war and practical military necessity prevented them from experiencing the full brunt of Patriot vengeance.[77]

Every Loyalist officer or gentleman who fell into rebel hands experienced captivity differently. Revolutionaries evaluated the personal honor of each of their prisoners to determine who merited the indulgent treatment owed to gentlemen and who had forfeited his right to respect. Deliberations sometimes included the highest ranks of the Continental Congress and Army, and George Washington personally interceded in dozens of cases. The captivity of David Mathews, William Franklin, Cadwallader Colden Jr., and others demonstrates both the pliancy and the power of honor. A gentleman's word of honor not to escape was expected to secure him as tightly as chains, since the risk of public shame and dishonor would "be worse than death." Yet Loyalists and Patriots were engaged in an irresolvable cultural battle between "true" and "false" honor, intermixed with the legal ambiguities of rebellion, treason, and retaliation. Thus, while both sides desperately sought to maintain the customs of gentlemanly privilege for themselves, the entire system was jeopardized by men who believed that they held the moral high ground. Elite Loyalist prisoners refused to accept the legitimacy of their paroles and escaped, while Continental authorities disregarded official commissions and negotiated agreements to retaliate against gentlemen prisoners for their alleged crimes. Rebel militias ignored military culture entirely when they enacted summary judgment on their unfortunate Loyalist prisoners. That the system of parole and exchange survived at all is a testament to the faith people placed in such cultural conventions. Even with so many violations, there was no viable alternative except chaos.

For Loyalist gentlemen, the personal nature of the insults they experienced in captivity was a bitter consequence of their political death. Revolutionaries employed close confinement and even shackles to demonstrate the transformation of gentlemen into dishonored criminals. As will be explored in the next chapter, it was precisely the personalized nature of their mistreatment that encouraged Crown supporters, led by William Franklin and other aggrieved gentlemen, to seek vengeance.

3

Revenge

IN 1778 THE GENERAL Court of Massachusetts banished Edward Winslow, heir to one of the oldest families in Massachusetts. Less than a year later, the politically dead Loyalist returned to his homeland in command of a fleet of more than a dozen frigates, sloops, and schooners. Winslow's raiders plundered coastal communities, preyed on rebel farms, and carried off livestock and provisions from the Long Island Sound to Cape Cod. The Loyal Associated Refugees, as the group was known, broadcast their actions and justified their cause in several handbills, newspaper notices, and a long-winded pamphlet printed by James Rivington. They described the abuse, insults, imprisonment, confiscation, and other dishonors as a "long train of evils" that had "laid a foundation for the most justifiable revenge." "The sword is drawn," declared the Refugees; "we will never resign our claims but with our latest breath."[1] George Leonard, Winslow's childhood friend and captain of the flagship *Restoration,* enticed Loyalist recruits to join the refugees with promises of "profit and honour."[2] The predatory raids would turn the tables on the rebels and provide Loyalists a chance to take back stolen wealth and pride and to restore their independence as men. The Loyal Associated Refugees and scores of other groups like them believed they would reclaim their honor through vengeance.

Not every Loyalist agreed that Winslow and his men were on the honorable path. Loyalist spokesmen like the Anglican Reverends Samuel Seabury and Charles Inglis preached against the moral and spiritual dangers of vengeance. British commanders and some Loyalist officials feared that violent

{76}

reprisals would exacerbate the violence and prolong the conflict. Yet Edward Winslow and other hardliners like William Tryon and William Franklin were convinced that armed retaliation was the only way to restore the Loyalists' honor and their rightful place in the colonies.

The Loyalist debates on revenge, or what a prominent South Carolina Loyalist referred to as "retributive justice," reveal the striking tensions and contradictions within eighteenth-century concepts of masculinity, the legitimacy of violence, and the conflicting demands of honor culture, gentility, and Christian principles. On the one hand, within genteel culture, vengeance was regarded as a "savage," unchristian, and unmanning passion. Nevertheless, honor demanded that a gentleman respond appropriately to insults and abuse to "make oneself whole." The tension between what Bertram Wyatt-Brown called "primal honor," which valued strength and martial glory, and "genteel honor," which celebrated civility and refinement, can be seen throughout the revolutionary Atlantic. Anglo-Americans navigated these fluid conventions and drew on both sets of principles, no matter how paradoxical or hypocritical they might appear to modern observers.[3] Loyalist gentlemen were caught between competing notions of honor and manhood.

To make matters worse for the Loyalists, the revolutionary press interpreted every act of armed loyalism as an expression of criminal vengeance. Regardless of uniforms or British commissions, Patriots considered all Loyalists politically dead and dishonored members of their respective states who could not honorably bear arms for another country. As David Ramsay explained in 1789, Loyalists "were considered by the whig Americans as being cowards, who not only wanted [i.e., lacked] spirit to defend their constitutional rights, but who unnaturally co-operated with strangers in fixing the chains of foreign domination on themselves and on their countrymen."[4] By the end of the war, Loyalists had earned the reputation of America's most treacherous enemies. In 1783, "Civis," an anonymous contributor to the *Boston Evening-Post*, wrote that the greatest share of blame for the entire war belonged to the "the malignant tories, who were among ourselves." It was the Tories, argued Civis, who provided the bad counsel to the king and encouraged the British to punish the colonies. "How obstinate, how spiteful, how murderous, have these domestic incendiaries been!" They burned "homes, churches, publick buildings, and even whole villages" and committed "innumerable murders."[5] According to the revolutionary press, Tories butchered old women in their homes, led Indigenous warriors in frontier massacres, and provoked the enslaved to turn on their masters. Lust for vengeance transformed the Loyalist—morally, spiritually, and at times even racially—into the antithesis of the brave Patriot and the honorable white man. Whig propaganda argued that Loyalists were unnatural corruptions of Americans who were too incompetent or cowardly to fight with honor. As Thomas Paine wrote scathingly in 1776, though a Tory "may be cruel, never can [he] be brave."[6]

Loyalist deliberations on the morality of armed retaliation and Patriot accusations of bloody Tory vengeance again reveal both the pliancy of honor in eighteenth-century culture and its direct impact on the progress of the war. While some prominent Loyalists felt it was more prudent to allow the Crown to restore order, other Loyalist gentlemen embraced the cause of armed loyalism as honorable, manly resistance against oppression. Both sides in the conflict believed their actions were fully justified and blamed the other for initiating the deadly cycle of attacks on people and property. Yet the Loyalists were caught in an impossible position. If they stayed out of the conflict or retreated, their adversaries mocked them as cowards; if they won a victory, the press blackened their names as thieves and murderers. Armed loyalism intensified the ongoing Patriot campaign to dishonor the internal enemy and juxtapose revolutionary justice and humanity against Tory atrocity. In the Patriot press and imagination, politically dead but formerly respected gentlemen like James De Lancey, John Butler, William Franklin, and others became pirates and killers who abandoned the rules of civilized warfare. Despite their attempts to counter Patriot claims of Loyalist brutality, they became among the most intensely despised enemies of the American Revolution. The Whig press successfully discredited armed loyalism even in Whitehall, where parliamentarians called on British commanders to restrain the violence of the Crown's American supporters. Rather than restore their political life in American society, the actions of armed Loyalists only deepened their dishonor in the eyes of their fellow Americans.

The resoundingly successful propagandistic image of vengeful Tory monsters persisted for generations after the Revolution and colored the depiction of the Loyalists in both history and popular memory. Even the normally sympathetic Lorenzo Sabine, writing in the mid-nineteenth century, described the "horrid warfare" of "predatory bands" that "speak of Tory guilt . . . in tones, which will ring in the ears of men for centuries to come."[7] The early twentieth-century historian Claude Halstead Van Tyne, while also trying to be evenhanded, admitted that he could "understand why a Tory was 'a devil in human shape' in the eyes of the patriots." Van Tyne argued that the Loyalists engaged in "acts of war which especially aroused the hatred" of revolutionaries. While the British and those involved in "great campaigns . . . were regarded as honorable enemies . . . the men who harassed and worried the country by petty attacks came to be hated in the most virulent way."[8] Considering the volume of anti-Loyalist writings from the Revolution, historians could be forgiven for seeing the war through a Patriot lens.

With more immediate examples of insurgencies and asymmetrical wars in the latter half of the twentieth century, American historians began to see armed Loyalists in more nuanced shades. William H. Nelson and Robert M. Calhoon both dismissed the idea of the vicious Tory outlaw motivated only by personal gain and vendettas. Instead, the ranks of armed Loyalists contained everyone from localized "agrarian radicals," who fought against their Patriot landlords, to those who took up arms to preserve their vision of law and order, and, indeed, to those Loyalists who sought to "unleash terrible vengeance on the rebels." The guerrilla wars of the twentieth century demonstrated that partisan conflict "involves terror inflicted by informal bands of insurgents," and neither Loyalists nor Patriots could be singled out as more or less ruthless when both were caught up in the violence.[9] Likewise, John Shy argued that "there was little difference between Loyalists and rebels in terms of organization, tactics, or the use of terror." Even so, Shy writes that Loyalist militia units "regarded retribution as their principal function" and later referred to Loyalists as "bitter, angry people bent on vengeance."[10] Harry M. Ward's examination of the "banditti" in the American Revolution describes them as being composed of Loyalists who were, again, motivated primarily by "revenge and greed."[11] The evidence provided for ascribing such motivations solely to the Loyalists is thin and again reflects the stubborn longevity of the Tory stereotype born in the Patriot press. T. Cole Jones demonstrates that revolutionaries invoked revenge, the law of retaliation, and the principle of *lex talionis* perhaps even more often than the Loyalists.[12] Nonetheless, it was the Loyalists, in both history and memory, who acquired the reputation of bloodthirsty, vengeful killers.

Some Loyalists did advocate strongly for revenge against their enemies. Wolfgang Schivelbusch argues that the "instinct for revenge is as elementary as thirst or sexual desire," and Loyalist gentlemen, and their Patriot adversaries, shared this seemingly natural impulse. But even if they understood that "the law of retaliation" was something primal, it was also within a man's rights to reclaim his individual honor and restore the body politic with violence. James Simpson, a prominent Loyalist and former attorney general of South Carolina, wrote to Sir Henry Clinton in May 1780 that the Loyalists in his region were "resentful of their past Injuries, [and] . . . are clamourous [sic] for retributive Justice." Charles Stewart longed for "the day of retribution," and Joseph Galloway wished "every rebell [would] receive his deserts." John Blackburn relished the idea that Sir John Johnson would "have his Revenge," while the young Henry Nase, who had escaped impressment into the Continental Army and joined the King's American Legion, wrote that he looked "forward to that hastening period when the Law of Retaliation shall take place." In 1780, the Reverend Jacob Bailey articulated the value of the Loyalists' sentiments to Samuel Peters. "It is true private revenge without any view to redress and reform discovers [i.e., reveals] a faulty disposition," he wrote, "but a proper resentment upon certain occasions may be attended with public utility."[13]

Yet politically dead gentlemen had no way to respond effectively to being dishonored or driven from their homes by crowds and committees. There was rarely a single person to challenge, and there was no legal process for redress unless the British won the war. The Loyalists were therefore trapped in a kind of impotence that, according to eighteenth-century thought, might unhinge their rationality. Should the opportunity present itself, Loyalists also had to be wary of how they retaliated against their enemies. In the genteel culture of the eighteenth century, anger needed to be restrained.

True gentlemen did not lose their temper, regardless of the situation. Men of standing felt "resentment" at a slight or insult, which was, in the words of Nicole Eustace, "a quintessentially masculine form of anger both because of its association with reason . . . and because of its link to honor." Blind rage was thought to express the "animalistic, the criminal, the insane."[14] "The Instructor" who wrote to the *Pennsylvania Gazette* in 1754 argued that "Anger and Revenge, when once enter'd, are very powerful: And the rational Man must exert his whole Force of Reason in Combat with them or be overthrown."[15] Revenge was therefore only suited to the primitive world or the frontier, where there were no laws or authority. Dr. John Perkins of New England explained in 1765 that vengeance "must be condemned in a Christian Country," reminding readers that "revenge seems to be the Rod of Justice in the Hands of savage Nature to keep the People in Awe and afford the Subject some little Degree of Security."[16] Revenge was thus presented as both a racialized and degenerative passion that could transform even a decent gentleman into an irrational monster.

These ideas are reflected in the works of playwrights and novelists of the early modern period. Shakespeare's plays are filled with tragic scenes of brutal revenge that turn ostensibly moral people into their own antithesis. Hamlet's quest for vengeance spirals into tragedy; Coriolanus, the great Roman general, joins his former enemies to wage war on his own city. The list of Elizabethan and Jacobean revenge plays is long, and each one warns of the transformative effect of vengeance.[17] Although it was a topic considered by essayists and moralists of the eighteenth century, the genteel literary world did not focus much on vengeance. One notable exception is Edward Young's drama *The Revenge* (1721), wherein an enslaved Moor exacts a terrible vengeance on his Spanish master. Again, this presents revenge as a brutal impulse, where the vengeance-seeker is neither European nor Christian.[18] In the generation after the Revolution, revenge became a popular subject among the Romantic authors as they explored the human passions. Lord Byron's Venetian aristocrat, Alp, in *The Siege of Corinth* (1816) is a "fiery convert" to revenge, "a renegade" who forsakes his countrymen and joins the Ottoman Turks to destroy his own people, who slighted him. Magua, in James Fenimore Cooper's *The Last of the Mohicans* (1826), serves as a prime example of "savage" vengeance, and a later work, *Wacousta* (1832), by the Canadian author John Richardson, follows the same theme and tells the tale of an English aristocrat so consumed with his lust for revenge that he is physically transformed into a terrifying Indigenous warrior.[19] In eighteenth- and early nineteenth-century literature, revenge was something ancient, primal, and animalistic. It was practiced by the low-born thug or the foreign-born alien and was deeply unchristian. This body of literature, written throughout the English-speaking world, demonstrated that revenge brought no honor to a Christian gentleman but instead transformed him into his bestial opposite.

Though revenge might be an unmanning passion, elements of "primal honor" still played an important role in elite eighteenth-century masculinity, regardless of its seeming incompatibility with Christian principles and civility.[20] Indeed, some eighteenth-century thinkers observed a kind of vengeance that arose not from wrath but from masculine pride born from civilized society. This did not mean that prideful vengeance was excusable, but, because it was an outcome of competition within genteel ranks, it was perhaps less blamable than its bloodthirsty cousin. The duel, for example, was not a hot-blooded act of vengeance for an insult but a deliberate way to channel resentment and settle accounts. Samuel Johnson noted that rational men "who could have conquered their anger are unable to combat pride." Social pressures caused aggrieved men to "pursue offences to the extremity of vengeance, lest they should be insulted by the triumph of an enemy." Frank Henderson Stewart describes this as "reflexive honor," in which members of a group are compelled to defend or assert their right to respect and maintain their place in the hierarchy. Aspiring gentlemen had to balance competing notions of politeness and Christian teachings with the demands to defend their manhood. Bernard Mandeville neatly summed up the competing forces, writing that while "Religion commands you to leave all Revenge to God, Honour bids you trust your Revenge to no body but your self." Christianity, he asserted, was "built on Humility, and Honour Pride."[21]

These tropes and contradictions are reflected in the advice given to refugees in the Loyalist press and from the Anglican pulpit. In a sermon titled *A Discourse on Brotherly Love* (1777), the Anglican clergyman and Loyalist chaplain Samuel Seabury condemned the idea of revenge and compared it to "the impetuosity of mighty waters [which] will drive us headlong down its furious current; bearing away all the little remains of principle, overwhelming the feeble restraints of reason." Though the Loyalists had been badly abused, revenge would leave them "unsatisfied with any thing but the destruction" of their enemies. He advised his listeners and readers to reject the "inordinancy," the "lust," "the bitterness of malice and revenge" and follow "gentle, benign and humane propensities . . . [to promote] peace, unity, and concord among the brotherhood of men."[22] Charles Inglis, a fellow clergyman of the Church of England, echoed these statements and admitted that, although his flock had suffered dreadful persecution and loss at the hands of their adversaries, he did not want to "kindle Resentment" or "widen a Breach," "but to recommend Earnestness, Fortitude and Perseverance." "For they were not Enemies," he explained, "who occasioned those direful Scenes. They were Brethren and Fellow Subjects." Yet these Loyalist preachers were not pacifists. Both men encouraged loyal refugees to enlist in provincial regiments and extolled the virtues of Christian soldiers to defend the weak and preserve lawful authority. The restoration of a just peace, not revenge, was the object of war; healing, not vengeance, was every Christian's duty.[23] Not every Loyalist preacher agreed.

Simeon Baxter, a "Licentiate in Divinity" of the Church of England imprisoned in the Simsbury copper mine, composed a sermon to justify taking deadly revenge against the Continental Congress. Quoting from the story of Samson in the book of Judges, Baxter instructed his readers and listeners on the necessity of the "law of retaliation," which was a "law of nature." When asked why he slew the Philistines, Samson replied, "What they have done unto me, so have I done unto them." Samson, Moses, Samuel, and the other champions of Israel, according to Baxter, "never alleged the command of God for what they did, but defended themselves upon the plea of retaliation." Therefore, Baxter contended, the Loyalists were justified in taking revenge on Congress because "the doctrine of killing tyrants and their adherents is not murderous, but truly Christian." The times called for drastic measures, yet the Loyalists lacked heroes to carry out God's will. There was "no Moses, no Ehud, no Samuel . . . with a Patriotic dagger to do

84 DISHONORED AMERICANS

justice upon our tyrants." This may have been a veiled slight against many of the Loyalist elite who fled the scene of battle for the safety of England or New York, but the main reason, according to Baxter, was that men did not "truly understand the laws of God, nature, and civil society," nor did they realize the extent of the societal collapse around them. When "social liberty ceases, and natural liberty revives . . . every man is a soldier, a Moses, a Samson, and may, without incurring the guilt of murder, kill those uncircumcised Philistines." Baxter argued that Loyalist revenge aligned with Christian principles to defend the weak and absolved his listeners and readers from the dishonor of acts that society would consider cowardly or criminal under normal circumstances, "since we live in evil times." The vengeful preacher admonished men who were unwilling to "use secret practices" or to "kill their oppressor with a dagger in the dark." The cause of justice superseded all other concerns, including the idea that an honorable man should meet his enemies openly. "We have rights of civil society to restore; we have honour, virtue, and religion, to maintain," he wrote. "Let us therefore take the first prudent opportunity to revenge our wrongs."[24] Polite gentlemen needed to transform into avengers, or civilization itself would be lost.

No other Loyalist professed such extreme rhetoric in defense of armed retaliation, but as the conflict progressed, the calls for manly action and revenge printed in Loyalist newspapers increased. The works of Jonathan Odell, the Loyalists' most prolific poet, exhibit a hardening attitude as the conflict intensified. His "Song for St. George's Day," published as a broadside in the spring of 1777, cheered on loyal Britons and extolled them to let "Vengeance arm your Hands!" "Seize and Destroy!" the poet cries. At this early stage in the conflict, with New York firmly in British hands and with Crown forces mustering for an invasion of rebel territory from Canada, his calls for vengeance are more rhetorical flourish than sincere calls to action. Odell reminds his readers in the next stanza, "Let Pity melt in British Eyes / Let Mercy still be shown," and throughout, the song repeats, "But let not Havoc reign! / The Brave alone, in Triumph, know / Soft Pity's tender Pain."[25] Odell distances himself from the idea of unrestrained violence but admits to the necessity of revenge to engender a martial spirit. As a member of Parliament declared in the House of Commons in 1775, revenge was "unchristian . . . yet how rarely do we find the human soul possessed of a sublime heroism, without this alloy!"[26]

By 1779 Odell was less mollifying. Continental forces had defeated and captured Burgoyne's army, the British had abandoned Philadelphia, and the French had entered the war. All of this happened, according to many Loyalists, while Parliament and British commanders dithered. The British war plan also shifted from the North to the South, a move that left many Loyalists in New York questioning the wisdom of British leadership.[27] In "The Congratulation," Odell's bitterness and anger are clear as he exults in recent rebel and French losses. Hoping that the Loyalists might finally have their moment, Odell writes: "Myriads of swords are ready for the field / Myriads of lurking daggers are conceal'd / In injured bosoms, dark revenge is nurst [sic] / Yet but a moment, and the storm shall burst."[28] The call for restraint and pity from his previous writings is replaced by visions of swift justice. The Loyalist frustration with the war can also be seen in a fanciful script for a "Prologue to the Tragedy of the Revenge" printed in the *Royal Pennsylvania Gazette* in March 1778, just prior to the British evacuation in June. "Away with Grief," cries the narrator. "Our God shall be REVENGE."[29]

Loyalist gentlemen who spoke openly of revenge believed firmly that their reprisals were natural, legal, and divinely sanctioned, but they also consciously framed their sentiments in the language of restraint and justice. Edward Winslow's Loyal Associated Refugees declared that their actions were "warranted by the Laws of God and Man, to wage war against their inhuman Persecutors," but they assured readers that their retaliation would be "devoid of passion and resentment, and free from every unworthy or vindictive motive."[30] The New Jersey Loyalist Lieutenant James Moody took pains to refute the devilish reputation he had acquired as a successful partisan leader.[31] In his narrative, Moody describes an oath he supposedly required his men to take before they embarked on their missions. Renouncing malicious vengeance, they swore to respect property, to protect fellow Loyalists, and "in case of our taking any prisoners, I will endeavour to treat them as well as our situation will admit of."[32] The Maryland Loyalist Captain John Ferdinand Dalziel Smyth of the Queen's Rangers avowed that even considering the brutality he suffered, it "would be unworthy of the

British arms to retaliate cruelty, and it is far from my disposition to wish it."[33] Nevertheless, British and Loyalist officials deeply mistrusted armed refugee intent.

The prominent Loyalist Andrew Elliot of New York was among many who feared the potential bloodshed revenge could unleash. In early 1779, he advised British commanders that "it will be dangerous to use Refugees but as the Commander in Chief directs and to him alone they should look up." In other words, it was essential that British officers always have control of the Loyalists. If they were allowed to operate under their own commanders, it would "produce disagreeable consequences in times when revenge and necessity go hand in hand and England aims at conciliating more than conquering."[34] Most British officers agreed with Elliot, but hardline Loyalists resented the perceived timidity and inaction of British commanders. Loyalist gentlemen presented themselves as sensible, humane individuals who were attacked by heartless rebels for their loyalty and were now let down by British leaders. In any war, this idea of justifiable retaliation can quickly degenerate into a cycle of atrocities. Even George Washington admitted that while the "Obligation arising from the Rights of Humanity, and claims of Rank are universally binding," that obligation dissolved if enemy cruelty demanded retaliation.[35] As the Reverend Charles Inglis wrote in 1780, "Civil Wars are always more cruel and more barbarous than foreign Wars, and more destructive to Morals." In a war between neighbors and kin, he wrote, "personal Revenge and Animosity mingle and kindle up the soul to tenfold rage."[36]

British commanders wanted to avoid the brutality and destruction Inglis described. In 1775, General John Burgoyne explained to the House of Commons that he understood his duty was to deliver the "correction of the state," not indulge in the "impetuous impulse of passion and revenge." He did not anticipate a problem with achieving that goal, because "there is a certain charm in the very wanderings and dreams of liberty that disarms an Englishman's anger."[37] Burgoyne's tone of a "generous enemy" may have appealed to a British audience eager to restore peace and commerce, but this gentle spirit was not what many Loyalists in America hoped for in their British commanders.

By 1778, Loyalists in and around New York City had split into two loose factions: moderates, who hoped for reconciliation, and hardliners, who wanted the British to crush the Revolution and punish the rebels.[38] Hardliners openly resented the British strategy. James Parker lambasted William and Richard Howe as the "fatal brothers" who, through their inaction, "brought many of the best [Loyalists] . . . to destruction & death."[39] Joseph Stansbury, a prolific Loyalist penman, attacked General Henry Clinton for his lethargic response to rebel expeditions in 1779. "For revenge let the Loyalists bellow," declares Stansbury's fictionalized general: "I swear I'll not do more / To keep them in humour / Than to play on my violoncello."[40] William Franklin held a similar view and wrote that "many of the Loyalists in America think they have Reason to complain not only of Slights and Inattentions, but of Ill-usage, from those who ought to have favoured and encouraged" the friends of lawful government. After his release from imprisonment in Connecticut, William Franklin became the leader of the hardline Loyalist faction in New York. Franklin, along with Governor William Tryon and others, advocated violent and sustained attacks on rebel-held territory to force Congress to a negotiated settlement. Sir Henry Clinton, the British forces' overall commander from 1778 to 1782, initially refused to consider Loyalist plans for intensifying the conflict, fearing that they would lead to "a system of war horrid beyond conception."[41] Despite Clinton's misgivings, the British defeat at Saratoga—and especially the French entry into the conflict—compelled the British to deploy every man they could get.[42] The conciliatory attitude of British commanders had worn off and was replaced with a greater willingness to use the Loyalists and engage in what Major Patrick Ferguson described as a "degree of severity, which would not have been justifyable [sic] at the beginning."[43] The emergence of determined armed Loyalist hardliners after 1778 transformed the American Revolution into an even bloodier internecine conflict and provoked a furious reaction in the revolutionary press that shaped the Loyalists' infamous place in American memory.

All warfare is communication through violence,[44] but Loyalists had little control of their intended message beyond the battlefield. In any modern conflict, media spin accentuates one side's virtues and condemns the enemy's cruelty or mocks its ineptitude. The campaign to dishonor

Crown supporters intensified with the rise of armed Loyalist resistance, and the dominance of the revolutionary press in most of America during the conflict ensured that this version of events prevailed. Patriot reports built on existing tropes of Loyalist dishonor and vacillated between tales of pitiful Tory incompetence and murderous banditry. This marked the final stage of political death for many patrician Loyalists who took up arms or held government positions. The revolutionary press crafted a Tory monster: a former gentleman unhinged and transformed by vengeance into a pirate or a barbarian. Loyalists, of course, deeply resented such characterizations, but there was little they could do to combat the accusations. Tales of bloody Tory violence provided powerful grounds for Patriot retaliation and caused the conflict to degenerate into what Charles Royster refers to as a "vendetta war."[45] Such tales also confirmed the deep misgivings of British commanders who feared unleashing Loyalist vengeance.

Loyalists underwent almost supernatural metamorphoses in the Patriot imagination. Lieutenant Colonel Thomas Brown, the principal villain in David Ramsay's 1785 history of South Carolina, purportedly transformed from an English gentleman, newly arrived in the colonies, into a physically and morally disfigured enemy to liberty who tormented civilians, hanged "beardless youth," and handed his prisoners off to be tortured by his "Indian" allies. In 1811, Hugh McCall presented a similar picture of Brown's cruelty, writing that the Loyalist's "feelings had long been banished from his remorseless bosom, and their place inhabited by a fiend of darkness." Nineteenth-century American novelists and historians could not imagine a rational cause for Tories like Brown who "gloated in revenge."[46] Just like witches, the internal enemy of the seventeenth century, the Loyalists of the American Revolution were imbued with an evil that could only have come from the devil.

According to the Patriot press, Loyalists' treachery stemmed from their weakness. In the first two years of the conflict, revolutionary newspapers depicted Loyalists as laughably ineffective and poorly led. Far from being a military threat, the Loyalists who fled to the British in 1775 and 1776 were noted only for their insignificance. The *Connecticut Gazette* reveled in the fact that "the Refugee Tories are taken but little Notice of by either Party," while another publication described the Loyalists "as sheep in the fold"

REVENGE 89

who forced the British to "listen to their lamb-like bleatings."[47] Similarly, the Loyalists who flocked to New York City after its capture were equally derided as "poor Devils . . . wandering about the city like lost sheep."[48] The Loyalists blindly followed their masters, were easily corralled, and were too impotent to change their circumstances.

Such passive or impotent traits correlated with popular stereotypes of enslaved African Americans and other minorities. A Connecticut newspaper ridiculed the "Loyal Fencible Americans" of Worcester, Massachusetts, formed in late 1775, for consisting of "some *head tories,* a few negroes, and some Scotch Rebels and Convicts." Virginia's Loyalist forces were described as "the poorest, miserable wretches" of the region and consisted of "black companies" led by "Scotch Tories."[49] The recurring refrain that Loyalists were all either of Scottish or African descent was a way for the Anglo-Protestant majority to malign the Tories as a mongrel or subhuman threat. The Scottish "rebels and convicts" reported in the newspapers invoked visions of furious, primitive Highlanders who fought to restore a hated Catholic king. Anti-Scottish sentiment was already a factor in Virginia, since Norfolk's powerful Scottish merchant elite held the Tidewater planters in its debt.[50] The repeated references to African American recruits in the Loyalist ranks pointed to the allegedly lowly status of most Crown supporters as well, but even more importantly, they highlighted the possibility of insurrection. Virginia Governor Lord Dunmore's proclamation of November 1775 promised freedom to those enslaved by Patriot masters if they fought for the British, a policy that earned the Scottish lord the moniker of "Negro Thief of Virginia."[51] The *Pennsylvania Evening Post* expressed horror at Dunmore's "cruel declaration" and within a week reported that roving bands of escaped slaves were taking revenge, with British blessing, on the families and property of white gentlemen. A group of fugitives allegedly attacked the home of Benjamin Wells, for example, where they "pillaged every thing valuable, such as bedding, wearing apparel, liquors . . . and carried off two Negro girls."[52] Such scenes horrified white Americans and, as Woody Holton argues, Dunmore's willingness to employ formerly enslaved and supposedly vengeful Black soldiers in Britain's cause pushed many moderate Virginians to side with the rebels. That Dunmore organized the Black volunteers into his "Ethiopian regiment," with uniforms emblazoned with the phrase

"Liberty to Slaves," helped transform colonial resistance in Virginia into an open rebellion with the underpinnings of a race war.[53]

As alarming as the prospect of a British-directed slave uprising might have been, widely publicized victories against motley bands of Tories, Scottish Highlanders, and African American allies at Great Bridge in Virginia on December 9, 1775, and at Moore's Creek Bridge in North Carolina on February 27, 1776, gave confidence to revolutionary forces. Both encounters involved ill-advised attacks across bridges against entrenched rebels. Reports characterized the Loyalist forces as little more than doltish cannon fodder for Britain. The Virginian commander at Great Bridge referred to the white Loyalists as "cattle," and the *Pennsylvania Ledger* reported that the victors shackled the "the worst of the tories" to enslaved men. Many of the Loyalists were considered too weak to be threatening, and a Patriot fighter noted that the "most stupid kind we discharge."[54] Revolutionary newspapers described the Scottish Loyalists defeated at Moore's Creek Bridge in much the same way. The Highlanders revealed their dim-witted brutality by charging across the bridge in "the most furious manner," and they were easily shot down by the Patriots, who "behaved with the spirit and intrepidity becoming freemen, contending for their dearest privileges."[55] The Loyalists at both Great Bridge and Moore's Creek Bridge were too incompetent to fear.

It took the Crown until late 1777 to see the logic of enlisting Loyalists to serve in properly trained and equipped provincial regiments, but British commanders were underwhelmed by the number of volunteers. Historian Paul H. Smith explains the disappointing turnout by suggesting that many Loyalists had already become disillusioned by the failure of British forces to protect loyal subjects. Perhaps, too, Smith argues, the "typical American Loyalist" was "conservative, cautious, abhorring violence" and was therefore "disinclined to commit himself boldly." Rather, he was content to leave the fighting to the British army.[56] Wallace Brown also sees "timidity and equivocation" as particular Loyalist traits. He points out that in the early years of the conflict, Crown spokesmen advised loyal subjects to remain passive and take no part in the struggle, only later to have British officials bemoan the Loyalists' lack of fighting spirit and unwillingness to enlist.[57]

The Loyalists saw things quite differently and blamed the British commanders' idleness and poor decisions for letting victory slip away. Loyalist gentlemen also resented how few opportunities there were to serve as officers. George Leonard wrote that so many Loyalists came from "a rank in life superior to the class from which the common seaman and soldier is taken" that many were unable to find suitable appointments and instead turned to privateering.[58]

Once British commanders began to take Loyalist regiments more seriously, they offered generous terms for enlistments that included the same pensions and gratuity for wounded officers that the British received. Nevertheless, Loyalist units continued to face considerable problems from what Paul Smith termed a "catalogue of inconsistencies." Loyalists in different regiments received wildly different signing bonuses, causing resentment and confusion, and Loyalist officers chafed at their junior status and lack of respect compared with their British counterparts. Despite these difficulties, by the end of the conflict the new policies produced several respectable Loyalist regiments with both Loyalist and British officers, such as the Queen's Rangers under John Graves Simcoe and the British Legion under Banastre Tarleton.[59]

The Loyalist press hailed such provincial regiments as agents of justice and retribution. In April 1778, the *Royal Pennsylvania Gazette* recorded with satisfaction that "the loyal refugees, who had formerly felt the effects of [the rebels'] lawless power . . . now rejoice to bring the culprits to justice." Describing acts of Loyalist resistance, the article details how the heroic Queen's Rangers surprised and defeated a party of rebel marauders harassing the New Jersey countryside, for which the grateful "inhabitants from all quarters flocked to them" to sell their goods to the Loyalists.[60] Likewise, the *New York Gazette* reported that a combined Loyalist force under John Graves Simcoe, Banastre Tarleton, and Oliver De Lancey surprised a band of rebels and "so briskly charged, that many of [the Continentals] forgot their Arms . . . and fled." Adding a comical nod to rebel cowardliness and bumbling, the newspaper recorded that the Patriot "Colonel . . . scamper[ed] off without his Breeches or Boots."[61] Such propaganda pieces were intended to show that the Loyalists could retaliate with honor in an organized and directed fashion.

92   DISHONORED AMERICANS

The Patriot press depicted Loyalist victories as terrible crimes, and specific Loyalist units and their officers became recurring villains in rebel reports. James De Lancey, the son of General Oliver De Lancey and leader of the Corps of Loyalist Westchester Refugees—or "De Lancey's Cowboys," as they were more popularly known—chafed at the dishonor Patriots attached to his name. He and his men operated in the murky area inhabited by both freebooters and uniformed combatants known as the "Neutral Ground" surrounding New York City. The region swarmed with foraging parties, guerrilla fighters, and simple outlaws who ravaged farms and houses. Both the British and Continental armies employed private bands that specialized in raiding and stealing cattle from the enemy. Though this was hardly honorable, it was a tactical necessity that both wounded the enemy's ability to wage war and fed friendly troops.[62] De Lancey, however, complained to Guy Carleton in 1783 that his men were unfairly blamed for all the abuses in the area. He fumed that even some of his fellow Loyalists "secretly endeavour to prejudice him" by blaming "every Irregularity committed . . . [on] the Refugees under his Command tho' most of [the crimes] have originated from other People who have no Connection with that Corp."[63]

As would be expected, Loyalist and Patriot newspapers spun the exploits of De Lancey's Cowboys in entirely opposite directions. In the spring of 1780, the Loyalist *New York Gazette* reported that a "successful incursion" by "Col. De Lancey" and "his loyal Band of Refugees" killed ten rebels and took thirty-seven prisoners along with "Trophies, consisting . . . of over one hundred Head of Cattle." The loyal band unfortunately lost "a brave Officer, Captain Fowler," who was shot from a nearby house, a cowardly act that "occasioned a severe Retribution—The House was immediately consumed to Ashes."[64] While the Loyalist press recorded this skirmish as a clean victory, the *Connecticut Gazette* described the same event as a "descent" by the "enemy's plunderers, commanded by Col. Delancey" who "did their King, not their country service, by burning two houses, in one of which was an old deaf woman who [*sic*] they let expire in the flames, and murdering five of the militia."[65] Interviews recorded with surviving witnesses in the early nineteenth century paint a different picture. De Lancey and his officers purportedly did their best to restrain their men, punish transgressions, and conduct their missions within acceptable limits of wartime behavior. Historian Catherine Crary judges that De Lancey's Cowboys, acting under British orders to carry out forage missions and other raids, did not deserve the reputations that history heaped upon them.[66]

Revolutionary efforts to recast Loyalist success as ruthless Tory vengeance were strikingly effective. This phenomenon can best be seen in the aftermath of the Loyalist victory at the Battle of Waxhaws in South Carolina on May 29, 1780. Around 150 Loyalist cavalry of the British Legion under Lieutenant Colonel Banastre Tarleton caught Colonel Abraham Buford's 400 Continental regulars and militiamen in the open. Even at such a disadvantage, Buford refused to surrender, and Tarleton's force charged. At ten yards the Continentals fired a volley that killed several officers and dozens of horses, but the Loyalists broke the Patriot line. Tarleton recorded years later that his men then attacked the rebels with "a vindictive asperity not easily restrained," killing 112 and badly wounding another 150.[67] The Loyalists lost only 5 men. The *New York Gazette* printed Tarleton's brief account of the clash, in which he trumpeted his victory and declared that his men "had attacked and cut them to Pieces." According to Tarleton, this engagement, combined with the British victory at Camden, convinced the backcountry militias to join the royal forces.[68] In fact, the effect was quite the opposite.

The Battle of Waxhaws became a tale of vengeful Tories murdering surrendered Patriots. The story spread quickly by word of mouth and became the accepted version of events until the twenty-first century. Writing in 1785, David Ramsay noted how this "barbarous massacre gave a more sanguinary turn to the war." More impassioned than ever, Patriots were fired by a "spirit of revenge [which] gave a keener edge to military resentments."[69] "Tarleton's Quarter" became a battle cry and the justification for brutal rebel reprisals on Loyalists. At the Battle of King's Mountain, for example, Patriots fired on several white flags from the surrounded Loyalists and executed numerous prisoners. This was but one instance in the cycle of revenge and reprisals in the southern theater's civil war.[70] According to Jim Piecuch, the Battle of Waxhaws was a lopsided Loyalist victory, but it was not a massacre. Nor did the Loyalists breach the rules of war. Regardless, revolutionaries managed to turn their resounding defeat into a moral victory that justified further acts of Patriot retaliation. The success of this narrative undid the fleeting morale boost provided by the Loyalist victory and severely hampered the British war effort in the South.[71]

The most hated Loyalists were those who crossed the racial line to fight alongside, and allegedly incite, Indigenous warriors on the frontier. Loyalists, Indian agents, and Britain's Indigenous allies understood a rebel frontiersman to be anything but a civilized and honorable foe. Yet, as with all acts of armed loyalism, the Patriot media controlled the narrative during the war and framed rebel violence as just retaliation for "Tory and Indian" atrocity. Some Loyalist writers defended or even applauded the Haudenosaunee and Anishinaabe ways of war, and other Loyalists, like the reviled Walter Butler, lamented the damage done to their reputations in the bitter conflict.

The Loyalist alliance with Haudenosaunee, Lenape, Wyandot, and other nations provided potent fuel for Patriot charges of Loyalist dishonor. Loyalists such as the Indian agent and interpreter Simon Girty stand out in American memory as "double traitors who had forsaken both their country and their race."[72] Whereas in previous conflicts the threat of Indigenous resistance to European encroachment served as a racially unifying force for religiously and ethnically diverse settlers, the Loyalist alliance added a new and terrifying element to the American understanding of frontier violence. Loyalists were purportedly masters of disguise who transformed at will to blend in with their settler kin or lay in ambush with their Indian allies. Like their counterparts on the East Coast, frontier Loyalists were presumed to be engaged in a great conspiracy to defeat the rebellion and massacre innocents in the process. According to reports, Tories roamed the backcountry with "the Indians" or lurked as fifth columnists in settler forts. Frontier Loyalists "fired up the Indians" to kindle "a spirit of hostility against us," reported the *Connecticut Courant*.[73]

The Battle of Wyoming stands out as another one-sided Loyalist victory that became a massacre in Patriot media. On July 3, 1778, Colonel John Butler, with around one hundred rangers, and Chief Cornplanter (Kayéthwahkeh), at the head of several hundred Seneca, Cayuga, and

Onondaga warriors, took positions outside Forty Fort in northern Pennsylvania. Colonel Zebulon Butler, a cousin of the Loyalist Butler, unwisely marched his mostly untrained militia out to meet the enemy, and in the ensuing firefight the Patriot militia panicked and became easy targets for their enemies. The combined Loyalist and Haudenosaunee force killed more than three hundred militiamen in the rout. A letter from Obadiah Gore Jr., who was away serving in the Continental Army during the devastating loss, described the effect of the raid on his family and the tight-knit community: "I lost three [of my] own brothers . . . and two brothers in law . . . our families were all driven out from this settlement. . . . Our buildings all burnt and our household furniture and clothing all carried away or destroyed."[74] Though the Loyalists and Haudenosaunee warriors only killed combatants, news quickly spread that Tories and Indians slaughtered both surrendered militiamen and civilians.

Published accounts of the battle suggested that the perpetrators were in fact "supposed to consist of Tories chiefly," and another article declared that most of the raiders were actually "Tories, painted like [Indians]" and that only the officers were dressed in European uniforms. According to the same reports, the Loyalists ambushed the Patriot militia after luring them from the fort under a flag of truce. Like the British Legion at Waxhaws, the treacherous Loyalists violated the conventions of civilized warfare. The article claimed that John Butler, in a final act of horrible savagery, ordered his men to take what captives they could "and shutting up the rest in the houses, set fire to them and they were all consumed together." This was a complete fabrication but helped encourage readers to search for some "speedy and effectual measures . . . to punish and extirpate these monsters in human shape" who betrayed their own families and their race out of vengeance.[75]

The allegations that the Loyalists and Haudenosaunee warriors murdered civilians in cold blood had profoundly violent consequences. In October, Patriot forces attacked and burned several Haudenosaunee villages in northern New York. News circulated among Loyalists and the Haudenosaunee that rebel soldiers, in their own quest for vengeance, murdered children found hiding in a cornfield at the village Onoquaga.[76] This, like other rebel atrocities committed against the Indigenous nations, was never reported in the newspapers. In retaliation, John Butler's son Walter and the Mohawk leader Joseph Brant (Tyendinaga) descended on Cherry Valley, New York, in November of the same year. Seneca and Mohawk warriors and, as some alleged, Loyalist rangers killed thirty-two civilians in the attack.[77] Published reports provided macabre details of the "inhuman barbarities"—scalping, decapitation, and dismemberment—committed against defenseless civilians.[78]

Reports of the massacre at Cherry Valley fired revolutionary resentment but also caused deep concern among British commanders and policy makers. Edmund Burke and William Pitt both delivered scathing speeches in Parliament deploring the use of Indigenous allies against the rebels.[79] The Swiss-born governor of Quebec, Sir Frederick Haldimand, knew the importance of these alliances and the effectiveness of the raids, but he reproached Colonel John Butler after the incident at Cherry Valley for "such indiscriminate vengeance," which was "useless and disreputable . . . as it is contrary to the dispositions and maxims of the King."[80] On previous missions Haldimand had stressed the need for restraint. Writing to Colonel John Peters in 1778, Haldimand advised keeping the number of warriors to a minimum and "to take special care that proper persons of your appointing . . . shall accompany them upon all occasions in order to prevent entirely all acts of cruelty or Inhumanity."[81]

Captain Walter Butler, the commanding Loyalist officer at Cherry Valley, took most of the blame. Guy Carleton once described Butler as a "pretty genteel man," but his name was now synonymous with one of the most publicized atrocities of the war.[82] Butler denied responsibility for the massacre in a letter to General Philip Schuyler published in newspapers, instead placing the blame on the rebels for provoking his Haudenosaunee allies: "I have done every thing in my power to restrain the Indians in their fury, from hurting women and children, or killing the prisoners who fell into our hands, and would have more effectually prevented them, but they were much enraged by the late destruction of their village Onohoghguago [Onoquaga] by your people." For Butler, the atrocities were explained by a longer history of outrages committed by the revolutionaries. Nevertheless, Butler assured the Continental general that he would continue to try to check his allies, as it was "beneath the character of a soldier, to wage war on women and children." Yet immediately following that statement, Butler invoked the threat of indiscriminate retaliation. "[B]e assured," concluded Butler, "that if you persevere in detaining my father's family with you, that we shall no longer take the same pains, in restraining the Indians from making prisoners of women and children."[83] Butler wanted to have it both ways: to continue to be respected as an honorable officer and gentleman and to preserve his most effective threat and weapon.

Butler adopted a more remorseful tone when he encountered the gentlewoman Hannah Lawrence Schieffelin on her journey through Canada in 1780. He explained "with horror and regret" that "his most strenuous exertions were ineffectual to restrain the fury of the Savages, and that he had more than once [had] tomahawks raised over his own head in attempting to rescue their destined victims." As in his letter to General Schuyler, Butler blamed Patriot atrocities for firing the warriors' zeal. In particular, he noted the genocidal rhetoric of the revolutionaries who "threatened to exterminate" the whole "race of Indians" if they did not return to their villages. He also blamed his rival Joseph Brant for the massacre, making a racially charged accusation that the Mohawk leader "was infected with the contagious spirit of cruelty and guilty of actions that redound to his dishonour." Schieffelin seemed to accept Butler's version of events but was aghast at frontier violence "destined to dishonour the British cause by the most barbarous violations of faith and humanity."[84] In November 1781 the *New Jersey Gazette* reported with grim satisfaction that "Captain Walter Butler and eight others were killed and scalped" by Oneida warriors allied with the revolutionaries.[85]

Despite the repeated charges of atrocities in the Patriot newspapers, frontier Loyalists continued to support their Indigenous allies against the rebels and, like Walter Butler, defended their reputations and actions. To them, Patriot charges smacked of hypocrisy. Rebel frontiersmen committed atrocities against noncombatants, took scalps, and reportedly even skinned slain Indigenous warriors to make grisly souvenirs. Congress also did its best to court alliances with the Indigenous peoples on the frontier, and they were occasionally successful. The Oneida threw their support behind

98 DISHONORED AMERICANS

Congress, a decision that sparked a civil war within the Six Nations.[86] Indeed, the Virginia Loyalist James Parker, incensed at the inactivity of British generals in New York, applauded "the example of Butler and Brant" and suggested that the regular British army would do well to "try a little irregularity."[87] Simply put, the raids were effective; they damaged Patriot morale and deprived the enemy of valuable materiel.[88] The correspondence between officers in the field and Daniel Claus, the deputy Indian agent for the Six Nations, testifies to this fact. Just one raid in 1778 on German Flatts destroyed the rebel granary and the winter's supply of beef for the entire garrison. Such raids, wrote the Loyalist agent, "must be severely felt by the Rebel Army."[89]

Peter Oliver, the affluent Massachusetts Loyalist, also defended the Indigenous style of warfare in his *Origin and Progress of the American Rebellion* (1781). "It is true," he wrote, "he [an Indigenous warrior] doth not discover what is called english [*sic*] Courage, of standing undaunted in the open field to be shot at." Rather, "an Indian prefers the Mode of fighting behind a Tree, or skulking in Bushes." Yet, according to Oliver, the "Indian can undergo the most excruciating Torture, without a Groan." As for scalping, Oliver wryly observed that "taking the scalp off a dead Man . . . will not give any great Pain" and reminded his readers that the New England militia had scalped fallen redcoats at Lexington, another insinuation that the Patriots, not the Loyalists or their allies, began the cycle of violence. Oliver dismissed the criticisms poured out against the Native warriors by asserting that "every Nation has something peculiar in its Mode of War," and furthermore, "the Definition of Courage is Arbitrary."[90] Oliver grasped honor's essential pliability in a way that most of his contemporaries could not.

Stories of Tarleton and his vengeful Tory cavalry, or of Butler and his rangers, stand out in historical memory, but the revolutionary press devoted far more ink to covering the depredations of Loyalist irregulars and privateers who allegedly indulged their appetites for plunder and revenge. The Marquis de Chastellux reflected popular opinion when he described the British army as a "hurricane which destroyed every thing in its passage" but "was followed by a scourge yet more terrible, a numerous rabble, under the title of *Refugees* and *Loyalists* [who] followed the army, not to assist in the field, but to partake of the plunder."[91] This reputation followed the Loyalists throughout the war. New York governor William Tryon's devastating raids on the Connecticut coast in July 1779 were conducted mostly by British regulars, but newspaper reports blamed Loyalist irregulars for the worst carnage. The *Connecticut Courant* called Tryon "the Tories kind protector" and erroneously reported that the governor was at the head of "three thousand Refugees and Tories." The prospect of an army of vengeful plunderers led by "a detestable salamander" sent by "the vice regent Satan" was terrifying for coastal communities.[92]

In reports of the British destruction of Fairfield, Patriots accused Loyalists of indiscriminate violence. Priscilla Lothrop Burr wrote that her sister fell victim to Tory raiders even though Governor Tryon had personally provided her with a protection document. Loyalist militants "Damned her and tore [Tryon's protection] to pieces in her hand, and instantly set fire to the house & swore that if she offered to put it out they would Stab her to the heart." Burr noted, too, that "our Tories were treated with no more respect" by the Loyalist raiders, who "abused old Mrs. Rowland very much, Draged her about by the hair of her head, tore her cloaths of[f], and swore they would kill her."[93] Similar reports of such senseless violence filled revolutionary newspapers in the weeks after the raids, prompting a sharp reaction in both America and Britain. The British commander-in-chief Sir Henry Clinton worried that such depredations would cast him as a dishonorable "buccaneer," and he eventually relieved Tryon of command.[94]

Despite Clinton's misgivings about buccaneering, thousands of Loyalists did in fact finance or personally join in privateering expeditions, though they were usually small-scale affairs that targeted rebel shipping. Refugees in New York regarded privateering as one of the only ways to earn a living, restore their personal honor, and, because opportunities in the British military were limited, strike back at the rebels. Loyalist captain George Leonard advertised that privateering was "an undertaking where profit and honour are inseparably blended." Thousands of refugees and British soldiers crowded New York City; everything from housing to firewood was thus in short supply and could be ruinously expensive. Adding to the hardships was

Parliament's Prohibitory Act, which, until October 1778, barred all trade with the rebellious colonies, and this included New York and its Loyalist merchants.[95]

Evert Bancker Jr., the head of one of the most prominent merchant families in New York City and a former government contractor, lost much of his estate to the rebels, while British soldiers pilfered what he had left.[96] Once the Crown lifted the prohibitions against shipping from the city in October 1778, Bancker and many like him began to fit out and bankroll privateering vessels, while the rank and file risked their lives in the crew. John Porteous, a Loyalist merchant, converted his firm's trading ship *Elegante* into the fittingly rechristened privateer *Vengeance,* and a group of Loyalist women even bankrolled *The Fair American.* The *Royal Gazette* celebrated this last vessel as an example of how the "insolence and obstinacy" of the rebels served to "excite the indignation of the Fair Sex."[97] Privateering was an opportunity open to all Loyalists.

A captured prize could both restore a gentleman's finances and elevate his status. The Connecticut refugee Joel Stone recorded that having "expended all my money [and] . . . run considerable in the debt of my friends . . . determined me to venture on the hazardous practice of privateering." Stone served aboard at least two ships as a "captain of marines" beginning in January 1779. Although shipwrecked once, by the end of his brief seven-month career as a privateer he had acquired "a sum not only sufficient to discharge the chief of my accumulated debt but also to enable me by the aid of my friends to resume my former employ in the mercantile [*sic*] business and hire a convenient store for the purpose in the city of New York." His privateering activities provided him with the means to earn a less hazardous living, earned him respect among the other New York merchants, and led to his marriage to "a young woman of a good family." No longer destitute, he became a captain in the New York militia and the head of a household and a business.[98] Privateering was his path to credit and honor.

As a result of such success stories, privateering became one of the chief pursuits of New York's Loyalists, but it also came with significant risks. Loyalist ships might be captured or destroyed or could come home empty-handed with no return on investment. "[R]eturning without a prize," wrote one privateering agent, "was almost equivalent to a total loss of the

Vessel."[99] But if the risk was great, so was the potential reward. James Simpson explained that the prizes from a single cruise could enable adventurers "not only to emerge from Indigence and obscurity, but to rise to a great degree of opulence."[100]

As with any action undertaken by armed Loyalists, the Patriot newspapers branded refugee privateers cutthroats and thieves. Baltimore's *American Journal* described Loyalist privateers as "piratical villains, called refugees," while another Whig publication despaired that the Loyalists' "small piratical fleet . . . a force which ought to be *despised,* [could] harass and perplex our Eastern seas."[101] Patriot newspapers published alarming reports of coordinated attacks on island communities in the Long Island Sound and on the Massachusetts coast. In 1779, George Leonard's "invincible tory armada" attacked Nonamesset Island, Nantucket, and Martha's Vineyard. The "Royal Sheep-stealers . . . pretended to act under commission from the Commander in Chief of the British forces," but the article alleged that the marauders raided without authority and sought only revenge and plunder. When vengeful Tory raiders landed at a farm on Nonamesset, they reportedly "threatened to kill the family that lived there, because the d—d rebels had been killing them." The Loyalists stole everything they could find, even "some chalk and old grindstones," and killed the cattle they could not take away. To highlight the depth of the raiders' betrayal, the lengthy article included the names of Loyalists spotted in the band and their local origins: "a Foster, belonging to Plymouth; one Uphan . . . of Brookfield . . . a Slocum, and two Sissons of Newport," and so on.[102] These were not alien Hessians or redcoats but their own sons and cousins. Such attacks continued, with the *Providence Gazette* reporting a similar scene of "between 50 and 60 Refugees" who plundered the isolated community on Fishers Island in the Long Island Sound.[103] The raids persisted until the very end of the conflict, with the last refugee privateers reported in March 1783, long after the provisional peace of November 1782.[104] To the readers of the Whig newspapers, the vengeful Loyalists would simply not give up.

Of all the armed refugees and privateers, none were as infamous as the Board of Associated Loyalists, commanded by William Franklin. Formed in 1781, the Associated Loyalists claimed they would provide "comfort to those now suffering under the iron [rod] of rebel oppression," find "the means of procuring a comfortable support, instead of becoming a useless burthen to government," and "make the enemy feel the just vengeance due to such enormities" the Loyalists had suffered.[105] In early 1782, New Jersey militiamen killed an Associated Loyalist named Philip White. The Loyalists claimed this was yet another summary execution, while the Patriots reported that they killed White when he attempted to escape. Frustrated at British commanders' refusal to act and reeling from the surrender at Yorktown months earlier, Richard Lippincott, a Loyalist captain, sailed to Patriot-held New Jersey with a rebel prisoner named Joshua Huddy, made a landing, and hanged him. Lippincott affixed a note to the hanging corpse that declared the Loyalists would not "suffer without taking vengeance for the numerous cruelties" and "further determine to hang man for man as long as a refugee is left existing." The note concluded with the terse yet chilling declaration: "Up goes HUDDY for PHILIP WHITE."[106]

This brutal act of vengeance is infamous in the history of the American Revolution, but it was not unique. In 1779, the Loyalist partisan Richard Smith left a similar note on the corpse of New York militiaman John Clarke near Goshen, New York. Smith shot and killed Clarke in retaliation for the execution of his father, Claudius Smith, another infamous Tory raider. Smith's note declared that "we are determined to hang six for one, for the blood of the innocent cries aloud for vengeance."[107] For Richard Smith and Richard Lippincott, the grisly act of pinning notes to their victims was an attempt to both settle accounts and clearly communicate with their enemy. The Loyalists did not seek random vengeance but retaliated on specific rebels. Affixing notes to corpses provided terrifying proof of the refugees' sincerity. Though some Loyalists considered this a cruel necessity, other Loyalists regarded such actions as criminal banditry that dishonored their cause.

When news of Huddy's execution reached Washington, he personally demanded that Clinton turn over the Loyalists responsible, or "a British Officer of equal Rank must atone for the Death of the unfortunate Huddy."[108] When Clinton refused, Washington ordered the execution of Captain Charles Asgill, a young British officer selected by lot from among the prisoners. This sparked a furious controversy, and Congress eventually abandoned the proposed retaliation after the French foreign minister intervened on the captain's behalf. Histories of the "Asgill Affair," with its transatlantic cast of well-known characters, often overshadow the response from British commanders who were also furious at the Associated Loyalists. Clinton ordered an investigation and had Lippincott arrested and put on trial, though it was commonly believed that Franklin had ordered the killing.[109]

Richard Lippincott made his court-martial as much a debate on the hard-line Loyalists' philosophy of retaliation as it was a trial for the murder of Joshua Huddy. In Lippincott's opening statement, he presented himself as one victim among many, one who had "long since been proscribed and attainted by the Rebels" and now served as a volunteer "without pay & without Rank" against "His Majesty's Enemies on unequal conditions." The accused defended his role in the execution of Huddy on two grounds. He argued first that the Associated Loyalists executed Huddy not from "enmity towards him as a Man" but rather as an act of self-defense against rebel persecution. Since "Huddy . . . had himself executed several Loyalists," he was "the fittest object for Retaliation." Secondly, Lippincott argued that he had adhered to the Associated Loyalists' declaration to take "just Vengeance" against the rebels and that he was following the verbal command of William Franklin. His arguments evidently persuaded members of the court-martial, who found Lippincott not guilty of Huddy's murder. Nonetheless, the execution of Huddy destroyed Franklin's reputation among British commanders. He was never officially punished for his role, but according to his biographer Sheila Skemp, the controversy "did more to ruin Franklin's name than anything he ever did."[110]

The debate over the honor and justice of this act of vengeance caused an irreparable rift between the Loyalists struggling to keep Britain in the fight and Sir Guy Carleton, the new British commander who was anxious to defuse the situation with the Americans and extricate Britain from her former colonies. To end the cycle of revenge, Carleton refused to consent to any further raids by the now notorious privateers. The Associated Loyalists, to the British commanders' relief, disbanded out of frustration in August 1782.[111] The Marquis de Chastellux recorded the "shame and indignation" of the Huddy case, writing that the "English General" was "unable to enforce

104   DISHONORED AMERICANS

discipline in his own army" out of fear of "irritating Governor Franklin and his envenomed board of loyalists."[112] Like the popular depiction of Britain's Native allies, the vengeful Loyalists had become uncontrollable.

The Loyalists of the American Revolution faced a unique moral quandary. They were caught between two poles of honor culture—the primal masculine demand to retaliate against their enemies for insults and injuries and the Christian, genteel injunction to prevent further bloodshed and restrain their passions. British commanders viewed armed refugees with suspicion and were fearful that vengeful Loyalists would deepen and prolong the conflict. Some Loyalists, such as Simeon Baxter and William Franklin, obviously felt justified in violent retribution, while others, like Samuel Seabury and Charles Inglis, wanted to limit violence in hopes of reconciliation. In the end, regardless of the approach Loyalists took, they lost both the military conflict and the propaganda war.

According to Patriot logic, Loyalist privateers, partisans, and provincial soldiers were all incapable of fighting honorably. Not only did they support an unjust cause but they also betrayed their country and were treacherous cowards who did not fight like men. Events like the massacres at Wyoming and Cherry Valleys, the continuous guerrilla campaigns and looting in the Neutral Ground and elsewhere, and the macabre notes pinned to the victims of Loyalist vengeance helped the Patriots construct their image of ruthless Tory monsters. This was a powerful and lasting archetype that persisted, in fiction and in history, for generations after the war. The novelist Lawrence Labree affirmed in 1851 that "our worst foes were not the English, nor their savage allies," but rather the "tories [who] were equally cruel and bloodthirsty, and often added to their other atrocities, the most unpardonable treachery."[113] In 1890, Harold Frederic described "the wanton baseness and beast-like bloodthirstiness [of] . . . native-born Tories." "Beside them," the narrator continues, "the lowest painted heathen in their train was a Christian, the most ignorant Hessian peasant was a nobleman."[114] While Patriots could retaliate against their former countrymen out of a spirit of righteous indignation, the Loyalists, it was argued, fought out of base, criminal vengeance. Revenge was a racialized passion that transformed

Loyalists, sometimes in spirit, sometimes in appearance, into corruptions of honorable white manhood.

Throughout the conflict, British leaders were concerned about the potential of Loyalist violence to deepen the conflict and stain the honor of individual commanders. Even while the British sought to employ more Loyalists to fill their dwindling ranks, they tried to rein in their activities. This led to deep frustrations among Loyalists who believed that they were fully justified in defending themselves against Patriot insults and attacks. Yet there was no consensus on this point, even among Loyalists. Hard-liners like William Franklin argued that honor demanded just revenge, while others like Andrew Elliot were deeply troubled by the bloodshed. Loyalist gentlemen and British commanders were never united in their goals, nor did they have a consistent outlook on the morality of their tactics. These divisions, caused in part by the cultural ambivalence toward the honor of revenge, contributed to the ineffectiveness of armed loyalism. Loyalist gentlemen already struggling with their political death gained reputations as murderers and thieves. William Franklin, Thomas Brown, James De Lancey, Edward Winslow, and Walter Butler were implicated in some of the most brutal atrocities of the war. Deserved or not, the reputation of the Loyalists in the American Revolution was forever stained, and all Loyalists shared the dishonor. With the Treaty of Paris and the British capitulation in 1783, Loyalist gentlemen had to begin the search for honor in defeat.

4

Loyalist Honor

"WITH THE CONSCIOUSNESS OF having done right," wrote the exiled Loyalist Lieutenant Colonel John Peters, "I can look with disdain at the triumph of successful Villainy." In 1785, the once-prominent gentleman was in England, separated from his family in Cape Breton, and living on government stipends and the charity of his friends. He was angered, grief-stricken, and bewildered at the injustices of the rebel victory and the "scandalous treatment" he and others received from British officials who refused to acknowledge the Loyalists' contributions and suffering. Yet Peters still argued that his allegiance to Britain was the honorable decision. Even though he and his family lost everything and had been driven from their homeland forever, Peters assured his readers that "I wou'd do it again if there was occasion."[1] Stoicism in the face of defeat, and vigorous activism against the injustice of their situation, became the basis of Loyalist honor for men like Peters in the aftermath of the American Revolution.

Defeat and loss pervaded the exiled Loyalists' postwar experience. Perhaps sixty thousand Crown supporters and their households left the United States, but no one is certain of the numbers.[2] Individually and collectively, the exiles had to find some way to rationalize the catastrophe and explain their role in it. Few Loyalists accepted that American rebel prowess had overcome the mighty British Empire. Instead, they pointed to British mismanagement and naïveté, along with the generals' failure to make better use of the eager Loyalists. But the refugees faced a fundamental problem: they could blame the British for their defeat all they pleased, but they

{106}

still relied on the British government to rebuild their lives. This was a bitter truth for the Loyalist refugees as they floundered in the years after the Revolution without a home, caught between America and Britain without being part of either.[3] The Loyalists needed to prove that they had done all they could in the war to justify their claims on the government. Their honor and manhood, as well as their families and fortunes, were at stake.

To make sense of their situation, and to present their side of the story in the campaign for both financial compensation and moral recognition from the British government, the Loyalists produced hundreds of personal narratives and collective histories. On the surface, the Loyalist claims might appear to present tales of emasculated and defeated people humbly seeking help from the Crown. By the standards of the period, exiled Loyalist gentlemen were indeed dependent on others, and to an extent, they hoped government officials would be swayed by compassion for "suffering, emasculated subjects."[4] Yet the wrenching stories found in the claims and the narratives represent more than victimhood. As John Peters argued, it took great courage to face unmanning insults and to leave one's family unprotected in rebel territory to join the royal standard.[5] The seemingly unbearable indignities could have ended with a public recantation and apology, but by highlighting the fact that the Loyalists willingly endured this suffering for their king, the narratives transformed what men might construe as failures into expressions of honor and manly resolve. The claims were not simply plaintive requests for monetary assistance from emasculated, defeated men but were claims to respect that rested on their virtues as Loyalists.

Through their histories, memoirs, and official claims, the refugees constructed a founding myth that articulated, to themselves and others, the tenets of Loyalist honor and identity. Though there were ideological elements involved, Loyalist honor was not a set of intellectual arguments but a simple moral and sentimental position built on the ideas of duty and obligation. Loyalists presented themselves as worthy, honest men who had worked hard to build their homes and fortunes in the New World, who restrained their passions in the great upheavals, and who obeyed the law. They were not unlike wholesome English country squires who served their community, provided some much-needed refinement to their bucolic surroundings, and lived simply compared to their metropolitan cousins.

108   DISHONORED AMERICANS

Loyalist men willingly sacrificed everything they had built—their house-holds, their social standing, their influence over others—for the British constitution. They were therefore ideal, manly British subjects who fol-lowed their king into bitter defeat. In the aftermath of the conflict, exiles regarded their loyalty and honor as one and the same, and they demanded that their distinct right to respect be acknowledged by the British state.

Throughout their campaign for recognition from the British govern-ment and people, the Loyalists invoked honor's function as a claim-right, "a right that something be done by another."[6] In other words, the Loyalists' identity as honest defenders of the British cause granted them the right to be treated with honor by the state and by everyone from the king to members of their own households. This assertion of their masculine claim-right was a common thread throughout the Loyalist experience of defeat, their search for compensation, and the final ordeal of resettlement and reconciliation, which will be explored in the next chapter. The Loyalists believed the Crown was duty-bound to restore their former privileges, re-spect, and property equivalent to what they had lost, not simply as a reward for their service and sacrifice but as a recognition of their moral status as Loyalist gentlemen. Such claims did not go uncontested, and powerful Brit-ish officers like William Howe and John Burgoyne questioned the existence of Loyalist honor, leading to very public and acrimonious disputes with some leading refugee spokesmen. Though individual claims were written with customary, even formulaic, expressions of deference, their claim to a special right to respect compelled some Loyalist gentlemen to aggressively challenge Parliament and the British public to live up to their obligations. The Loyalists made restoring their manhood into an imperial concern.

Loyalist writers in the postwar years were adamant that a handful of misguided British officials lost America. Wolfgang Schivelbusch argues that nations experience defeat through stages of collective mourning and renewal. In the initial stage, a defeated people fall into a "dreamland . . . in which all blame is transferred" to the failed leadership.[7] Loyalists regarded timid British military commanders and feckless parliamentarians as the culprits for Britain's defeat. Joseph Galloway argued that the Loyalists' virtues "taught them to look up to Government to take the lead in suppressing [the rebellion]," but they found that the British authorities in the colonies "were daily giving way to new usurpations, without any exertion to prevent it." Furthermore, individual Loyalists could do little, since they "were disarmed, [and] the most obnoxious of them imprisoned." To make matters worse, they could not fully participate in the ideological struggle since the "loyal presses were restrained, some of them seized and destroyed . . . [and] Publications in favour of Government were publicly burned." Meanwhile, "republican presses teemed with speeches of their friends and allies in parliament, and letters wrote from their colleagues in faction in England . . . all tend[ed] to lead the people into a rebellious opposition to Government." British officials dashed any hope of subduing the rebellion, according to Galloway, by sending an ill-timed and wrongheaded peace commission to North America that only emboldened the American rebels and set them directly on the path to winning independence.[8]

The British government's shiftless response and diplomatic bungling joined equally disastrous military policies. If, as Schivelbusch argues, "the deployment of armies on the battlefield is the classic manifestation of collective self-confidence," then the Loyalists were deprived of this from the earliest stages of the war. According to Galloway, the rebels "were arrayed in arms by voluntary associations, and there was moreover a regular armed force under the Congress to support them." In stark contrast, "the loyalists . . . were without a head, and without weapons." Throughout the conflict, Loyalists were not effectively employed as soldiers, and those who were often felt insulted at British commanders' arrogant high-handedness. The Crown's political ineptitude and military incompetence led to defeat, but this did not lessen the Loyalists' virtues, according to men like Galloway.[9] The Loyalists had done all they could to uphold their personal honor and remain faithful to the king. The loss was not owing to any deficiency in Loyalist manhood; it resulted from impotent British leadership.

The Treaty of Paris, signed by American and British diplomats in 1783, only exacerbated Loyalist feelings of betrayal. Many Loyalists hoped to fight on after the Yorktown disaster in 1781, but the British government and treasury were exhausted. Facing a global conflict against France, Spain, and the Dutch Republic, the British Parliament—and eventually the king—accepted the American victory.[10] The Treaty of Paris recognized American independence, secured fishing rights for American sailors on the Grand Banks, and established generous borders for the new nation. An independent United States was difficult enough for Loyalists to accept, but the fifth article of the treaty struck them as a faithless and cowardly surrender. Rather than demand the return of Loyalists' confiscated estates as a condition of peace, the treaty simply stated that "Congress shall earnestly recommend it to the Legislatures of the respective States to provide for the Restitution of all Estates, Rights, and Properties, which have been confiscated." Furthermore, the Loyalists "shall have free Liberty to go to any Part or Parts of any of the thirteen United States and therein remain twelve Months unmolested in their Endeavours to obtain the Restitution of their Estates."[11] To Loyalists, this was an incomprehensible injustice. It seemingly ignored their suffering and permitted the states to keep the Loyalists' illegally seized property. Refugees scoffed at the proviso that they could return to the scene of their persecution and dishonor with only the rebels' promises to protect them.

Patriot newspapers gleefully reported on grief-stricken Tories and their apparent abandonment by the British in the Treaty of Paris. An article in the *Connecticut Journal* recounted that "many of the Loyalists affect not to believe our accounts. . . . However, their faith of the important truth, is to be read distinctly in the countenance of the tories." Furthermore, "offers of land in Nova Scotia, the promise of six months provisions, and other tokens of royal favours, have no influence in dispersing the melancholy gloom which has taken deep impression on their faces."[12] Patriots must have been gratified to read that the "Loyalists . . . boldly d—n their King for 'a Turncoat.'"[13] The *Connecticut Courant* reported that "the vile miscreants of tories were so exasperated that they trampled *their most gracious* King's proclamation under their feet, with the utmost scorn and contempt." "Finding themselves duped by a government on whom they reposed the highest confidence in," continued the article, "they are become desperate even to madness," but this was the "just reward of their demerits."[14] To Patriot readers, accounts of friendless refugees highlighted once again the perfidiousness of the British government and the gullibility of Loyalists. Indeed, many Loyalist gentlemen shared these sentiments.

Loyalist exiles in East Florida who suddenly found their refuge ceded to Spain were among the most demoralized. "A Planter," writing from the St. Johns River, implored his former countrymen to feel pity rather than malice toward the "unfortunate Loyalists in America": "The man that is steeled against such forceable impressions, is a monster, that should be drove from the circle of cultivated society." The Loyalists had been "sacrificed to the ambition of their enemies, expelled [from] their native country, and thrown upon the wide world, friendless and unsupported." British promises, the planter wrote, "have been violated in every instance; and that national faith, which we had been accustomed to look upon as sacred, basely bartered for an inglorious peace." After being so "betrayed and deserted," it was time, he argued, "that the Loyalists should think for themselves, and not trust to a people who have so repeatedly deceived them, and whose national honor is sunk beneath contempt." Rather than go to the British for assistance, the planter suggested that since the "brave and the virtuous will ever find patrons and protectors," it would be better to bring their case to the new states "and to set forth in decent and manly terms the nature of their sufferings."[15] Valiant manhood, he hoped, would always be respected, regardless of politics.

The feeling of betrayal is palpable in other Loyalist writings. In his official narrative to the commissioners, Joel Stone called the treaty "unjust," while a Georgia Loyalist delivered his sentiment more strongly, declaring that he "shall ever . . . remember with satisfaction that it was not I [who] deserted my King, but my King who deserted me."[16] Mather Byles Jr., the exiled Boston clergyman, struck a more sardonic and stoic tone. In a letter to his sister, he described watching the ceremonial disbanding of some provincial regiments in Halifax, Nova Scotia, "immediately upon which I bought a cheese & a Frying-Pan; the latter, because I concluded all *Broils* would be at an End; & the former, because after cheese comes Nothing." Byles followed his attempt at humor with an expression of Christian fortitude. He could endure his suffering, he wrote, knowing that "in Heaven [he would] have a better & enduring Substance, where the Sons of Violence can afflict no more . . . & where those faithful Ministers who have steadily adhered . . . to their solemn ordination-vows of Loyalty to the King, will meet their Reward."[17] Byles put his faith in God, not in the British government.

While Byles took consolation in a clear conscience and the promise of heavenly rewards, the Connecticut exile Joshua Chandler believed that the cause of Britain's defeat lay in the immorality of the English. The aging Yale graduate was shocked at the decadent manners and customs he encountered in London. He referred to England as "this Great Sink of Pollution, Corruption and Venality." "This Kingdom," he despaired, "without a miracle in its favor must soon be Lost; you can have no idea of their Corruption, of their Debauchery and Luxury; their Pride; their Riches; their Luxury has Ruined them; it is not in the Power of Human Nature to Save them." To that excoriating assessment of the English, he added that even men whom he assumed were the Loyalists' allies, such as former prime minister Lord North, were "in Favor of the Democratical Part of the Constitution to the Ruin of the Monarchical." To Chandler, like many others, it was clear that the British were the architects of their own defeat and the ruin of the Loyalists.[18]

Loyalists were caught in a quandary. They were certain of the honor, justice, and righteousness of their allegiance but torn by resentment toward British authorities who either did not appreciate the extent of their suffering or were perhaps unworthy of the Loyalists' sacrifices. To work out these issues, some of the most literary-minded Loyalists, such as Joseph Galloway, Alexander Hewatt, Peter Oliver, Samuel Peters, and Jonathan Boucher, wrote lengthy histories to explain Britain's defeat and defend the Loyalists' part.[19] Without exception, each writer agreed that the rebellion had been incited by a small group of demagogues who whipped a gullible people into an emotional frenzy, even though the colonists should have been perfectly happy in their rich country.[20]

Samuel Peters saw the Revolution as a war of religion, contending that the spirit of rebellion from the English Civil Wars had persisted in the "darkness of superstition" among the bigoted Congregationalists of New England. The Connecticut-born Peters recorded outrageous tales of his countrymen's fanaticism, such as fining an Anglican clergyman who ran to escape the rain on the Sabbath. According to Peters, the New Englanders' peculiar religious devotion compelled them to "cheat the King of those duties, which they say, God and nature never intended should be paid. From the governor down to the tithing-man," Peters charged, "they will aid smugglers, resist collectors, and mob informers."[21] Regardless of their advantages and comforts, Peters asserted that the New Englanders had always been religiously and culturally disposed to rebellion and republicanism.

The former Speaker of the Pennsylvania House of Representatives, Joseph Galloway, also saw the connection between the Roundheads and the Revolution. "If the pulpits of the sectaries in England in the year 1641, resounded with sedition," he wrote, "the pulpits of the Congregational Independents and Presbyterians, from Nova Scotia to Georgia, rung with the same flagitious doctrines."[22] Jonathan Boucher, writing almost two decades later, agreed with Peters and Galloway that radical dissenters had played a major role in the rebellion, but what united all of the colonies into conflict with Britain was much more complicated. Indeed, Boucher wrote that it was a "marvellous, romantic, and incredible" fact that the people of Virginia and Maryland would follow the New Englanders, "for whom they entertained an hereditary national disesteem," into civil war. The true cause, argued Boucher, was that the colonies were "planted in imperfection." "A possibility of their future defection," he wrote, "was not foreseen; nor of course, guarded against." The imperial authorities "either saw not, or heeded not, the latent mischief, till at length it broke out with a force that was irresistible." The Loyalist chroniclers generally agreed that although the Revolution had deep cultural roots, it was, in the end, completely unjustifiable.[23]

Since the Loyalists contended that the Revolution was not ignited by actual oppression, the writers looked to the revolutionary leaders as the true initiators of the war. Loyalist writers depicted the Patriot leadership as either fanatical dissenters or, just as often, as scheming, self-interested men. Through their demagoguery and charisma, this small group managed to delude the people of America. Peter Oliver devoted lengthy portions of his manuscript dissecting and lambasting the character of some of the most prominent revolutionaries. Samuel Adams "was so thorough a Machiavellian, that he divested himself of every worthy Principle, & would stick at no Crime to accomplish his ends." These crimes included deluding John Hancock, whose "Mind was a meer [sic] tabula rasa," and hijacking his fortune to support the rebellion. Benjamin Franklin "was a Man of Genius, but of so unprincipled an Heart, that the Merit of all his political & philosophical

114 DISHONORED AMERICANS

Disquisitions can never atone for the Mischiefs which he plunged Society into." John Adams was characterized as a petty tyrant, possessing "an Acrimony of Temper" which "settled into Rancor & Malignancy—by having an absolute Authority over Children" when a schoolmaster. James Otis had ruined his law practice "by drinking & by Passion." These invectives painted the revolutionary leadership as a sort of rogues' gallery of men guided by the worst defects gentlemen could possess.[24] Indeed, both Joseph Galloway and John Peters wrote that the deceitful rebel faction had intentionally thwarted any attempt at reconciliation, and despite Congress's protestations of loyalty, "the Bankrupts, dissenting Teachers and Smugglers [in Congress] meant to have a Serious Rebellion, and a Civil and Religious separation from the Mother Country."[25] Thus, deep-seated religious and political distemper, along with the structural weakness of authority in the colonies and the demagoguery of the dishonorable rebel leaders, explained how the rebellion erupted. The upheaval became unstoppable, a fact the Loyalists emphasized to underscore their courage in standing against such overwhelming odds.

Explaining the causes of the rebellion and Britain's defeat was helpful in exonerating the Loyalists, but to restore their honor, the exiles had to make Parliament and the British public aware of their unjust postwar situation. The refugees again found their champion penman in the former Pennsylvania assemblyman Joseph Galloway. While fighting his own battles for compensation, Galloway published several pamphlets that articulated the Loyalist cause and presented solutions for restoring faith and honor between Britain and her American refugees. His 1783 pamphlet, *Observations on the Fifth Article of the Treaty with America,* called on the British government to compensate the Loyalists for their material losses. His argument focused on the impossibility that the fifth article of the Treaty of Paris would convince the American states to return confiscated property. Galloway argued that since the property had already been sold under the seals of the individual states, which were now recognized as legal entities by Britain through the treaty itself, it would be impossible to restore the actual estates. In any event, the "Loyalists, who are subject to those attainders and confiscations, can therefore of right, and in justice, look up only to Great Britain for a compensation." Any idea of returning to the United States to purchase back their property was delusional, because the politically dead Loyalists would face the "implacable resentment" of their former adversaries and would be subjected to *every insult, and even death itself.* Besides," Galloway asked, "where are men, who have forfeited all they possessed on earth, to find money to repurchase their property[?]" Galloway succinctly stated what most Loyalists surely thought: that Britain had "purchased peace with the property of the attained Loyalists."[26] The work of Galloway and others had a significant impact on British parliamentarians who passed the Compensation Act in July 1783, which established the Loyalist Claims Commission.[27]

The Royal Commission on the Losses and Services of the American Loyalists was a remarkable moment in British imperial history. Parliamentary debates about the Loyalists and their compensation were saturated with invocations of national honor. Maya Jasanoff argues that the Claims Commission represented an early example of government taking on the role of a welfare provider, and that is certainly worth noting. But she also argues that the Loyalists were making a demand not unlike the one their rebel adversaries had made at the beginning of the conflict—to be treated as full citizens of the British Empire and enjoy the same rights as Englishmen. In the end, Parliament never declared that the Loyalists were entitled to compensation based on their rights as British subjects or citizens. Rather, the claims were acknowledged because "the honor of the nation" was at stake. As Edmund Burke explained, the Loyalists "had no claim upon [the British government] founded in strict right," but Parliament would consider the claims for the sake of "honor and justice" and to exhibit "a new and noble instance of national bounty and generosity."[28] The Loyalists insisted, however, that their claims were centered on their rights—if not as British citizens, then as loyal and honorable men who had earned their distinct right to respect. Their actions and suffering in the war placed a moral duty on the Crown. As Joseph Galloway succinctly stated in his 1783 pamphlet, Britain was "bound by the principles of moral, as well as of political justice."[29]

The Loyalists pointed to the compensation the British government had provided for losses suffered in the Jacobite rebellions earlier in the century as precedent, but the situation of the American Loyalists was unique. The sheer scale of the process, both in terms of the investigation and the compensation recommended, was unprecedented, but so too was the uncertain status of the Loyalists in British law. Even the wealthiest Loyalist in the colonies could not vote for a Member of Parliament, and Loyalists' rights within the empire were not entirely clear. Nonetheless, most parliamentarians understood that some restitution was necessary to maintain, as Galloway put it, "the social compact."[30]

The structure of the claims process, and the requirements of individual claimants, favored formerly wealthy and connected Loyalists. Literacy, or access to someone literate, was a basic requirement, since claims had to be submitted in writing. Witness testimony was also a vital component in the claims process, and those Loyalists with more extensive personal connections could produce more prominent witnesses, like governors and generals, who were taken seriously by the commissioners. In the first round of claims investigations, Loyalists had to attend a hearing in London personally. This disqualified thousands of people who lacked the means to travel and support themselves in England. In the end, middling and wealthy white men dominated the commission's time in London as well as a later commission sent to Nova Scotia and New Brunswick in 1786. Of the 3,225 claims fully examined by the commission, the majority were submitted by formerly landholding men, and of the 468 white women who submitted claims, most did so on behalf of deceased or absent husbands or fathers. These women were often unable to provide accurate valuations of the lost property and received little restitution.[31] The compensation of the Loyalists was not a recognition of their citizenship but an acknowledgment by the commission of the important place of gentlemen householders within the empire.

In the patriarchal world of the eighteenth century, it is not surprising that the claims commission would favor landholding men, but even with their advantage, Loyalist gentlemen resented the burden of proof the commissioners placed on claimants. For their part, the five men appointed to run the commission were tasked with the unenviable chore of determining appropriate compensation for the Loyalists while representing a deeply indebted imperial state reeling from defeat. The initial Compensation Act included a deadline of March 25, 1784, for the Loyalists to submit their claims. Because of the vast distances involved and the inability of many Loyalists to travel to England to submit their testimony in person, the government enacted another claims commission to be held in British North America with a deadline of May 1786. The sheer number of claims, and the extensive supporting material required, created a massive backlog for the commissioners, who were also required to engage in bureaucratic and investigative due diligence that some Loyalists found insulting. Yet Loyalist spokesmen and agents understood the necessity of demonstrating refugee transparency and honesty, no matter the seeming indignity. The "more justice and less fraud," argued the Reverend James Stuart, "the more will Government be able to bestow upon . . . our suffering Brethren." Thus, he advised the commissioners, that "every man's claim be his Rank or Character what it will, ought to be enquired into as strictly as the lowest."[32] To assist in their work, the commission sent the barrister John Anstey to the United States to investigate the situation Loyalists faced during the conflict and, just as importantly, to determine what things actually cost in the colonies at the outset of the war. Initially suspicious of the Loyalists' claims and narratives, Anstey's findings confirmed their version of events. Although the Loyalists as a group tended to exaggerate the monetary value of their losses, there was very little outright fraud.[33]

Even with careful documentation and Anstey's findings, the eventual compensation fell far below what the Loyalist gentlemen had expected, and some felt betrayed once again. The commission only considered losses suffered directly on account of the claimants' loyalty, not those resulting from the depredations of British soldiers or from fire or other disasters. Merchants and professionals received a smaller percentage of their claims than landowners, likely because it was simply easier to determine the value of real estate as opposed to professional losses documented in inventories and account books. Lost debts were disallowed. Regardless of occupation, the Pitt government determined that the British treasury could simply not afford to compensate the Loyalists pound for pound. Instead, Loyalists who bore arms would receive 40 percent of their accepted claims, and everyone else would receive 30 percent. Despite Joseph Galloway's passionate invocation of Britain's "sacred obligations" and the sad reality he described of destitute Loyalists dying "of broken hearts" while others were "driven by their

118 DISHONORED AMERICANS

extreme distress, into insanity, and from insanity, SUICIDE," the average Loyalist gentleman received 37 percent of what he claimed.[34] This led Peter Oliver to lament bitterly the fact that they were "obliged to put up with every insult from this ungrateful people the English." "Blessed are ye, who expecteth . . . nothing," he fumed, "for ye then will not be disappointed."[35]

Though Loyalists could not rely on the claims for their economic salvation, there was a moral weight embedded in the process that went beyond simple financial restitution. In many ways the claims provided a public forum for individual Loyalists to have a direct conversation with their government through the submission of narratives, wherein they could account for the more intangible losses suffered in consequence of their loyalty. The narratives were an opportunity for Loyalists to construct their own sense of honorable manhood exemplified in their suffering and services. Collectively, the claims formed a macro-narrative that all white Loyalists could share. As Keith Mason argues, even with the repetitive "banality" of their language, the claims contributed to a common Loyalist identity that was particularly strong among the elite.[36] And while most narratives and depositions dwell on the trauma of insults, displacement, and suffering families, Loyalists told these stories not as expressions of helpless emasculation but as proof of a manly willingness to undergo any trial for the sake of loyalty. Through their personal narratives and the macro-narrative they formed, Loyalists defined who they believed they were, expressed what they valued, and accounted for their role in the defeat.

Most narratives submitted to the claims commission were very short, amounting to little over a page that summarized the claimants' experiences, services, and losses. These were accompanied by witness statements and supporting documentation, such as certificates from British officers, deeds, records of confiscation from the American states, and other types of evidence. Some Loyalists, such as Joel Stone, John Peters, James Moody, and John Connolly, penned much longer memoirs to add to their case. Moody and Connolly even published their narratives for the London print market in the hopes of garnering popular support for their own claims and the Loyalist cause in general.[37]

Memorials submitted to the claims commissioners tended to follow a standard template found in a helpful pamphlet published in 1783. The anonymously authored pamphlet was meant to guide the refugee claimants through the process, and it provided instructions on how to format the memorial, items to include in the supporting inventories and schedules, along with stipulations for acquiring written witness testimonials. Included in the suggested language for the memorials are basic expressions of humility that followed eighteenth-century conventions. Most gentlemen would have been aware of the expected displays of deference, so it is interesting that these instructions were included. Perhaps the Loyalist agents feared that the refugees' provincial manners or their sense of outrage and assertiveness would embarrass the cause. In any event, nearly all the claimants followed the pamphlet's rubric and began their memorials by stating that they "*Humbly Sheweth. . . .*"[38]

The longer Loyalist narratives expanded on this customary expression of humility. John Connolly, in perhaps the lengthiest Loyalist narrative published in the 1780s, apologized for any appearance of "unavoidable egotism" and hoped that it might "be overlooked in mercy to the misfortunes of one who is at least conscious of having acted with good intentions, and from principles which he believed were descriptive of a loyal subject, an honest man, and a man of honour." James Moody likewise averred that though he was once "a plain, contented farmer," it was only "the importunity of his friends" that compelled him to compose his narrative. He at least would keep his tale brief, rather "than to make a pompous display of any supposed merit of his own." John Peters characterized his narrative as a response to another gentleman's queries. He did not intend "to boast of my Exploits by complying with your request: but, to relate my Story in Simplicity." Despite their professions of humility, these gentlemen Loyalists also portrayed themselves as remarkable men who were sharper, wittier, and more honorable than their ragged adversaries.[39]

The Loyalist narratives, whether short official submissions or longer memoirs—even those written decades later—present strikingly similar elements. The Loyalists describe an idyllic prewar existence and glowing prospects, then turn to their grim determination in the face of overwhelming odds before providing accounts of their endurance, suffering,

120 DISHONORED AMERICANS

and loss.[40] In general, Loyalist narratives and memorials present a few recurring personas. Some Loyalists portrayed themselves as refined martyrs who were set upon by the unruly, unwashed mob. Other Loyalists depicted themselves as wily foxes that had outwitted the ham-fisted agents of Congress. The most gripping Loyalist narratives went beyond the templates and showcased adventurous men with the requisite blend of strength and sensibility thought to be possessed by the first class of gentlemen. Regardless of how they presented themselves, the Loyalists intended to demonstrate how deeply unfair it was that such honorable men were so badly used.

Loyalist authors rarely missed an opportunity to indulge their nostalgia and recount the ideal colonial world of the country gentleman that the Revolution destroyed. James Moody was "a happy farmer, without a wish or an idea of any other enjoyment, than that of making happy, and being happy, with a beloved wife, and three promising children." He was a moral and independent family man "clear of debt, and at ease in his professions." Joel Stone, from a more modest background, was a farmer's son turned successful trader in partnership with "a Merchant of great trade." His dignity and work ethic were visible in the "confidence and esteem of all my Neighbours and the public in general." No retired gentleman, Stone was building his fortune, and "by dint of an unwearied diligence and a close application to trade I found the number of my Friends and customers daily increasing and a fair prospect of long happiness arose to my sanguine mind."[41] Both John Connolly and John Peters wrote of their advanced education—Peters attended Yale, and Connolly "received as perfect an education as that country could afford." Wherever these two settled on the frontier, civilization seemed to spring up around them. Connolly helped establish new settlements in western Virginia and valiantly assisted Lord Dunmore in his war with the Shawnee in 1774. Peters left Connecticut for New Hampshire, where he established mills and farms, and then moved west to New York and was "appointed by Governor Tryon to be Colonel of the Militia, Justice of the Peace, Judge of Probates, Register of the County, Clerk of the Courts; and Judge of the Court of Common Pleas: Here I was in easy circumstances, and as Independent as my mind ever wish'd."[42] Independence, industriousness, and respectability formed the core of the Loyalist's prewar honor.

Gentlemen Loyalists relied on witness testimonies to support their claims to prewar gentility and advancing careers. Nehomiah Marks testified that Amos Botsford of Connecticut "lived as genteely as any Man in New Haven." Moreover, "he seemed to be in full as much Business as any young Man of the Profession and seemed arising very fast." Another witness, Daniel Lymans, agreed, testifying that Botsford "was in considerable Practice [and] Was amongst the first Lawyers . . . had the fairest Prospects, he lived very well and seemed to be laying up Money."[43] These were subjective observations that described appearances of wealth and gentility, but such witness testimonies were important in determining what property the Loyalists owned before the war, their place within their former communities, and the power they radiated with their homes and finery. Simply having witnesses testify on a man's behalf was evidence of his connections and influence.

Ideally, witnesses were to attend and give their statements in person, but written and notarized statements were also acceptable. Perhaps one of the most interesting witness statements was submitted on behalf of Reverend Samuel Peters of Hebron, Connecticut. Charles Wattles, a former friend and neighbor, described "Priest Peters" as "a Gentleman greatly beloved by all his Acquaintances," one who "built a grand house on his Estate" and "lived in a genteel and splendid Manner." Wattles, like the majority of Connecticut, had supported the Revolution, and therefore his assertions that Peters and his family were "industrious and indefatigable to Subject America under the power of the King of Great Britain" must have held significant weight. Indeed, a letter of support from a man who signed off with "I shall live and die your political Enemy" underscores the fact that the Loyalists relied on former contacts in their homelands, be they friend or foe, for evidence to secure their claims.[44]

Once the Loyalist gentlemen established that they were either men of property or had been on the sure path to prosperity, they moved on to describe their stalwart character as Loyalists. Joel Stone declared that he "was fixed in my resolves rather to forego all I could call my property in the world than flinch from my duty as a subject to the best of Sovereigns [and] sooner to perish in the general Calamity than abet in the least degree the enemies of the British Constitution." Connolly "decided instantly, and resolved to

122   DISHONORED AMERICANS

exert every faculty in defence of the royal cause." Moody "resolved to do any thing, and to be any thing, not inconsistent with integrity—to fight, to bleed, to die—rather than live to see the venerable Constitution of his country totally lost." Amos Botsford was less florid in his declaration, stating that his loyalty "rendered himself obnoxious to his Country," while most other claimants simply listed the sufferings they experienced "on account of" or "in consequence" of their loyalty.[45] Like their descriptions of property and the idyllic past, the refugees' expressions of their undying loyalty fit a common pattern with few variations. A picture of an archetypal Loyalist gentleman was coming into focus.

At this point, most Loyalist narratives turn to a discussion of the insults, losses, and violence they suffered. In another context, these might have been confessions of masculine failure, but the wounded patriarchs were sharing their misfortunes both to highlight the extent of the suffering they were willing to endure and to reaffirm that this suffering was on behalf of the king. Munson Jarvis first recalled his inability "to supply his Family with meat, Drink or Clothes" and then described being driven from his home, leaving "his Family behind to the mercy of the Rebels who they stript of every necessary of Life." Timothy Hierlihy's "Wife, and nine Children were left in a great Measure destitute of the necessaries of Life" on account of his political choice, while Lieutenant Hugh Fraser's family was "stripp'd of every thing by Gen'l Gates's Army."[46] Edward Jessup's career as a Loyalist officer left his "Large family . . . exceedingly distressed by means of the Loss of his property."[47] Such examples fill page after page in the claims and narratives. These men followed their conscience and their king, and in the process, they ruined their households and their status as patriarchs and providers. Applying the paternal analogy of the king as the father of his people, the Loyalists' failures were the king's as well, since he and his government were unable to protect his innocent subjects.

In addition to their losses and suffering, the Loyalists also went to great lengths to describe their services to the Crown, though not all Loyalists had to bear arms to be considered worthy servants of the king. Men like Amos Botsford, Evert Bancker, and Joshua Loring served as government agents in a variety of tasks, from provisioning soldiers to surveying and allocating lands for refugees. In what must have been one of the more eyebrow-raising narratives, Dr. Isaac Moseley described how he and his confederates spent the war disguised as Patriots in Connecticut, all the while delivering provisions into the hands of lurking British ships.[48] For many of the wealthiest gentlemen, it was enough that they had forfeited their estates and become refugees. Clergymen like Jonathan Boucher and grandees such as former governor Thomas Hutchinson of Massachusetts lived out the war in England yet worked to influence government policy.[49] Other Loyalist officers, who served under arms but did not see much action, distinguished themselves by obeying orders and keeping their men in line. Such officers found a written testimony from a general added significant weight to their Loyalist claims.[50]

Loyalist narratives occasionally included tales of gallantry and heroic resistance to rebel mobs. These episodes added memorable drama to the narratives and demonstrated the Loyalists' manly virtues. John Peters described the tragedy of civil war and his deep feelings as a gentleman soldier when he found himself at the end of rebel bayonet. The wounded Peters realized that his opponent was an "Old School fellow & Playmate and a Couzin of my Wife's: Tho his Bayonet was in my Body, I felt regret at being obliged to destroy him." John Connolly explained how unimpressed he was at the rebel who held a pistol to his head. The veteran Loyalist declared that "I had been so long learning to despise danger . . . that [I] was not easily to be intimidated." In a scene worthy of a modern action film, Connolly grappled with his armed opponent while briefly fending off another twenty rebels at his door. Such superhuman feats are rare in the narratives. Self-styled Loyalist heroes more often presented themselves as wily foxes than British-American lions. Peters, for example, explained how he tricked his enemies by leading them into "an Ambuscade whereby [the British] took and killed near 150 Rebels." John Connolly wrote that he "secretly frustrated the machinations of the Republicans" to win over Indigenous nations. Even "while I received [rebel] thanks," he "procured assurances from the Indian chiefs to support his Majesty, at all events, as his Majesty's most faithful friends and auxiliaries."[51]

Perhaps the most gripping tales of sly and stealthy Loyalist heroics are found in James Moody's narrative. Moody portrayed himself as a Loyalist avenger, slinking behind enemy lines to intercept Washington's dispatches,

124   DISHONORED AMERICANS

capture cruel committeemen, and rescue imprisoned Loyalists—all while maintaining the moral rectitude of a gentleman. Moody's tales were so fantastic that the second edition of his printed narrative included testimonials from a variety of respectable commanders and gentlemen who assured the reader of the narrative's truth. In a particularly dashing sequence of events, Moody attempted to gain access to a jail in some unnamed "country town" to free a captive Loyalist. He first posed as a Patriot soldier, delivering one of his own men as a prisoner to the jail. When that failed because of a standing order to refuse entry to anyone after dark, Moody tried to cow the jail-keeper by announcing who he really was, warning the guards that "I have a strong party with me, and if you do not this moment deliver up your keys, I will instantly pull down your house about your ears." The Loyalists struck up the "Indian war-whoop" and the jailer "obsequiously conducted Moody to the dungeon."[52]

With such men on their side, how did the British lose? For that, the Loyalists blamed Britain's military leaders in America.

Loyalists took great risks in publicly blaming British generals for the defeat. Two bitter and often public feuds between prominent Loyalists and British commanders display the stakes and rancor involved in determining culpability, and both disputes centered on questions of personal honor. Joseph Galloway took on British general William Howe, and John Peters battled with John Burgoyne in parliamentary inquiries, in the back channels of political influence, and in the court of public opinion. The American exiles attempted both to vindicate the conduct and integrity of the Loyalists and to demonstrate how the defects in the generals' characters led to the disaster at Saratoga in 1777 and the failure of the Pennsylvania Campaign in 1777–78. The Loyalist writers argued that the generals were intemperate, vain, foolish, and even cowardly. These concerted attacks on British authority figures by Loyalist gentlemen underscored just how assertive the leading refugees became in defeat. To Galloway and Peters, and doubtlessly many other Loyalists, America was lost because of the deficient martial prowess and deep character flaws of Burgoyne and Howe.

The disputes began even before the war was lost. As a refugee in London in 1779, Joseph Galloway anonymously published a pamphlet titled *Letters to a Nobleman on the Conduct of the War in the Middle Colonies*, which, he wrote, intended to reveal "the shameful misconduct of the American war" and refute General William Howe's claims that his reversals were the fault of the administration's lack of support and the strength of the "almost universally disaffected" colonists.[53] Galloway attacked Howe on almost every page and compared the general's defeat in the middle colonies to Britain's victory in the Seven Years' War in Canada, "a country of thick woods, full of vast mountains, high precipices, and strong defiles" defended by "French veterans." And yet it was conquered by "an *Amherst* and a *Wolfe*," who, Galloway sniped, were "unconnected with party, prized their own honour, and devoted their lives to the interest of their country and the glory of their Sovereign." Britain's loss of Philadelphia was a result of "the military indolence and misconduct of men, who have sacrificed to party and faction their own honour, the glory of their Sovereign, and the dignity of the nation."[54] This was a stinging rebuke for a general whose reputation had already been skewered by gossip about his tawdry affair with the married Elizabeth Loring.

According to Galloway, the overwhelming might of British arms should have ensured victory. Over forty thousand British soldiers "commanded by able and experienced officers" were pitted against a force of eighteen thousand rebels "seduced into arms" and led "by men destitute of military skill or experience; and, for the most part, taken from mechanic arts or the plough." British soldiers were trained and led by gentlemen, yet they succumbed to lesser men. The eventual failure of the British in the northern colonies, save for the occupation of New York City and Long Island, was entirely the fault of the "British General [Howe]" who "was left to his own judgement in forming and executing his plans in every instance [except in assisting Burgoyne] and by that neglect sacrificed a British army, and involved his country in a degree of disgrace it never before had experienced." In the end, Galloway asserted, the seeds of defeat were found in Howe's "want of wisdom in plans, and of vigour and exertion in the execution."[55]

126 DISHONORED AMERICANS

Galloway provided a litany of examples of bungling: instances when Howe pointlessly delayed his army, overestimated rebel strength, and failed to arm American Loyalists. To make matters worse, after "thousands" of Loyalists "took the oath," "the Royal faith, pledged for their safety, was shamefully violated. The unhappy people, instead of receiving the protection promised, were plundered by the soldiery. Their wives and daughters polluted by the lustful brutality of the lowest of mankind." In response to these outrages, Howe "was indolent and neglectful in putting a stop to these cruelties," which disheartened the Loyalists and gave the Patriot press unmatched propaganda material. Galloway presented example after example of poor planning, abysmal leadership, and moments of "unparalleled absurdity" where Howe turned overwhelming advantage into failure. In a final rebuke, Galloway declared that neither Howe's superiority in arms, men, and equipment nor "the distress of the loyal inhabitants, the millions he was wasting, the prospect of glory, nor the duty he owed to his Sovereign and the nation, could prevail on the general to desert the delusive pleasures of the long room and the Faro table."[56] Galloway was not alone in his frustrations. London printers published a torrent of twenty-five pamphlets blasting Howe over his failures in America.[57]

Howe defended himself vigorously and published his own pamphlet, which attacked both Galloway's "invidious assertions" and the honor of the Loyalists in general. Howe denied that "thousands" of Loyalists flocked to British-occupied Philadelphia and insisted that any Americans who came through the British lines did so not from principle but "to get possession of their houses and effects" or to do "us all the mischief they could, by sending out intelligence to the enemy, and inveighing the troops to desert, and smuggling . . . supplies for Washington's army." Local farmers fed the redcoats out of greed, not from any zealous attachment to the king. Far from describing the rebels as undisciplined rabble, Howe complimented Washington's troops for being surprisingly well disciplined, provisioned, and having "as good use of fire-arms, in general, as the King's troops."[58]

Howe never claimed to know the author of *Letters to a Nobleman*, but his frequent mention of Joseph Galloway, emphasized in italics, indicates that he was fully aware of the author's identity. Howe portrayed Galloway as a puffed-up provincial whose declarations of status and ability fell far short of his promises. The general claimed that he put great confidence in Loyalist gentlemen, but added, "I confess that I sometimes found myself the dupe of such distinctions." Howe alleged that the former Pennsylvania assemblyman only came into British lines after the resounding victory in New York and the subsequent "Proclamation of indemnity," thus implying that Galloway deserted his countrymen as British victory loomed. Howe "expected much assistance from a gentleman of [Galloway's] abilities and reputed influence" and entrusted him with a variety of posts and an annual salary of £770, but, he wrote, "I afterwards found that my confidence was misplaced." "His ideas," Howe continued, "were visionary [i.e., delusional], and his intelligence was too frequently either ill-founded, or so much exaggerated, that it would have been unsafe to act upon." Howe went on to allege that Galloway had "applied . . . for permission to raise a provincial corps of dragoons . . . chiefly from the county of Bucks in Pennsylvania, where he pretended to have (for he certainly had not) great influence," and failed in his task. On another occasion, the Loyalist gentleman promised to find five hundred loyal workers to erect fortifications around Philadelphia but could only produce "seventy or eighty." Galloway was constantly assuring the general of his "intimate knowledge" of the land and its people and insisting on their loyalty. When they did not materialize, Galloway simply stated that the Loyalists "were farther on."[59] In the general's narrative, Howe was impeded, not helped, by Galloway and other Loyalists who undermined the war effort with their unmanly greed and bad advice. A Loyalist was little more than a fawning huckster.

Howe's open attacks on the Loyalists' honor compelled Galloway to respond in kind. In a tedious 160-page document, Galloway answered Howe's refutations of his earlier pamphlet point by point.[60] Enough people evidently took interest in the dispute for there to have been several editions of Galloway's pamphlets, and in 1788 a Philadelphia printer published the entire collection as a single volume titled *A Short History of the War in America*. In the appendix, Galloway scolds Howe for not following "the example I had set you in my Letters; in which . . . I had confined my strictures to your 'professional conduct,' without suffering one syllable of personal abuse, or one hint at the defects in your private moral character . . . to escape my pen." This was entirely false. As seen above, Galloway clearly described Howe

128   DISHONORED AMERICANS

as a bumbler and a lazy gambler. Nonetheless, Galloway accused Howe of deserting "the field of decent and manly argument, and [taking] a mean refuge under the abuse of [Galloway's] private reputation." "A conduct of this kind," he added, "is the usual practice of the guilty, and the common weapon made use of to wound the innocent."[61] If Galloway felt better for defending himself in print, his nemesis Howe, even with the cloud of controversy hanging over him, remained a powerful figure in the British establishment for the rest of his life.[62] Galloway continued as an influential advocate and spokesman for his fellow refugees, printing several pamphlets in defense of the Loyalists' claims on the government. He never returned to Pennsylvania, and by the 1790s, he had retreated from public life. He died in England in 1803.[63] The dispute between Howe and Galloway faded but was never resolved.

An equally acrimonious argument took place between Lieutenant Colonel John Peters of the Queen's Loyal Rangers and his onetime commanding officer, Lieutenant General John Burgoyne, over their competing versions of the British disaster at Saratoga in 1777. Like the Galloway-Howe quarrel, this controversy called Loyalist manhood and honor into question, but it also had a profound impact upon John Peters's personal claims on the British government. Powerful and well-connected British officers were eager to protect their own reputations, and they dismissed Peters and his fellow Loyalists as grasping, cowardly, opportunistic provincials who lacked the moral fiber of their rebel adversaries. In the end, Peters's attempts to vindicate his actions and those of his fellow Loyalists at Saratoga failed, and his hopes of political rebirth were dashed entirely.

Though he has long been characterized as a foppish and incompetent dandy in the popular imagination, John Burgoyne enjoyed fame as a respected commander and playwright. Despite his military defeat and his unwise political allegiance with the short-lived Whig government that collapsed in 1783, Burgoyne remained an influential figure in British politics until his death.[64] John Peters, by comparison, was a relatively unknown provincial exile who provoked the ire of both Burgoyne and Frederick Haldimand, the military governor of Quebec. In 1779, Peters learned of Burgoyne's attempts to defend himself and blame his crushing defeat, in part, on "the ill Conduct of the Indians & Provincials on whom he found too late was no Dependence." Peters, who commanded the Queen's Loyal Rangers on that campaign, lacked the means to publish a printed response to Burgoyne. Yet his handwritten narrative provides an intriguing glimpse into the thoughts of a Loyalist caught between the demands of his personal honor and his desperate need for support from the very men who insulted him.

Peters argued that Burgoyne blundered his way to defeat, alienated his American supporters, and consistently ignored their advice. According to Peters, Burgoyne lost the allegiance of the Haudenosaunee allies when he threatened to hang any warrior who "carried on the War in their own Way." Peters neglected to mention that Burgoyne was responding to the murder of Jane McRae, the wife of a Loyalist officer. Nonetheless, the warriors were incensed and left the camp. While Burgoyne's high-handedness lost the army invaluable Indigenous allies, he also thoughtlessly sacrificed loyal American lives. Peters at first refused an order to take his men along the "Connecticut Road through Bennington" to secure supplies, knowing "the certain Danger & the Mountains between which they must pass." Burgoyne ignored his own subordinate officers' suggestion that Peters had a point and instead declared that the "Americans were Cowards and disobedient. [A]t this Colonel Peters told the General that . . . he was ready to obey his Orders but we shall not return." The resulting Battle of Bennington on August 16, 1777, found the British, Hessian, and Loyalist forces exposed to fire from "Rebels, secreted behind Rocks & Trees," who "killed in half an Hour above one thousand Men."[65]

Peters's anger becomes ever more palpable as the narrative continues. "The Provincials further say, that if Genl Burgoine [sic] had condescended to the Advice of those who knew the Country," he writes, "all America could not have tarnished his Glory, nor hurt or starv'd his Army." Furthermore, "the Provincials think themselves ill treated, as their Characters are wounded by the General for whom they went to die." In the same way that Galloway bristled at Howe's compliments of rebel prowess, Peters wished "that Gen' Burgoine would consider these Questions as he calls the rebel Americans bold & brave" and the "loyal Americans . . . cowards." This was too much for Peters and was evidence that the whole moral universe had been upended. After all, the Loyalists "had Courage to leave their Wives &

Children, their Friends & Property and turn Soldiers and go in the forefront of all his Army to receive the first Blows of the Enimy [sic] and be Guardians to Each Wing & Rear . . . when . . . the loyal Provincials . . . were killed ten to one of the royal Army." The final line of the letter is an ominous, if impotent, threat responding to Burgoyne's failure to acknowledge and reward the Loyalists: "Neglect is a Percecution [sic] that may be attended with equal bad Consequences to Insult or reproach."[66]

In 1780, John Burgoyne published his version of events in *The State of the Expedition from Canada*. It is a well-written and thorough defense of his conduct, one supported by transcribed examinations of his fellow officers and witnesses. Burgoyne's version of events does not blame his defeat on the Loyalists; rather, the provincials are shown as having little impact on events. Nonetheless, Burgoyne offers a very unflattering depiction of the Loyalists. That the damning testimonies came from several different sources made the aspersions even more cutting and seemingly credible.

Of deepest concern to John Peters were Burgoyne's charges that he had abandoned his post on the eve of the surrender. In his own records, Peters maintained that "the General gave Leave to Peters & others to return to Canada" and "700 went off to Canada with out Loss" rather than be captured by rebels.[67] In Burgoyne's transcript of his court-martial, the general asked Lieutenant Colonel Kingston: "If any party did make its way to Canada, do you not suppose it must be that party of provincials that ran away while they were employed to repair roads, and that were never heard of afterwards?" Kingston answered that any who escaped were "likely to have been that party." Since Peters had explicitly stated that he returned to Canada, this was a direct stab at his character, placing him in the ranks of deserters and not of wily servants to the Crown. Since no action was ever taken against Peters as a deserter, these statements are puzzling and may have been included simply to cast doubt on the Loyalist's character. Kingston further denigrates the Loyalists as "not disciplined" and comments that a "very great part of them were such as I should have placed very little dependence upon."[68]

In his lengthy "Review of the Evidence," Burgoyne shared his own opinions of the "professed loyalists" in his army. In his estimation they were entirely unfit for military duty because the "various interests which influenced their actions rendered all arrangement of them impracticable." His evaluation of the provincials under his command would undoubtedly enrage any American Loyalist:

> One man's views went to the profit which he was to enjoy when his corps should be complete; another's, to the protection of the district in which he resided; a third was wholly intent upon revenge against his personal enemies; and all of them were repugnant even to an idea of subordination. Hence the settlement [of] who should act as a private man, and who as an officer, or in whose corps either should be, was seldom satisfactorily made among themselves; and as surely as it failed, succeeded a reference to the Commander in Chief, which could not be put by, or delegated to another hand, without dissatisfaction, encrease or confusion, and generally a loss of such services as they were really fit for, viz. searching for cattle, ascertaining the practicability of routes, clearing roads, and guiding detachments of columns upon the march.[69]

To Burgoyne, the Loyalists were tedious provincials who spent more time squabbling over the dubious honors of their junior ranks than they did fighting their common enemy. Even some of the best Loyalists under his command were incapable of behaving like gentlemen soldiers and suffered from the same ungovernable spirit as their rebel counterparts.

Burgoyne concluded his thoughts on the Loyalists by undermining the entire basis for their claims on the British government. "I only maintain that the interests and the passions of the revolted Americans concenter in the cause of the Congress," he wrote, "and those of the Loyalists break and subdivide into various pursuits, with which the cause of the King has little or nothing to do."[70] In other words, though the Patriots might be rebels, they at least fought for a cause, while the Loyalists fought for themselves. John Peters and the Loyalists had a particularly obstinate opponent in John Burgoyne.

Peters's personal quarrel with Burgoyne continued for years, and while he obviously loathed the general, he depended on Burgoyne's attestation of his services to submit a formal claim to the British government, a

132   DISHONORED AMERICANS

document Burgoyne refused to provide. Peters was both insulted and seemingly helpless in this case. Because of the gaping chasm of rank and culture that separated the two men, the Loyalist could not take on Burgoyne alone. Nine years after Saratoga, Peters composed a letter asking for help from his "only Patron," Sir Guy Carleton.[71]

Guy Carleton, Lord Dorchester, served as military governor of Quebec until Burgoyne's promotion to command of the Saratoga Campaign in 1777. Insulted at being passed over in favor of a subordinate officer, Carleton demanded his recall to Britain, and Sir Frederick Haldimand took over as governor in 1778. Carleton returned as commander-in-chief of British forces in America in 1782 to direct the evacuation of the British army. Loyalists admired Carleton, and though he was in and out of favor with the government, he was one of the few British commanders who actively stood up for the refugees. Jonathan Odell lauded his "mild command," and many Loyalists wrote to him upon his return to America and afterward in the hopes of special consideration and assistance in redressing wrongs committed by other officers.[72]

The rough copy of Peters's letter is an emotionally charged document, full of redactions and rephrasing as Peters struggled to find the balance between assertiveness and impudence, deference and self-defeating timidity. Peters's central claim was that he had "inlisted 643 Men" and yet "General Burgoyne did not deliver to me my Commission and I believe it was owing to the various disasters under which the royal Army laboured."[73] Years after these events, however, Burgoyne still had not issued a certificate testifying to Peters's rank and services. A signed commission from Burgoyne was essential proof of Peters's activities in the war, without which he could not apply for an officer's pension. Perhaps just as importantly, without the commission Peters could not receive public acknowledgment of his loyalty to the Crown. The lack of a commission was very likely an intentional insult, calculated to prevent any preferment for the former Loyalist colonel. Burgoyne's sin of omission in this case prevented Peters from even beginning his quest for political rebirth.

"I know myself under greater obligation to you than to all Mankind besides; this truth I have owned Since 1776 and will continue to own as long as

I live," wrote Peters, before arriving at his bitter point. "I had full faith in the Promises of British Ministers and British Generals. Upon that faith I acted without expecting to meet with deception, neglect & contempt from those I served with my Mind, my Person & Property." His tone changes sharply here. "Sir, I have at last discovered that I was once blinded by the Dazle [sic] of British Honor vested in the hands of certain British Officers, whose maxim has been to make no Difference between evil Servants & good." Peters could only conclude that these slights were "designed while in America": "[Burgoyne] was fond of my services while he was to receive the Glory of it." Now, Peters reported, without Carleton's help, he would "despair and die in wretchedness with my numerous family."[74]

Rather than end on such a pathetic note, Peters drew on Carleton's own potential piques and rivalries by including the Swiss-born general Frederick Haldimand, who replaced Carleton as governor of Quebec in 1778, as another conspirator in the scheme to undo the Loyalist. "While in Canada [Haldimand] said that he would take care & prevent me having half pay or any other favour from the King for no other Reason known, than that because he Supposed me to be the Author of . . . [a] Petition to himself to be Signed by the Loyalists in Canada," wrote Peters, "but I have reason to Suspect my greatest crime consisted in my being born in New England & not in a Hut in the Mountains of Switzerland."[75] Haldimand evidently despised Peters, and he even demoted the colonel to a captain of an invalid company and refused to provide any employment for Peters's sons. In the end, "General Haldimand refused a certificate of my Loyalty & Services, tho' they had been so conspicuous for Ten Years past."[76]

These disputes weighed heavily on Peters. As a gentleman he could not silently abide such treatment, especially considering what he had sacrificed for the British government. Yet his opponents were too powerful and his resources too limited to carry on a campaign like Joseph Galloway's. With both of his former commanding officers refusing to provide certificates on his behalf, Peters could not make an effective claim for compensation. His disfavor was also felt by his Loyalist sons and his entire family. For as much as Peters defended his honor and that of the Loyalists in general, he was at a fatal disadvantage in this contest. His quarrels with Burgoyne and

134 DISHONORED AMERICANS

Haldimand reveal how faction and hierarchy were inextricably linked in the Loyalist claims process. Peters died in 1788, never achieving the satisfaction he so desperately sought.[77]

It is unclear what impact these disputes between Loyalist gentlemen and British commanders had on the claims process, but there is evidence that individual tales of Loyalist heroics and suffering had some positive impact on the wider British public. The Loyalist macro-narrative of stoic, honorable men who endured the loss of their families and fortunes can be glimpsed in a poem by Mariana Starke, the English author of some of the first travel guides to France and Italy.[78] In *The Poor Soldier; An American Tale: Founded on a Recent Fact* (1789), Starke tells the story of Charles Short, a "Carolina loyalist." Starke's sentimental poem follows the standard Loyalist narrative pattern exactly, with the only innovation being the introduction of a feeling young gentlewoman named Felicia who sets out to save the Loyalist from his misery.

Felicia first comes across Short begging in the street:

> A Soldier's garb the mournful Object wore
> A wooden-leg, stern Honour's badge, he bore
> Dire Famine in his hollow cheek was seen
> But placid Resignation mark'd his mien.

Short has lost everything but accepts his lot with a clear conscience, knowing that he has done right. Once Felicia learns how this former gentleman came to such a pitiable condition, she cannot help but echo the Loyalists' cry:

> Ungrateful England! Shall the Man whose blood
> Flow'd, at thy bidding, in a copious flood;
> Who left his happy Cot, his fair domains,
> To war for thee on Carolina's Plains,
> Shall he in vain solicit thy relief,
> And die from meagre want and pining grief?[79]

Short's career began in a golden land of plenty, where he minded his "fruitful Farm" and lived the patriarchal dream with his faithful "Tenants" and "pure Wedlock's hallow'd joys." Then came the "deathful banner" of war at which "domestic Comfort fled / And dark suspicion came in Concord's stead / The Brother now against Brother rose / And dearest Friends were turn'd to deadliest Foes." Short chooses loyalty "to my Prince and Albion's interest true" and joins the British army, eventually evacuating his whole family to New York. There he is met by unspeakable tragedy when marauding Hessians burn his family alive in their home. Left "Unman'd, distracted, void of all relief, / Silent [Short] stood, a monument of grief." After this trauma, Short fights recklessly for the British, until his mournful encounter with his rebel brother dying on the battlefield. His family dead and his world destroyed, Short is finally wounded and crippled on the battlefield. The shattered gentleman travels to England but is ignored by his former commanders, until Felicia uses her resources and influence to give the poor soldier a comfortable place to die.[80]

The Poor Soldier is a well-designed piece of poetry, intended to jerk tears from a feeling, genteel audience. Written after the conclusion of the Claims Commission's work, it would have been of little political use, yet the Loyalists would have identified with the story. The fact that it was penned by a young English gentlewoman indicates that the macro-narrative of the Loyalists was known by and had an impact on the wider public. The character is a good, honorable man who did everything that was expected of him as a gentleman, a husband, and a loyal and brave soldier. For his virtues he is rewarded with nothing but tragedy and abandonment. It was a perfect encapsulation of the Loyalists' self-perception. As late as 1797 the exiled Reverend Jonathan Boucher brooded in his history of the Revolution that "loyalty and loyal men gained nothing but honour, either by their superior prowess, or superior skill."[81]

The exiled Loyalists experienced the trauma of defeat as a people adrift, as refugees caught between the nation that exiled them and a government that had, for some, seemingly betrayed them. In this trial, the Loyalists articulated their idea of honor, defended the justice of their cause, and asserted their rights as worthy men within the empire. Most Loyalist refugees agreed that a combination of wicked and ambitious colonists, raised in a republican, dissenting culture, had been victorious because of weak colonial administrators and the defective manhood of the generals sent to quell the rebellion. The Loyalists argued that they had done all they could in support of British arms, despite the charges of men like Burgoyne and Howe. To the refugees, the British government was responsible for losing America and the Loyalists' estates. The king and Parliament sacrificed the property and livelihoods of their loyal American subjects for peace, and the Loyalists were determined to make the government understand its obligation and provide compensation.

The Claims Commission dominated the hopes and fears of Loyalist gentlemen eager to reclaim their status as honorable patriarchs. Though the refugees tended to be disappointed by the compensation they received, parliamentarians held up the commission as a shining example of British faithfulness and compassion. The British government did not compensate the Loyalists based on their rights as citizens but out of concern for the honor of the British state. The Loyalists regarded themselves as important members of the empire who were owed compensation because of their honor, which they defined in simple, sentimental terms of steadfast duty. They contrasted their honor, built on restraint and manly stoicism, with the corrupt passions of the rebels and the foppish, indolent, and ungrateful character of Howe and Burgoyne.

In the war's aftermath, Loyalist refugees had the opportunity to compose narratives for official record and public consumption that together created a consistent depiction of the honorable Loyalist gentleman. This was an identity and a distinction, they argued, earned through toil and sacrifice. Though their role in the war was never fully acknowledged, and though they were even attacked and denigrated by prominent British officers, the narratives they constructed during the early years of their exile shaped the Loyalists' political rebirth.

5

Political Rebirth

I N LATE 1782, JOEL Stone's family urged him to return home. The Loyalist had fled his Connecticut hamlet of Judea in 1777 and found sanctuary in British-occupied New York. There he served as a Loyalist recruiter, a privateer, and a militia captain. In his absence, the Connecticut government declared him politically dead and auctioned his confiscated property. Whaleboat men captured Stone on Long Island and hauled him to the Fairfield jail, but the wily Loyalist escaped. Despite all of this, his brother assured Stone that "the inhabitants of Judea wish you to return." Stone did not doubt his brother's sincerity, but he had good cause to be wary of returning. The former neighbors who apparently invited him home were among the same people who had forced Stone to flee, broke into his home, and abused his sister. Stone replied that he was "much obliged to them for there [sic] good opinion of me, and wish as sincerely there was an end to malice, & I could happily spend my days with them."[1] Both men knew that would not be easy. Even if the Connecticut government permitted the Loyalists to return, Stone could not expect it to rescind the property confiscations. Nor would the government protect returnees from further insult.

Nonetheless, the terms of the Treaty of Paris included the freedom to pursue lawful prewar debts and permitted Loyalists "to remain twelve months unmolested" in the United States in their attempt to regain lost property. Though Stone likely knew his chances of success were slim, he returned very briefly "to try what I could do among my original debtors." Before the war, Stone was a rising merchant and shopkeeper. His official Loyalist claim includes a ledger containing the names of hundreds of debtors who together

{137}

owed him over £2,000. Stone needed the money badly, but there was more at stake in his audacious attempt to collect. Debts were a matter of honor.

Stone may have intended this visit as a test to see whether he could, in fact, live among his former neighbors—or whether they would refuse to pay and continue to dishonor him. He recorded that his "former friends" treated him "with respect but from those of the populace who deemed me criminal to their principles I met a quite different treatment." Stone does not specify whether the resentful Patriots were the same people who owed him money, but the justice of the peace warned Stone not to pursue his "book debts as the populace being still enraged against me the consequences might be dreadful." When the locals learned of Stone's presence and intentions, he "received solemn warning from the mob to leave the province within forty-eight hours." He went into hiding to finish making copies of his account books before returning to New York.[2]

If Stone had any serious intentions of returning permanently to Connecticut, this final dishonor dashed those hopes. His debtors had evidently decided that the Loyalists' political death would continue. They owed him nothing. Neither could Stone rely on the courts for redress. Another Connecticut Loyalist, Amos Botsford, tried to pursue his prewar debtors but was informed that the state government would "not suffer [a Loyalist] to maintain a Suit for recovering a Debt." The best a Loyalist could do was hire a lawyer who, rather than engage in futile court proceedings, would prevail upon the debtors' sense of honor and fairness. As Sally Hadden has demonstrated, such efforts produced mixed results at best. John Hancock, for example, died owing the Loyalist Harrison Gray a personal debt of £1,000 that he refused to pay. Mather Byles Jr. noted wryly in 1786 that citizens of the new republic had "a rooted Antipathy to paying their just Debts" since "it is certainly inconsistent with the Liberties of a free People to be obliged to pay them at all."[3] Patriots' refusal to pay their prewar debts to Loyalists was one final act of dishonor, one last clear message that a Tory was not a man worthy of respect.

Stone carried the bitterness of this and other dishonors for the rest of his life. Six years later, while he languished, destitute, in a tent on the banks of the St. Lawrence River, Stone refused his family's entreaties "to leave

that distant wilderness and come again to live in his native country to better himself and his friends." Even if he could return and live safely with
his family, Stone would never be whole. Thirty years later, he lamented to
a passing British aristocrat in Upper Canada that he had "not seen one of
them [his family] since 1783." "That is wrong," he said, "very wrong. I know
it is, but yet I cannot bring myself to go there, and I read & dwell upon the
history & discussion in Parliament from 1765 to the present day with a mix-
ture of sincere sorrow & astonishment at the Events."[4] For Stone and other
Loyalists like him, the personal repercussions of the American Revolution
were inseparable from the imperial schism.

By the late 1780s, however, it was possible for all but the most "notorious" Loyalists to return to their homelands. Silvanus Bishop, another Loyalist who lived not far from Stone in Litchfield County, returned in 1790 after
a few years of exile in New Brunswick. He bought back his former home
and in 1804 was selected as a grand juryman, a vote of confidence that confirmed that he had indeed been fully reintegrated as a respected member
of the community. Genteel custom worked to bury the Tory stigma, while
time and discretion evaporated any local memory of the Loyalists except
a few exiled archvillains. By the mid-nineteenth century, an orator at the
county's 1851 centennial could assert confidently that Litchfield "never furnished the enemy with any Tories."[5]

This final chapter is not intended as a retelling of Loyalists' reintegration into the early republic nor of their resettlement in Canada. It is rather
an examination of how exiled and returning Loyalists navigated the social
complexities of the postwar period.[6] The high politics and legislation of
the day were crucial in both paths toward political rebirth, but Loyalists
were made whole again first through the intercession of their social networks and local communities that acknowledged their right to respect.
Exile and reintegration were very different journeys, but they both relied on
honor culture's capacity for peacemaking, reconciliation, and community
building. Much of this book has explored honor and dishonor in the context
of insult, upheaval, war, and violence, but as Linda Pollock argues, honor
was experienced more often as "an ethos of unity and harmony" in which
men and women worked together to protect the reputation and rights of

140 DISHONORED AMERICANS

their family and ensure its place in a wider hierarchy. It was through these relationships that Loyalists could begin the process of political rebirth. Genteel families and social networks in the United States embraced the essential pliancy of honor to forgive and reintegrate Loyalists into their own ranks, and they then leaned on American legislators to see the wisdom of putting the war behind them and embracing a spirit of forgiveness. Despite some vociferous opposition in the newspapers and legislatures, and as capricious as the process could sometimes be, many gentlemen Loyalists were reborn at home as American citizens. This meant abandoning the Loyalist identity and focusing instead on their status as honorable and useful members of their families and communities.[7]

Comparing the rationales of men like Stone, who chose exile, with those who opted for reintegration provides revealing insights into the nature of elite honor culture and the persistence of Loyalist identity in the postwar years. Rebecca Brannon argues that Loyalists were guided by a "brutal calculus of self-preservation" in the postwar world.[8] For some exiles, that calculation involved more than money, though personal finances and property were always vital factors in their decisions. Loyalist gentlemen determined whether to attempt reintegration or to migrate elsewhere in the British Empire based on which option seemed most likely to lead to their political rebirth, that is, the restoration of their honor and status. For some, reintegrating into their homelands and communities was essential. Exile seemed a far worse fate than the passing sting of atonement and admitting fault. As Bertram Wyatt-Brown observes, for gentlemen, "kinlessness and solitude" were "the twin dangers to be avoided at all costs."[9] For other Loyalists, supplicating their former enemies, even if it meant returning home, seemed like another unbearable humiliation.

The previous chapter explored Loyalists' articulation of their identity as uniquely honorable men. Even if they endured disrespect from British officials, Loyalists who accepted exile, especially those who considered themselves gentlemen, could not simply abandon that identity. Exile was traumatic, but migration permitted Loyalists to focus on reconciliation in their own way and on their own terms, without fears of reprisal or further insult. They could maintain and even deepen their Loyalist identity surrounded by other like-minded people and pass on their identity to a new generation. Under British rule, they received recognition and compensation for their sacrifices and they did not have to resign themselves to living under republican governments. They could still work to reestablish ties with their homelands, families, and social networks in the United States, if at a distance. As will be shown, many exiled Loyalist gentlemen in Canada reconciled with their homelands and repaired their social networks without having to experience the abasement seemingly demanded by reintegration. Exile, for these Loyalists, was the honorable path.

Returning Loyalists did their best to act contrite and put the conflict behind them. Exiled Loyalists embraced their wartime experiences and sacrifices as their exclusive sources of honor. The Loyalists' drive to restore their status in exile again reveals the oppressive elements of gentlemanly honor culture in the Atlantic world. For all his refinement and politesse, the gentleman's status and self-worth depended on the obedience of others, and his honor was conspicuous because of pervasive degradation in society. From different backgrounds and with varying levels of influence, the exiled Loyalists explored in the second part of this chapter could be caustically demanding of their wives and children, their servants, and the enslaved, and they were often surprisingly combative with their superiors. Loyalist men in exile believed they were owed a special right to respect. This was the exiles' last chance to reclaim the social and economic power they once had. If they failed, all that was left was shame, destitution, and the final triumph of their enemies.

Political death annulled the citizenship of Loyalist gentlemen in the former colonies and stripped them of their rights to own property, lead households, pursue their economic interests, and influence public affairs. Patriots dishonored the Loyalists by transforming them—legally, culturally, socially, and sometimes physically—into the antithesis of gentlemen. Loyalists lost their right to respect, their honor, as elite white men. As will be seen, these losses, however painful, were temporary. Once the wartime fervor abated, family networks and governments returned gentlemen to prominence wherever they settled. Political rebirth was the complex and often multigenerational process that restored the Loyalists' status and

142 DISHONORED AMERICANS

public life as authority figures, householders, and honorable patriarchs. Whether that involved the survival of their Loyalist identity was a decision that each man and his family had to make.

Loyalists chose exile over reintegration for a variety of reasons: economic incentives, ideological devotion, personal resentments, the lasting pain of insults and wounds, and no small degree of stubborn pride. Loyalist regiments and other military units settled new lands in Canada together. Thus esprit de corps and the honor of the regiment also played a likely role for soldiers in accepting exile. Like Falstaff marching to battle, even if some Loyalist soldiers wished to return, honor pricked them on to exile.

Other Loyalists could not return to the United States even if they had wanted to. Branded "notorious conspirators," high-ranking collaborators like Joseph Galloway of Philadelphia, who served as an advisor to General William Howe in the Pennsylvania Campaign, or Joshua Loring, the reviled Boston Loyalist whom many blamed for the wretched state of American prisoners of war, would never find peace in the United States. In Massachusetts, William Brown, who was declared "politically deceased" by a New England newspaper in 1774 for serving as a mandamus councillor and then officially banished in October 1778, found his attempts to return rebuffed in the postwar years. Even when the Massachusetts legislature passed an amnesty act in April 1787, enough legal and social hurdles remained for men like Brown that return was not feasible.[10]

Loyalists implicated in wartime atrocities faced even more daunting challenges to any reconciliation or reintegration. The New Jersey Loyalist Richard Lippincott, whose very public reprisal killing of Joshua Huddy in 1782 set off an infamous transatlantic controversy (see chapter 3), knew there was no way he could ever return to the United States. He eventually settled near present-day Toronto, where the tale of Huddy's extrajudicial killing was passed down through the family as a courageous act of justice for the murder and mutilation of Lippincott's brother-in-law. A later Canadian historian described Lippincott's land grant in Upper Canada and "his superlative example of loyalty and devotion," along with his "bitter enmity toward the United States," as the basis of a prosperous and long-lived

POLITICAL REBIRTH 143

provincial dynasty and Tory ideology that "raised 'loyalism' to the level of divine injunction."[11]

Likewise, Colonel John Butler of New York went into exile with his rangers along the Niagara River. In the immediate aftermath of the conflict, Colonel Allan MacLean, the commandant at Niagara, reported that Butler's men, implicated in several frontier atrocities including the Wyoming Valley massacre, believed "they could not expect the shadow of justice" in New York. Butler explained that his men "would rather go to Japan than go among the Americans, where they could never live in peace." As late as 1792, American newspaper descriptions of Niagara Falls recorded that the lands on the Canadian shore were "settled chiefly by the noted Col. Butler's rangers; a corps, which, in the time of war infested the frontiers." The article included an ominous postscript: "No subject of the United States is permitted to pass the river."[12] Both Lippincott and Butler knew that in losing the war, they had lost their place in the former colonies forever.

Loyalists like these were right to be wary of the immediate postwar period in the United States. It was not a safe place for Loyalists, especially those who had fought alongside Indigenous warriors on the frontier. Butler's rangers and others like them were doubtlessly on the minds of the "principal inhabitants" of the Mohawk Valley who published a resolution against those who "with a malicious pleasure . . . wantonly sported with the lives of helpless women and children; numbers they have scalped alive, shut them in their houses and burnt them to death." They declared that the Loyalists had "killed thousands of cattle and horses that rotted in the fields" and burned "more than two million bushels of grain" along with farms and homes. They had "tomahawked and scalped" children and left "three hundred widows and above two thousand orphans in this county." The people of the Mohawk district would never permit "these merciless fiends" to return, even if they "have washed their faces from Indian paint, and their hands from the innocent blood." Their former neighbors had transformed, morally and racially, into the worst enemies, and there was no coming back.[13]

Such sentiments were printed regularly in American newspapers in 1783. An article in the Boston *Evening-Post* asked readers, "Do not your spirits rise with indignation and your very blood curdle in your veins, at the idea of those wretches . . . returned to live amongst you?" "Can you detach the

144   DISHONORED AMERICANS

idea of a robber, an incendiary, or a murderer, from one of their names?" Since the peace treaty permitted the return of the Loyalists, even if just briefly, the author proposed forming "general associations to render their situation . . . so uneasy, that they will prefer a voluntary banishment to a proposed return. . . . Like Cain of old, they will carry their mark in their foreheads; let them be avoided as persons contaminated with the most deadly contagion, and remain as their just demerits 'vagabonds upon the face of the earth.'" Evidently, some vengeful Patriots took such advice quite literally. A mob in Fairfield, Connecticut, branded the returning Loyalist Peter Guire with "GR" on his forehead, forever marking him as the king's property. This was an extreme example of what could happen to Loyalists attempting to return while passions were still aflame.[14]

While the fifth article of the Treaty of Paris permitted Loyalists to return to attempt to restore their property, and the sixth article prohibited any further persecution, local governments actively worked against any returning Loyalists in the months following the war. Several communities in Connecticut, for example, forbade the return of Loyalists on pain of imprisonment and deportation.[15] The townspeople of Stratford formed a committee to prevent "whole shoals of Tories . . . flocking over from Long Island, and other parts within the enemy's lines." The committee's resolutions, published in the *Connecticut Journal,* were unequivocal, stating that until there was some direction from state authorities to do otherwise, "we do pledge our honor, to each other, that we will exert ourselves, in the most proper and strenuous manner, to drive off and expel all such persons who shall make the attempt to regain that settlement . . . in this town, which they have utterly and forever forfeited." The announcement included the names of several Loyalists who had attempted to return and specific committee orders that each leave the state within a few days and never again "walk the streets of Freedom."[16]

Yet even during this intense phase, a returning Loyalist's experience might be more negotiated and contingent on family networks and connections than diehard Patriots would care to admit. Stephen Jarvis, a lieutenant in the Queen's Rangers from a prosperous Connecticut family, risked both arrest and an angry mob when he temporarily returned to his former home in Danbury to marry his fiancée, Amelia Glover, after a seven-year delay.

POLITICAL REBIRTH 145

Through his father, Jarvis acquired "leave from the American Government" and arrived at his childhood home in late May of 1783. Unfortunately, the return of the prodigal Loyalist caught the attention of several companies of militia gathered in the town for muster day. A family friend and a Continental dragoon warned the family of the danger, and Jarvis's father went to investigate. He returned in alarm and announced that they were coming. Jarvis put on a brave face in his narrative. His family "might perhaps see me die, but they should see me die like a soldier," he wrote, claiming that he told his loved ones, "I'll dispatch as many of them as my two pistols and my Sword will acquit me in doing."[17]

Instead of a bloodbath, the following scene reveals the power of family and collective honor as a peacemaking force. Jarvis's father and brother rode off to alert the authorities, while the Loyalist remained with his female relatives. When the militia arrived and entered the home, Jarvis retreated upstairs and "for a short time [there was] great confusion, the females imploring for mercy." Whatever the Jarvis women said had the desired effect: "the Mob became more tranquil." They negotiated with the militia and worked out an agreement. At the insistence of his sisters, Stephen Jarvis came downstairs to speak with the militia. "I saw many who I knew," he recorded, "and offered my hand. Some shook hands with me and others again damned me for a dam'd Tory, others charging me with cutting out prisoners' tongues." The militia leader assured Jarvis that they would not harm him, but that "if you are seen within thirty miles of [Danbury] by sundown you must abide the consequences." With the arrival of family, friends, and neighbors as well as a small contingent of Continental dragoons, the militia agreed to allow Jarvis to stay the night for an impromptu marriage, after which the newlyweds would leave.[18]

The next morning the sheriff returned with a crowd to arrest the groom despite his official passes and the deal brokered earlier with the militia. Barricaded in his bedroom with his bride, and with the Continental dragoons again acting on behalf of the Loyalist officer, Jarvis placated the militia by tossing them a dollar to drink to Amelia's health. The gathered townspeople reciprocated and shared a "bottle of bitters" raised to the bedroom window in a basket. With the mood lightened, the mob reportedly declared the local Tory "a dam'd honest fellow," and Stephen and Amelia went on their way.[19]

146   DISHONORED AMERICANS

The Jarvis experience points to both the intense feelings of the immediate postwar period and the role of family and collective honor in reconciliation. The militia's behavior bears some similarities to the custom of the charivari, or rough music, in which a community expressed their displeasure at a marital mismatch or some other form of nuptial transgression. Yet the Jarvis family network closed ranks around its own to prevent violence or insults. Jarvis described his father as "a great Tory" and his uncle as "a great Whig," but in practice these apparent political divisions did not undermine solidarity within this genteel family's network; they strengthened it.[20] The Jarvis men called upon their influential friends, while the women of the family exercised their power as conciliators and negotiators. Whereas during the conflict Patriot mobs might insult or brush aside women associated with Loyalists, in this postwar scenario, they accepted the intervention of the Jarvis women. Stephen Jarvis was not saved because the militia recognized his honor. Rather, the militia members accepted his place within a family that had an acknowledged right to respect within the community. Though this was a dramatic example of the power of family honor, similar processes occurred throughout the United States as Loyalists returned home.

Returning Loyalists were not just a family matter. They posed a complex set of problems for the new republic and became a point of heated debate in the immediate postwar period. Opponents in state legislatures echoed many of the arguments found in the newspapers at the time. Allowing the Loyalists a place in the new nation would be a grave injustice, they insisted, and an insult to the Americans who died or risked everything for independence. Furthermore, returning Tories could work as a fifth column in favor of Britain and sap the moral purity of a republic built on virtuous citizenship. Such anti-Loyalist sentiment continued throughout the 1780s, but every historian who has examined the process of reintegration notes that passions cooled quickly in the mid-1780s, leading to more openness to Loyalist reintegration. As early as 1782, Henry Laurens predicted this situation and advised the Penn family to "give decent Time for recovery and deliberation" and await "a cooler hour" before seeking compensation for losses, a time when the exiled family could "expect much more magnanimity of the Citizens of Pennsylvania."[21]

As the anger abated, proponents of "moderate republicanism" and reintegration, such as Aedanus Burke in South Carolina and Alexander Hamilton in New York, argued that the principles of the Revolution demanded reconciliation with former enemies. Confiscation and the legal persecution of all but the most loathsome Tories, argued Burke, came from a place of weakness, and forgiveness reflected confidence and strength. At issue was the very concept of citizenship, who defined it, and who could take it away. Not every Loyalist was a diehard partisan fighter or an elite collaborator. Many were simply trapped in occupied territory and did what they needed to survive, while others were mere "trimmers" with no real ideological convictions who hedged their bets until a clear victor emerged. Then there were the religious pacifists, such as some Pennsylvania Quakers who refused to take oaths or bear arms for either side. Though the harsh penalties inflicted on such figures may have been justified during the conflict, in the war's aftermath, moderates like Governor George Clinton of New York regarded further Loyalist persecution as "private vengeance" that was corrosive to a nation built on rational laws and individual rights. Benjamin Rush likewise denounced the Pennsylvania Test Acts, which stripped otherwise honorable men of their citizenship without trial, as tyrannical. For men of property sitting in state legislatures, the treatment of the Loyalists in the American Revolution presented a very dangerous precedent. If governments could seize Loyalist property and cancel their citizenship without trial based on populist clamor, what might happen to unpopular men in the democracy's future? The delegates at the Constitutional Convention agreed unanimously to ban attainder in the United States lest it become a tool of some demagogue or the tyranny of the majority.[22]

For Alexander Hamilton, the Loyalist question and the states' mercurial responses also underscored the deficiencies in the Articles of Confederation that risked the honor of the United States on the international stage. Article 4 of the Treaty of Paris obliged Congress to permit the recovery of all debts; by the notorious fifth article, Congress agreed to "earnestly recommend" that the states restore the Loyalists' rights and property; and article 6 prohibited any further legal prosecution. State refusal to abide by these treaty stipulations threatened to undermine the new nation and risked the entire postwar settlement with Britain. Hamilton, writing as "Phocion," insisted that if the individual states could ignore treaty obligations based on their own sovereignty, then "would not all the powers of the confederation be annihilated and the union dissolved?" In addition to the constitutional weakness this exposed, state refusal represented a "wilful [sic] breach" that would provide Britain with justification to also ignore the treaty. Moreover, "the little vindictive selfish mean passions of a few" who sought to punish and profit from the expulsion of the Loyalists would lead to "a loss of [national] character in Europe." Just when the United States sought to take its place in international relations, European states would regard Americans as a "people, destitute of government, on whose engagements of course no dependence can be placed." Supporters of reintegration, like Hamilton, had their eyes on the bigger picture: the United States as a sovereign state whose principled laws and treaty obligations superseded state and local concerns.[23] The moderates argued that the fate of the Revolution depended, at least in part, on reconciliation with the Loyalists.

The actual process of Loyalist reintegration differed among the states, but the intercession of family and social networks was the consistent factor that permitted Loyalist political rebirth throughout the new nation. Friends and family provided testimony that acknowledged returnees' right to respect and vouched for their value to society. No gentleman could live in a community that dishonored him. This would be an intolerable situation for the man himself, but it would also be corrosive to the whole community. Edward Rutledge took assurances from the fact that no one would ever endure such a scenario, musing that the government of South Carolina hardly needed to intercede to prevent the return of particularly obnoxious Tories since "the People . . . will soon make their Situation very uncomfortable."[24] Finding prominent Patriot allies would, conversely, help smooth the path to a Loyalist's political rebirth. John Adams, John Jay, Henry Laurens, and other leading figures supported the return of their former Loyalist friends.[25]

Loyalists who had never fled to the British but instead rode out the conflict at home, under suspicion or even house arrest, faced an easier transition back to full membership within their communities. Thomas Ingersoll notes that in Massachusetts, such individuals "effortlessly regained their political rights." Joseph Tiedemann describes a similar phenomenon in Queens County, New York, where the predominantly Loyalist population found itself in a surprisingly strong position after British evacuation in 1783 and faced few serious problems.[26]

The situation was more complicated for the many wealthy Loyalists who remained behind in New York City. Although initially threatened with expulsion and attacked repeatedly in the press, the city's monied Loyalists soon found allies in the moderate ranks of the Patriot elite, including Alexander Hamilton. Expelling the Loyalists, Hamilton argued, would only enrich the British at the expense of the newly independent state. Such practical sentiment worked in tandem with the spirit of reconciliation and polite discretion built into genteel honor culture. As Judith Van Buskirk observes, in the aftermath of British withdrawal from New York, "like-minded, similarly educated, finely clothed people sought out their own kind with a vengeance." The genteel peacemaking impulse, in which both men and women played vital roles, quickly rekindled relationships, healed breaches, and smoothed over quarrels or pushed past injuries into oblivion. Family and social networks went about the delicate work of reconciliation in private even while anti-Loyalist sentiment dominated the newspapers. Eventual public appearances of Whigs with former Tories at a "dancing assembly," for example, inflamed republican outrage but demonstrated that the old genteel networks of New York looked after their own. Within months the radical voices in the legislature were replaced with moderates. There would be no return of confiscated estates, but legislation passed quietly in May 1784 that allowed former Loyalists to buy back their property. The legislature enacted some voting restrictions on returnees, but such punitive measures were temporary and were filled with exceptions and loopholes. By the early 1790s even exiled Loyalists supposedly disqualified from returning—such as Frederick DePeyster, who bore arms for the British as an officer in the King's American Regiment—quietly slid back into the elite ranks of New York society.[27]

Rebecca Brannon's study of Loyalist reintegration in South Carolina also demonstrates the central role of genteel honor culture in postwar reconciliation. Even though the state experienced some of the bloodiest internecine violence of the war, South Carolina offered clemency to most Loyalists who petitioned for reintegration if they were supported by strong testimonies from neighbors and friends. Brannon argues that "class solidarity" among

150   DISHONORED AMERICANS

the small ruling clique of planters "smoothed the way" to reconciliation. The South Carolina gentry could "identify and forgive each other" partly because of the "culture of agreeableness that a slave society created." Whether in South Carolina or in the elite culture of urban New York, private reconciliation was key to political rebirth. New York was divided by factionalism, whereas the more unified South Carolina planter class dominated the courts and legislature that ultimately enacted their wishes. "Law is a cultural artifact," writes Bertram Wyatt-Brown in his examination of Southern honor, and the smaller the "community in which it is administered, the more certain it is that the law will reflect the neighborhood will." Such was the case in South Carolina, where elite circles embraced an honor culture predicated on "communal solidarity."[28]

The reintegration process in South Carolina protected the honor of supplicant Loyalists and their extended families. A humbled Tory might receive a dressing-down from relatives, and he had to word his apologies carefully, but once he completed "the painstaking work of personal apologies and reconnecting frayed social networks," these efforts tended to stay private. In their official petitions to the state, former Loyalists sought ways to excuse their wartime allegiance and prove that they were, and always had been, honorable men who were valuable to their community. A few men claimed that they were too ill or too old to resist the British occupation. Youthful indiscretion was sometimes an effective excuse. Henry Laurens felt that South Carolina would extend clemency to young James Poyas "in consideration of his minority." Others claimed that they had made an error in judgment or had little choice but to accept commissions in the Loyalist militia to preserve their property or to feed their families. Southern gentlemen embraced a "selective, honor-bound fatalism" that perhaps made these admissions easier to swallow. Neither a judgment from God nor an indictment of their manhood, Loyalist defeat might be regarded as a reflection of the "arbitrary, morally blind, and indifferent" nature of fate. More practically, most reintegrated Loyalists in South Carolina recovered their estates, which played a valuable and productive role within a wider network of plantations. Henry Laurens's support for his nephew Elias Ball's reintegration involved sharing land and enslaved laborers. All these elements ensured that former Loyalists could expect their communities to support their return to South Carolina. In 1784, earlier than any other state, the South Carolina legislature passed an omnibus clemency act reintegrating most former Loyalists who applied.[29]

There were some strikingly successful examples of Loyalist reintegration that vindicated the political moderates and the assurances of genteel families that their formerly Tory sons were worthy members of society. In Massachusetts, the Loyalist Henry Van Schaak bought another exile's confiscated estate to replace his own, built a fine new house, and by 1787 was the selectman for his community and served as justice of the peace until 1807. William Paine, a prominent Worcester physician, returned from his exile in New Brunswick for a brief visit only to be encouraged to resettle permanently. He eventually founded the American Antiquarian Society. The former Connecticut Loyalist William Samuel Johnson was elected to Congress in 1785 and then to the first Senate in 1791. In South Carolina, the Loyalist officer Patrick Cunningham reclaimed his plantation and won election to the state house of representatives in 1792. His granddaughter Ann Pamela Cunningham Bird established the Mount Vernon Ladies' Association to preserve the home of George Washington.[30]

Other returnees were unable to shake the stigma of their former allegiance, a fact exacerbated by the intense politics of the early republic. Conservative Federalists tended to support returning Loyalists and champion their contributions to the new nation, while the Republican faction took advantage of anti-Loyalist sentiment when it could. John Porteous rode out the war in occupied New York and was a prominent investor in Loyalist privateering ventures. After the conflict, he became an active player in New York State politics for the Federalist party. In March 1795, a political ally warned him that a rival, Dr. Jonathan Moore, was spreading "infamous and groundless reports" intending to "defame and injure your reputation." Moore apparently declared to "everyone he meets or sees" that Porteous was "the damndest [sic] villain knave and rascal this side [of] Hell . . . that he believes you would rob and murder if you could do it and not be found out." Most importantly, Moore claimed that "during the last war you paid an immense sum of money to the Indians for the scalps of the Dutch people on the German flats" and that "you are a damned Tory." Porteous was by no means alone in having a genuine or alleged Loyalist past dredged up for his

152   DISHONORED AMERICANS

opponents' political gain, and the epithet "Tory" remained a potent insult well into the nineteenth century.[31]

There is no record of whether Porteous responded to these allegations, but his reintegration, like so many others, required him to endure such insults. To be reborn as an American citizen, a former Loyalist had to at least tacitly, and more often explicitly, disavow loyalism and admit in public or private that the Loyalist cause was dishonorable or at least foolhardy. Too young, too old, too ill, too many mouths to feed, too much property to risk, too conflicted and afraid of the war's outcome: these were all understandable excuses for failing to support the Revolution, but none was flattering. The reintegrating Loyalists most often presented themselves as meek and mild men who were hardworking and would serve their communities well, but they were not the heroic sort, nor were they in any way ideologically devoted to a cause other than the well-being of their country. In an honor-conscious society, such self-abasement might have been painful, but it was also necessary and indeed even laudable. As Linda Pollock observes, honor "was not something brought into play only in potentially violent confrontations" but was a communal force that could override individual pride. "Patience under provocation," Pollock writes, was regarded in the English Atlantic world "as a masculine virtue, not just, as is more conventionally claimed, as a feminine one." Behind the public recantations and petitions, whether in Connecticut or South Carolina, families and friends encouraged their Loyalist relatives to swallow their pride and devote themselves to family fortunes and social harmony. This may not have been a glorious path to political rebirth, but it was an honorable one. Any lasting stigma of political death, like that experienced by John Porteous, gradually faded, and the memory of the Loyalists in America slipped into oblivion.[32]

Loyalists who chose migration or were forced into exile saw the reintegration process very differently. The banished Massachusetts Loyalist Edward Winslow excoriated refugees who returned home as "giddy eccentric and discontented characters" who "made a voluntary sacrifice of their former honorable principles" and "meanly skulked into the United States." In a pair of addresses printed under the name "Tammany" in New Brunswick's *Royal*

Gazette in 1802, Winslow let loose two decades' worth of resentment against men he viewed as Loyalist apostates. The "order of Men who call themselves Loyalists," Winslow explained, chose "to plunge into the wilderness with their wives and children, rather than submit to the humiliating and degrading necessity of soliciting mercy from those whom they were in the habit of considering rebels." Gentlemen who gave up on the "laudable and manly" enterprise of building a righteous counterrevolutionary society debased themselves to become "hewers of wood and drawers of water" for their enemies. Most galling of all for a military man like Winslow, Loyalist officers who accepted reintegration were "compelled to consider the most meritorious actions of their lives as the most atrocious offences which they ever committed."[33]

Winslow's description of Loyalist reintegration is deeply gendered, sarcastic, and insulting, but it accurately captures the basic steps involved. To return to the United States and become a citizen, Winslow explained, such "contemptible and mercenary men" first had to negotiate "through their maiden aunts and other relatives for *leave to visit their* friends in the States." The supplicant had to remain "for some time in obscurity" and endure the humiliation of only being allowed in "company with elderly ladies, at their evening parties." Through the "persevering efforts" of their families, former Loyalists were presented "as deluded men, who never bloodied their fingers" in petitions to "a republican tribunal." Finally, "after a series of solicitations," the ex-Loyalists "were favoured with licenses to become citizens." Formerly proud Loyalist officers became "hucksters, grocers, auctioneers, etc. What became of their pride or their loyalty during these negotiations, is not for me to inquire," Winslow concluded. The old Loyalist observed that the transformation of the friends of government into the "subjects of Thomas Jefferson" had a corrosive effect on the morale of his province and "had a tendency to weaken that principle of duty, and to destroy that sense of shame . . . which ought to exist in the breast of every genuine loyalist, and every faithful soldier of the King."[34] In other words, the example of Loyalists returning home was catching on, and only honor and pride might convince those who remained in exile to hold the line.

Edward Winslow's diatribe against the dishonor of reintegration reflects the hardened sense of Loyalist identity that formed among a clique

154   DISHONORED AMERICANS

of elite exiles in the war's aftermath. Keith Mason argues that an inclusive Loyalist identity born from the shared experience of trauma and the privations found in refugee communities or garrisons rapidly dissolved after the Treaty of Paris. Black Loyalists, tenant farmers, frontiersmen, merchants, officers, planters, German and Dutch settlers, Scottish Highlanders, and others could not, Mason argues, be held together by the idea of loyalty as they dispersed and began to resent the British government as much the rebels.[35] Yet the identity of Loyalist exiles who viewed themselves as gentlemen solidified in the postwar years in a very distinct way. Like their counterparts who reintegrated into the United States, the exiles were focused on securing their status as gentlemen, but the recovery of their positions was inextricable from the maintenance of their identity as Loyalists. Postwar refugee settler loyalism centered on repeated recitations of past services and losses as well as statements of open commitment to the imperial connection as a moral imperative. Reform-minded settlers in the decades after initial settlement had to tread a careful, moderate path lest they be labeled "disloyal" and politically illegitimate.[36] Proof of service and sacrifice became the foundational sources of honor that translated into land grants from the Crown and, for the men explored in this chapter, wealth and influence. The Loyalist elite desperately needed British assistance, but rather than view this as dependence, they regarded their land grants and preferment as part of a reciprocal relationship with the imperial government. The gentlemen exiles believed it was their duty to order their new world, to replicate the values and manners of the British metropole, and to build a counterrevolutionary society built on respect for authority, both in public and in the home.

The previous chapter demonstrated how Loyalist narratives coalesced around the central trope of a brave, industrious martyr for the British Constitution. To this Edward Winslow added a blunter assessment of the qualities of Loyalist gentlemen: "irritable from a series of mortifications—scarcely cooled from the ardor of resentment—jealous to an extreme."[37] Preserving their distinctive identity and its exclusive privileges produced competitiveness and cutthroat political maneuvering in the years of initial settlement in Nova Scotia and Quebec. Men like Winslow and his small group of close friends believed that they alone had an exclusive right to authority and to the wealth that should naturally support their efforts to order the land and build their counterrevolutionary society.

Such an attitude was on display in what became known as the "Petition of 55," in which fifty-five Loyalist gentlemen wrote to Sir Guy Carleton to ask for land "sufficient to put us on the same footing with field-officers"—that is, five thousand acres each. Clergymen, merchants, lawyers, and other formerly prominent men attested that they did not ask for this land as compensation for their lost estates. Rather, since they were "Loyalists of the most respectable characters," they would be "highly advantageous in diffusing and support[ing] a spirit of attachment to the British constitution." The petition infuriated less prominent Loyalists, who responded with their own petition bearing six hundred signatures. The controversy also ignited a small pamphlet war in London.[38]

What most rankled the Loyalist counter-petitioners and pamphleteers was the elites' claim that their loyalty and honor was superior to such a degree that they had a right to be granted power over every other Loyalist in the province. The rank-and-file Loyalists argued that they, too, were dutiful, suffering Loyalists who had come to Nova Scotia under the belief that the lands allotted to refugees "were held out equally to all his Majesty's persecuted subjects." Their petition pulled no punches and stated that the gentlemen petitioners were in fact unworthy of the vast allocations and were instead plotting to force honest Loyalist settlers to "submit to be tenants to those, most of whom they consider as their superiors in nothing but deeper art and keener policy." A pamphleteer, probably the Reverend Samuel Peters, argued that the Loyalist elites schemed to elevate themselves to the ranks of a proper landed gentry, "to enrich themselves at the expense of the crown and their poor brethren in distress," and to lord over estates that they could "cultivate with vassals from Africa, Ireland, and America." The dream of the Loyalist elite, argued the opponents of the fifty-five, was to create not a counterrevolutionary society but a tyranny of upstarts and grifters.[39] The counter-petitioners argued that this plan represented a twisted kind of loyalism. If loyalty was the source of honor in the province, and honor was a claim to respect and dignity, then surely it

156   DISHONORED AMERICANS

accrued to all who suffered for it, not just those who felt they were owed special treatment because they claimed to be gentlemen. In the end, the government did not grant the fifty-five their vast estates.

This petition was indicative of a pattern of seemingly greedy or nepotistic behavior that led the historian Neil MacKinnon to characterize the Loyalist clique as a "parasitic coterie" of family networks. Such behavior offends modern sensibilities, and it also offended other Loyalist refugees, but the elites truly believed their rank and privileges were warranted and provided social stability. They were establishing the communal honor of a new colonial aristocracy upon which the fate of the whole society hinged. The Reverend Charles Inglis defended the petition by arguing that the gentlemen were in fact taking on a great task, reestablishing "habits of familiarity and friendship" while also undertaking the great expense of improving Nova Scotia's worthless tracts of forest. Edward Winslow explained his rationale for supporting the creation of the separate province of New Brunswick in similar terms of noblesse oblige. He told his good friend Ward Chipman that the idea of a Loyalist homeland came to him when a group of landless and abandoned soldiers implored him for help. Their pleas "almost murdered me," he said, and he realized that a new province, one that he and other members of the Loyalist elite could govern without interference from Halifax, was "the only possible means of effectual relief—and to contribute to that relief was my ambition and my motive." Nonetheless, a historian of Loyalist New Brunswick described the successful partition movement that established New Brunswick as a separate province in 1784 as an "old fashioned political battle . . . between competing elites."[40]

The competitiveness of the Loyalist elite continued in the new province. Opportunities existed for merchants and surveyors in the new land, but many Loyalist gentlemen who settled in New Brunswick were trained as lawyers. There would never be enough work for these men to all practice their genteel vocation. Government positions were therefore the only reliable source of income for gentlemen in the early years of settlement. Men vied with one another for positions and, to maximize earnings and prestige, they often held far more offices than they could effectively administer. Whether they acquired offices through nepotism or merit, Loyalist leaders routinely found their authority questioned.[41] Winslow's "irritable" and "jealous" Loyalists responded poorly to such challenges on their journey to political rebirth.

Amos Botsford was one such prominent Loyalist who stoked controversy as he attempted to build a new life and dynasty in New Brunswick. A Yale-educated lawyer with a flourishing practice in New Haven before the war, Botsford fled Connecticut in 1779 with his immediate family. As a well-connected gentleman, he quickly found government preferment in New York as a refugee agent and then as a settlement director in Nova Scotia after the peace. Botsford displayed his sense of entitlement to respect and authority in what one contemporary described as his "dictatorial style." Loyalist settlers accused him of lording over inferiors and British officials noted his surprising impertinence, with one official reminding the exile that he was no longer in Connecticut, where people "may reject and chuse another [Governor] when they please." Several disgruntled middle-ranking refugees drew up a petition charging Botsford with gross neglect of duty, conflict of interest, and peremptorily reassigning lands, presumably to his friends. When the British passed him over in the initial allocation of government offices in 1784, Botsford attributed this to the influence of more powerful Loyalist gentlemen petitioning in England, not to his own behavior. Nonetheless, this was only a temporary setback, and Botsford went on to hold several prominent government posts for the rest of his life.[42]

Botsford was not the only New Brunswick Loyalist to be accused of haughtiness and pomposity. An American visitor described Gabriel Ludlow, the mayor of Saint John, New Brunswick, as "aping the hauteur of the British," while Jonathan Bliss shuddered at the behavior of fellow gentleman Loyalist Jonathan Odell, whose "hauteur" was "so disgusting that he has become completely obnoxious."[43] The new powers entrusted to these men, combined with the memory of the insults and losses they had suffered during the war and their desire to repair their wounded manhood, may have produced this overweening behavior. Yet the displays of imperious manners were consistent with these Loyalists' beliefs that their refined honor required significant displays of deference from other men. That their fellow refugees rolled their eyes at such pretensions indicates people understood

158 DISHONORED AMERICANS

the spurious foundations of the gentlemen's authority—authority that the Loyalist elites thought was their natural right but could, in fact, simply depend on the whim of British officials.

Other Loyalist gentlemen reported their frustrations at the disrespect they encountered in their efforts to build an ideal society. The former Boston clergyman Mather Byles Jr. did his best to promote an orderly and deferential flock in Halifax, but he was sorely disappointed. He felt his honor impugned as he spent his days dealing with "the Rage of Electioneering, & the Violence of Party" coupled with the garrison community's "many drunken Mobs." They ignored Byles and his teachings, did not attend his services, and, most gallingly, disregarded his claim to privilege and authority in favor of other denominations—or seemingly embraced no religion at all. Much of this unpopularity owed to the Church of England's rigid customs. While locals raised Baptist and Presbyterian churches and supported their ministers, and itinerant Methodist preachers traveled healthy circuits, Byles and his fellow Anglican clergymen were supported by government subsidies and by the Society for the Propagation of the Gospel in Foreign Parts. Charles Inglis, consecrated as the first bishop of Nova Scotia in 1787, fussed over the fact that some clergy allowed churchgoers to sit where they pleased, a practice destined to "produce disorder and confusion," he wrote, and he ordered churches to maintain hierarchy by renting pews to individual families based on rank and respectability. None of this appealed to the settlers. Byles was therefore overjoyed when he received an appointment to the rectory in Saint John in New Brunswick, a colony governed by Loyalist gentlemen like himself. After leaving Halifax, he wrote that he had "been imprisoned" in the city, and "upon cool Reflexion," he continued, Halifax was "in every Respect, the most contemptible my Eyes ever beheld & I desire never to forget that the most irreligious People I ever knew were at the same Time the [most] ignorant, the most stupid, & the most unhappy."[44]

Not everyone who claimed to be a gentleman could so easily slide into the New Brunswick elite as Mather Byles. Upper Canada, another new Loyalist province established in 1791, offered brighter prospects for the middling sorts and resulted in considerable emigration from the Maritime provinces. The Loyalist settlers in Upper Canada received lands based on their losses and service, and many communities were structured on the military hierarchies of disbanded regiments. The names of bona fide Loyalists were kept on official rolls and were marked with the letters "U.E." for Unity of Empire, a hereditary distinction that privileged them over later migrants from the United States. Like their counterparts in Nova Scotia and New Brunswick, rank-and-file Loyalists in Upper Canada resented the pretensions of the officer class.[45]

Joel Stone considered himself a worthy and honorable man, but he was not part of any influential clique. His position as a captain in the New York City militia earned him a half-pay pension, but he struggled throughout the 1780s in exile. Without the wealth or influence of men like Amos Botsford or Edward Winslow, Stone failed in his attempts to procure a government position and instead initially settled in the refugee community of New Johnstown on the St. Lawrence River, where he opened a ramshackle distillery in a building constructed "from the forests standing." By 1790, Stone's entrepreneurial venture collapsed "owing to the singular Scarcity of grain," and he fell into debt. He lamented to a friend that his situation "embarrassed my mind & finances . . . to a degree of ruin."[46] Stone aspired to be a gentleman, but he could not support his claim. A year later Stone met John Graves Simcoe, the new lieutenant governor of Upper Canada, and his wife, Elizabeth Posthuma Simcoe, when they stopped at his little settlement further down the St. Lawrence. Mrs. Simcoe described Stone as "extremely civil," though she was uncertain of his status. When she offered "a dollar to the people" in the settlement, another settler advised her that "Stone was too much a gentleman to offer anything to."[47] While Stone's standing was understood by the other refugees on the St. Lawrence, Elizabeth Simcoe did not immediately recognize him as a gentleman.

Even if Stone did not cut the figure of a gentleman, he was still determined to claim his right to respect and the compensation he felt he was owed. This led to a drawn-out dispute with Sir John Johnson, who was formerly one of the greatest landholders in colonial America and a brigadier general of Loyalist forces. The British surveyor general, Samuel Holland, instructed Stone in 1787 that if he paid to survey the lands around a set of falls on the Gananoque River, a tributary of the St. Lawrence, he could then take legal possession.[48] Unfortunately for Stone, Johnson was the supervisor of

160 DISHONORED AMERICANS

Loyalist settlement and, seeing the potential value of the falls, made a claim to the same land. It was an ideal location to construct both grist- and saw-mills to serve the growing population in the region, and neither man was willing to back down. The correspondence between the men reveals that far from being intimidated in the unequal contest, Stone was determined not to lose what he saw as his last chance at political rebirth.

With the requisite combination of assertiveness and deference, Stone argued that while he "never presumed to doubt your [Johnson's] Rights," he was eager to "explain and defend my own rights . . . particularly in point of right to [my] just proportion of the King's Bounty in Lands." Stone refused Johnson's offer of one thousand acres further up the river and continued to argue his point. The lands, Stone said, were his by law, since he had paid for the survey and Johnson had not, and by right of his previous sacrifices. The baronet seemingly acknowledged the legality of Stone's claim and agreed to a compromise wherein they would each take a bank of the river. This moment marked the beginnings not only of Stone's successful political re-birth but also a period of social, economic, and political advancement. He had asserted himself against a much more powerful adversary and secured his reward. Johnson served as an absentee landlord of the east bank of the river, while Stone began operating a sawmill and a general store, which eventually grew into a set of mills, shops, and a British garrison, with Stone as the undisputed leader of the settlement until his death in 1833. An early twentieth-century historian described him as "a little autocrat . . . in his little kingdom."[49] Though denied a place among the Loyalist grandees, he nonetheless became a member of a new frontier clique.

During the American Revolution, Patriots stripped Loyalists of their status as householders and patriarchs. Dishonor meant unmanning: the rebels demonstrated Tory impotence by attacking and then confiscating their homes and ejecting or otherwise abusing Loyalist families and dependents for the sins of their patriarch. Resettled Loyalist gentlemen therefore went to great expense to rebuild their households, both as statements of their power in the refugee societies and as vindication of their political allegiance and their manhood. According to Ann Gorman Condon, the household was "the one area of life they [Loyalist men] could control and also the one area capable of positive response."[50] As will be seen, Loyalist householders could be bitterly resentful of wives, children, or the enslaved who did not acknowledge their right to respect.

The Loyalist elites, like their counterparts everywhere in the Atlantic, regarded their households as political units, and they were deeply anxious about continuing threats to their patriarchal authority in the reordered world. If the "bonds of affection" between ruler and ruled could be permanently severed, what would happen to similar bonds within families? Patriarchs in the new republic shared these fears, but for all the anxieties of Loyalist exiles or American citizens, the Revolution did not overturn the power of husbands and fathers. The sons of revolutionaries remained dedicated to traditional ideals of patriarchal rule, just as Loyalists were, and both built their family fortunes on the same foundations.[51] Indeed, Linda Kerber's concept of "republican motherhood," in which women inculcated civic virtue within the households of the early republic, does not alter the fact that men still needed to project the appearance of domestic mastery in order to have a place in public life, just as they had done in the colonial period.[52] Mark Kann argues that a "grammar of manhood" characterized the politics of the early republic, and the household remained central to the construction of male identity and honor.[53] The societies Loyalists settled were equally patriarchal but also suffused with the touchiness born of defeat and dislocation. British and Loyalist leaders sought to create a rigidly hierarchical political system in the new colonies to prevent any further republican calamities. In order for a Loyalist to be politically reborn as a gentleman with a public role in this new world, he needed to demonstrate his domestic patriarchal authority in a very public way. This meant stylish houses, a dutiful wife and children, and obedient servants and slaves. The Loyalists achieved this through the support of the British government and through reconnecting with their social networks in the United States.[54]

Elite Loyalist exiles fused notions of gentility with their loyalism. Particularly in the Maritime provinces of Nova Scotia and New Brunswick, this led to the construction of genteel manors, complete with parlors for sociability and rooms for dancing. Historians have pointed to the lavish spending on such impracticalities as one cause for the demise of the

162 DISHONORED AMERICANS

Loyalist city of Shelburne, Nova Scotia, which reached perhaps twelve thousand inhabitants by the end of 1784 only to contract dramatically to a few thousand humble residents by the 1790s.[55] More stability was to be found along the St. John River in New Brunswick. Here the closed oligarchy of perhaps two dozen families dedicated themselves to replicating and inculcating the genteel virtues they believed were lost in the Revolution. Even in the sparsely populated colony of Upper Canada, elite Loyalists built fine houses as expressions of gentility that took on even more power when contrasted against the log cabins and huts of the humbler refugees. Over the course of his resettlement at Gananoque, the otherwise thrifty Joel Stone built three increasingly ornate homes to keep up with his rising status.[56] The physical household was an emblem of status, a supposed beacon of order and civilization, and an expression of the respect the elite Loyalists expected from their neighbors.

Slavery played a vital role in the construction of many of these fine homes, especially in the Maritime provinces. Prominent Loyalists like Brigadier General Timothy Ruggles, for example, relied on his human property to reconstruct a version of his former New England estate in Nova Scotia. As demonstrated by Catherine Cottreau-Robins, he transplanted both apple seedlings for a new orchard and the very "landscape of slavery" from Sandwich, Massachusetts, to his new lands.[57] The Jarvis family were slaveowners in Upper Canada, and other prominent Loyalists who appeared earlier in this book—such as James De Lancey, Jonathan Odell, James Moody, and many others who resettled in the Maritimes—relied on the enslaved to clear the land and rebuild their world.[58] Slaveholding refugees imported the Northern slave system into the Maritimes and Upper Canada: the enslaved were presented as members of the household, subject to the authority of the patriarch. Between two thousand and three thousand enslaved people were taken against their will into the British colonies that became Upper and Lower Canada, Prince Edward Island, Nova Scotia, and New Brunswick, with most concentrated in the latter two provinces. Slaveholding Loyalists usually held one or two people in bondage, with a small minority of wealthy Loyalists enslaving five or more people.[59]

Because the honor of the slaver derived from the degradation of the enslaved, maintaining slavery in exile was not only economically important

POLITICAL REBIRTH   163

but also vital for the self-perception and presentation of white elites. On Prince Edward Island, settlers regarded slaveholding as an inseparable part of elite status, whereas in other parts of the Maritimes, slavery was more widespread among the middling sorts. As Harvey Amani Whitfield has shown, some Loyalists were so desperate to hold on to their enslaved people that they falsified and even destroyed manumission documents, cheating Black refugees out of their freedom. The cruelty of Loyalist household slavery, a system its proponents argued was benevolent and paternalistic, is revealed through runaway advertisements, court cases, oral histories, and the steady stream of people sold to plantations in the West Indies or back to the United States. Except for Prince Edward Island, the Maritime colonies never protected slavery through statute, and the institution was opposed by large segments of the population. Yet it persisted into the early 1820s owing to the influence of prominent gentlemen. Loyalist arguments for maintaining slavery in the Maritimes centered on white supremacy as much as on an economic rationale, and it remained a "distinct mark of respectability" with some elites. In response to this persecution, hundreds of free Black Loyalists chose to settle a new colony in Sierra Leone rather than continue to endure racism and discrimination from the white Loyalist majority, who were eager to restore their own status within an honor culture based in part on racial subjugation.[60]

The honor of a patriarch demanded obedience from everyone in the household, whether enslaved or free, and this included Loyalist wives. It would not be unreasonable to assume that marital strain would accompany the trauma of war, dislocation, and exile, and Loyalist gentlemen could be very severe with wives who did not live up to their ideals. Amos and Sarah Chandler Botsford, for example, had a dreadful falling-out. Though the cause is not recorded in their correspondence, it was serious and long-lasting enough that, even though she accepted blame and apologized profusely for the unnamed slight, her husband essentially banished her to live in a different community. Although it was expensive to maintain his wife elsewhere, Botsford wrote to his son that "it is however less troublesome to board her out than to keep her in the Family."[61] This would have been a very public rebuke. Mather Byles attempted to be tender to his suffering wife, Sarah Lyde Byles, but nonetheless became "convinced of the

164   DISHONORED AMERICANS

necessity of her being confined" to her bedroom for three weeks after she "made a great Racket about Nothing" which "alarmed the whole Neighborhood" in the dead of night. The very public scene caused Byles to reflect that "this memorable crisis . . . had such direct Tendency to *lessen* the Family in the Eye of the World, & indeed to make the poor Woman herself look *little*." She died in 1787, and Mather Byles was at least somewhat cheered that "her funeral was long & very respectable; a large Number of the American Refugees being dressed in Black & walking as Relations," which he interpreted as a testament to the esteem the community still held for his family. As no household was complete without a wife and mother, Byles, then in his fifties, remarried a year later.[62]

In 1789, Joel Stone's marriage to Leah Moore Stone of New York disintegrated in what he referred to as a humiliating "calamity." The couple's dispute began when he left her—pregnant and with their infant son in tow—to live with his family in Connecticut while he traveled to London in 1783 to present his Loyalist claim, and matters grew worse when the couple resettled in Upper Canada. Few letters survive between Joel and Leah from the years of their marital breakdown, but Stone's family commented on the drama. Stone's brother referred to Leah Moore Stone as "that Rib of the Devil," and his sister, Dothe, referred to her sister-in-law in her diary as the "evil ——."[63] The public embarrassment continued to mount for Stone when he learned from a friend in Montreal that "your quondam wife . . . is endeavoring to place you in debt wherever she can find that you have any credit."[64] Stone's honor and finances were being deeply tarnished by the affair. Leah returned to New York to live with her brothers, with Stone's small military pension as a stipend. Her angry husband placed advertisements in New York newspapers that give some hint of his understanding of the failed marriage. This was a painful but not uncommon practice in the event of marital breakups. In a draft, Stone declares that the separation was caused by his wife's "ungrateful conduct, and repeated demands" that "obliged me to enter into Articles of Final Separation."[65] His notice in the *Daily Advertiser* further blames his wife for the separation, stating that she "has impetuously requested and demanded a final separation from me." The notice was signed on May 25, 1789. It is plausible that Leah Moore Stone was exasperated with her husband's constant failures and missed her extended family and the life she knew in New York. In court documents, Stone alleged infidelity. The extant letters tell only Joel Stone's side of the tale. By 1791 Stone had effectively banished his wife to New York City to live with her family while he took full custody of their two children.[66]

It is tempting to connect these examples of patriarchal anger with the Loyalists' earlier experiences of public dishonor, but the evidence is too scant for such a diagnosis, however plausible. There is no indication that such marital breakdowns were endemic in Loyalist societies, and, at any rate, legally dissolving a marriage was exceedingly difficult in British territories. Divorce required a special act of the legislature, and the first successful divorce petition in Upper Canada did not occur until 1839. In the whole legal history of the province, only seven divorce proceedings ever made it to the Legislative Assembly of Upper Canada.[67]

The private correspondence of other genteel Loyalist couples demonstrates far healthier relationships. Edward and Mary Winslow, Jonathan and Mary Bliss, and Beverly and Nancy Robinson all show abiding concern, respect, and mutual love in the face of the material privation and the likely emotional depression of exile. The appearance of harmonious marriages was another important part of honor and sociability in elite circles that benefited husbands and wives alike.[68] This did not mean that women were expected to blindly obey their husbands. Rather, women took on a central role in the emotional and social life of refugee societies, and as G. Patrick O'Brien argues, they helped knit their communities together. Wives and daughters also wielded far more power within the household than men might admit. Mary Bradstreet Robie, for example, visited Massachusetts several times from her family's refuge in Halifax throughout the 1780s. Without the approval of her husband, Thomas, she arranged a marriage for her daughter, established business connections, and essentially did the reconciliation and repatriation work for her husband. Though deeply reluctant, Thomas Robie finally consented to his wife's plan and returned to Massachusetts in 1790.[69] The cases of Stone and Botsford therefore represent extreme, though not unique, examples of mortified husbands who punished their wives' failure to acknowledge their patriarchal right to respect. Both men exiled their wives as public assertions of their domestic power.

166   DISHONORED AMERICANS

While gentlemen Loyalists often found their domestic and public authority challenged in the new settlements, their correspondence reveals that they continued to rely on family and friends in their homelands for support. Letters and visits served as conduits for local and family news, for continued economic ties, and for the exchange of political ideas. As Jane Errington and G. A. Rawlyk have shown, these connections facilitated a loose political alliance between the elite Loyalist settlers in Canada and Federalists in the United States. Loyalists differentiated between their conservative American allies and their republican opponents, associating the radical violence of the Revolution with the Jeffersonians and any advancements in the fortunes of the new republic with the Federalists.[70] There was no dishonor for Loyalists to maintain relationships with the United States and do business with Americans, so long as they were the decent ones. Even in Edward Winslow's harangue against reintegration, he was careful to point out that his "remarks do not apply to . . . gentlemen in their trading capacities" who regularly visited the United States.[71] The fortunes of many Loyalist gentlemen depended on their continued cross-border connections.

As demonstrated in Stone's marital breakup, he leaned heavily on his family in Connecticut for emotional support, but his continued social connections were also pivotal in carving his new home out of the Canadian forests. News of Stone's settlement in Upper Canada drew several Connecticut men to the Gananoque River, where they cleared the land and built Stone's mill. His political rebirth in Upper Canada therefore signaled at least a partial rebirth in his former homeland as well. Stone became a contact for men looking for a brighter future, and with Stone's patronage they could apply for free lands in Upper Canada and settle permanently.[72] Though referred to as "Late Loyalists" by the Upper Canadian government, the men did not share Stone's diehard Loyalism. During the War of 1812, Stone arrested several of his countrymen for "treasonable practices" and later demanded an apology from American workmen for daring to celebrate the Fourth of July in his Loyalist community.[73]

Of all the reasons Loyalists maintained their connections, perhaps the most paradoxical was to provide an education for their children, especially their sons. Ann Gorman Condon refers to the next generation of Loyalists as "redeemer children," who "were expected to carry the torch" of genteel loyalism.[74] Loyalists raised their children with the Revolution ever on their minds. When Belcher Byles turned six and made "his first Appearance in Jacket & Trowsers," his father Mather Byles described how "he struts, & swells, & puffs, & looks as important as a Boston Committee-Man." When his daughter Betsey turned twenty-one and left the family home, Byles mused on his shrinking household, writing that "my Subjects are reduced to four. I expect the Example will spread, & that they will all, one after another, declare their Independence."[75] Before the next generation of Loyalists declared their independence, refugee parents worked to instill Loyalist political ideology in their children. It might therefore appear strange that such people would send their children to live and learn in the United States.

The Loyalist elite considered their ideology and their gentility inseparable, but only loyalism could be taught in rough wilderness settlements. Refinement had to be found through an education in more settled lands. A proper education was not simply a matter of academics, although that was certainly an important element. Rather, a genteel education consisted of the inculcation of tastes, customs, and mores that served to set men apart and distinguish them as leaders. The Reverend Charles Inglis explained that studying among fellow gentlemen provided knowledge and virtues that elevated men "above the common Herd . . . who never think anything Worthy of Pursuit but what pampers their appetites."[76] Loyalist elites and British governors like John Graves Simcoe acknowledged that the opportunities for a genteel education in any of the provinces were sorely lacking. Loyalist parents with the means and connections thus sent their children back to the United States to make them fit to take the reins of Loyalist government.[77]

The options open to Loyalists depended heavily on their networks in the United States. Joel Stone first enrolled his son William in a boarding school in Montreal during the mid-1780s, but after his marriage collapsed, he sent William and his daughter Mary to live with family in Connecticut until, Stone wrote, "I can rid myself of bad examples in my own family."[78] The Stone family was neither wealthy nor connected enough to provide William with a college education, but local schools in Connecticut, and the households of the extended family, were more refined environments than the frontier of the upper St. Lawrence River. The children stayed in Connecticut for several

168 DISHONORED AMERICANS

years, attending school and living in different households. In many ways this was a continuation of the old New England custom of "sending out," in which children lived in related households to attend school or apprentice, refine their manners, and build character in a less familiar environment.[79]

Stone visited when he could in the winters and kept up steady correspondence with his family to monitor his children's development.[80] Once William entered his teenage years, Stone's sister Rene Stone Hopkins wrote that William was becoming a problem and that she could not bear to become a "tyrant" in the typical joust of caregiver and teenager. She urged Stone to bring his son to Canada rather than let him stay in Hartford, where he risked falling in with "bad company or . . . trifling away his time . . . that would unman him forever."[81] Stone agreed, not least because he wanted to fashion his boy into a Loyalist.

William returned to live with his father in Gananoque and learn the family business—and the family politics. On a trip to Connecticut in 1803, William wrote to his father that the "people now begin to open their eyes, and see that Thomas Jefferson and Tom Paine . . . will not always lead the people as they wish." No doubt to his father's satisfaction, William explained that many of their relatives in Connecticut "are wishing that their property was under the King's Dominion."[82] Stone was proud of his son and groomed him to lead the next generation of Loyalists along the St. Lawrence. He secured William a position as customs collector at Gananoque and was giving the young man more responsibilities when tragedy struck: William Stone died in 1809. Stone's hopes shifted to his daughter, Mary, who married an enterprising Scottish merchant who eventually became the leading figure in the little community.[83]

Wealthier and better-connected Loyalists could call upon the networks of their alma maters to educate their children. Amos Botsford sent his son, also named William, to study first at a grammar school in New Haven, Connecticut, and then to Yale. Like Stone, the elder Botsford monitored his son's progress in as minute detail as he could from a distance, and he often wrote both to William and to the boy's teachers. The correspondence contains a great deal of advice and instruction, as was typical of genteel patriarchs of the time, who used rewards of fine clothes and money as incentives to encourage study and proper behavior.[84] When William entered

Yale in 1789, Botsford became even more interested in his son's progress (a situation resented by the young scholar, who responded to his father less frequently).

The elder Botsford was determined his son should receive the gentleman's education that Yale offered, but he was deeply troubled by the corrosive influence of revolutionary ideology he detected in his son's letters. Loyalist father and son agreed on most things but were at odds over the value of politeness, and especially deference, in the character of a gentleman. William, caught up in a new spirit of assertiveness and resistance to authority in the elite colleges of the new republic, argued that his father's antiquated ideas "were injurious" to his advancement in college politics. Amos mocked William when he complained about being passed over for some distinction. "[I]t seems your Sophimorical Honour and Dignity has been wounded, a great affair indeed!" he chided. "I clearly discover too much Obstinacy in your temper," Botsford continued; "if you cannot bear little disappointments it shews a great want of Philosophical Coolness."[85] Young William's behavior seemed alien, uncouth, and alarmingly republican to the Loyalist patriarch.

Amos Botsford determined to put an end to what he saw as democratic influences, explaining that a "youth should not be . . . proud, obstinate, haughty, foppish, nor ill-tempered; not given to Noise, Riot, drinking or debauchery." Instead, a young gentleman should be "complaisant, submissive to rule and good order, quiet . . . studious, respectful to superiors and obedient to the Laws of the Society [of] which he is a member." Fathers had given such advice for generations, but the revolutionary age, which to Loyalists had caused the collapse of divinely ordained hierarchy, sharpened the importance of such basic wisdom for Botsford.[86] When William sent his father a letter full of histrionics about a debt he had incurred, Amos scolded him once again, writing, "You are really too desponding at times . . . it does no good, you have a want of Philosophy." By embracing the sort of stoicism displayed by his Loyalist patriarch, Amos wrote, "you will find convenience to carry you easily along in Life."[87] These were words that Amos Botsford and many other Loyalists lived by, and he expected his son to follow this advice. William Botsford completed his studies in 1796 and settled in Saint John, where he practiced law and followed in his father's footsteps. He became

170 DISHONORED AMERICANS

Speaker of New Brunswick's Assembly and held several other judicial offices until his death in 1864.[88]

The cross-border education of Loyalist children represents one of the strongest examples of postwar reconciliation. There are no indications in any of the correspondence that Loyalist children were ever bullied or teased by their peers because of their fathers' loyalism. Whether they were middling sorts like the Stone children, living among relatives, or from prominent Loyalist families like the Botsfords, they were accepted as members of both American and Loyalist communities. Some elite Loyalist sons remained in the United States, such as Beverly Robinson III, who married into the wealthy Duer family of New York, but most returned to their Loyalist fathers in the Canadian provinces with their Loyalist identity intact. Ward Chipman Jr., for example, lived with his eminent Patriot uncle William Gray, and even when invited to stay and become an American citizen, he adamantly refused. Chipman's aunt wrote to the boy's father with this news "so you see he is a true son."[89] Loyalist children like these navigated their complex identities and strengthened their connections with their homelands even while they embraced loyalism. They completed both the process of reconciliation with their American families and their fathers' political rebirth.

The honorable path for Loyalists split after the Treaty of Paris. Reintegration, though seemingly impossible amid the early postwar rage, became a painful but remarkably smooth path for many white Loyalists as the decade wore on and tempers cooled. Reintegration meant abandoning their Loyalist identity, but it resulted in political rebirth as gentlemen in their homelands and as citizens of the new republic. Patriots and former Loyalists found lasting peace through thousands of personal acts of reconciliation within families and communities. In many cases, this spirit of reconciliation was mirrored in the legislatures or courts, and, eventually, American memory buried the civil war of the American Revolution. For other Loyalists, the wounds cut too deep, their anger remained too hot, their losses too severe, their names too infamous, and their sense of identity too strongly bound up with loyalism to submit to the demands of their former enemies. Yet even if they could never be reconciled to living under republican governments, exiled Loyalists could still find peace with their former neighbors and friends.

That such reconciliation and reintegration was possible is testament to the power of eighteenth-century honor culture. The experience of political death demonstrates honor's violent potency to punish transgressions and compel conformity through ritualized insult and shame. Political rebirth reveals honor culture's capacity for peacemaking, reconciliation, and the preservation of the family network. Both were communal decisions about hierarchy, about who could claim the special right to respect that was accorded to gentlemen. Whereas political death was a product of revolutionary fervor, political rebirth emerged from the routine functions of honor culture that maintained social harmony and elite control. Political death was traumatic, but it was not permanent. In the end, whether gentlemen Loyalists were reborn in the United States or in the British Empire, an entire structure of cultural, social, legal, and financial supports existed to restore these privileged white men to places of authority. Loyalists did not see this as assistance or dependence: it was their right. Whether in the United States or in the British Empire, gentlemen Loyalists were politically reborn because others accepted (or were forced to accept) their status and privileges. For many women, for the poor, for the enslaved, and for free African Americans, life in the reordered world was still marked by legal subjugation and few social privileges. But for Loyalist gentlemen, this was honor restored.

CONCLUSION

The Loyalist Puzzle

I N 1826, IN THE small town of York (now Toronto), the Scottish printer and reformer William Lyon Mackenzie launched a withering attack against the Loyalist elite of Upper Canada in the pages of his newspaper, the *Colonial Advocate*. According to Mackenzie, the hereditary distinction of "United Empire Loyalist," granted by Lord Dorchester in 1789 to American refugees, had become an "an engine of discord" that unfairly enriched "a particular and favoured caste or class of the population." The few elite Loyalists who dominated the politics and courts of the colony believed "themselves much better subjects, nay even a superior race to their American brethren" in the province, and even some "British settlers are . . . looked upon by these sub-aboriginals as intruders."[1]

Mackenzie was one of a growing population of new arrivals who found the government of Upper Canada economically stifling and outrageously corrupt. He labeled the small elite network the "Family Compact," a pejorative that remains the accepted shorthand for the Loyalist and British families that effectively ruled the colony until the union of the Canadas in 1841. By the early 1820s the United Empire Loyalists and their children constituted perhaps 20 percent of the province's population, though most of these were simple farmers who played little role in government. The majority of Upper Canadians were American immigrants, attracted to the British colony by cheap land and low taxes. Since the War of 1812, however, the government considered many of them disloyal aliens, and they were disqualified from participating in the political life of the province.

{173}

174 DISHONORED AMERICANS

This led to rising discontent among reform-minded Canadians who pushed loudly for political change and fair representation.[2]

The small Upper Canadian elite obviously did not regard their nepotism and political control as corruption. Instead, they believed that they had a special right to their privileges based on their Loyalist honor. They embodied the gentility and morality required to civilize the land and, just as importantly, they were the first line of defense against the corrosive republicanism of the United States. These families had earned their exclusive rights through generations of sacrifice, first in their suffering and exile in the American Revolution, then in their efforts to build their new colony, and most recently through their determined defense of Upper Canada in the War of 1812. They had constructed an honorable, counterrevolutionary society in North America that men like Mackenzie now threatened.[3]

Mackenzie would not acknowledge any rights that flowed from Loyalist pedigrees. In the weeks following his initial diatribe, Mackenzie, writing under the pseudonym Patrick Swift, narrowed his blistering offensive to specific members of the clique, printing their names "at full length—no blanks—no asterisks." According to Samuel Peters Jarvis, the son of the Loyalist William Jarvis and the grandson of "Connecticut's Loyalist Gadfly," the Reverend Samuel Peters, this breach of custom made "the insolence the more intolerable." Mackenzie unleashed the worst scorn on the Robinson family, who, he wrote, emerged from the "thieves, rogues, prostitutes, & incorrigible vagabonds" who settled Virginia in the seventeenth century. Such "Virginian nobles as the Robinsons," Mackenzie blasted, "were descended from mothers who came there to try their luck and were purchased by their sires with tobacco." It was in the swamps of Virginia that Tory "tyranny [was] engendered, nursed and practiced by those whose blood has been vitiated and syphilized by the accursed slavery of centuries." Upper Canadians could not allow themselves to be duped by such false gentlemen. "It is no loss of honour to submit to the lion," Mackenzie wrote, "but who, with the figure of a man, can think with patience of being devoured by a rat?" A week later Mackenzie wrote that his words had "operated upon our little York patricians nearly in such a way as if he had taken some of them publicly by the 'nose.'"[4] He was right.

CONCLUSION   175

For reformers, what became known as the "Types Riot" was a blatant display of the Family Compact's corruption and a confirmation of the violence that lay at the heart of their power. On the afternoon of June 8, 1826, Samuel Peters Jarvis led a small group of young lawyers and law students, all with direct connections to the Family Compact, in an attack on Mackenzie's printshop. They smashed the press and tossed the equipment into Lake Ontario. Across the street, John Beverly Robinson, the attorney general of Upper Canada, looked on with other government officials, but none intervened. The rioters were never criminally charged, though Mackenzie took the men to civil court, where he won £625 in damages. Mackenzie, undaunted, continued to print against the Family Compact and eventually led the unsuccessful Upper Canada Rebellion in 1837.[5]

Jarvis justified his seemingly lawless behavior in the language of honor. "As to the morality or immorality of the act, I am easy on that head," he wrote, "for I feel that I deserve more the respect of Society, and have more reason to respect myself, as an actor in the attack" than anyone who paid to read the *Colonial Advocate*. He admitted that the riot was "hasty and inconsiderate" and served as a "bad example" to the people, but, Jarvis argued, he had little choice. Mackenzie inflicted real pain on Jarvis's friends and threatened the reputations of their wives, mothers, and children. He and his friends acted "without any disguise or concealment of any kind, and in open day" for all to see and judge. Jarvis was a known duelist who had killed an opponent less than a decade earlier (for which Mackenzie had called him a murderer in the newspaper). Had Mackenzie been Jarvis's equal, he might have challenged him, but the gentleman and the editor were not equals. Far from reflecting sinister conspiracies or government corruption, the attack, according to Jarvis, was the proper way to treat a cowardly newspaperman and preserve the public good. Jarvis pointed to the fact that the £625 penalty levied against the rioters was paid through donations from the good people of York, who shared "the feelings of indignation under which we had acted," even though "they condemned, the rash, imprudent, and improper act, into which those feelings had hurried us." Like a duel, this gentlemanly violence was carefully structured to be simultaneously applauded and condemned. Such contradictions were not

176   DISHONORED AMERICANS

uncommon within an honor culture ordered by "a logic of its own which could dispel the paradoxes."[6]

The Types Riot was the continuation of the counterrevolutionary conflict and the process of Loyalist mythmaking begun in the American Revolution. The Upper Canada elite were haunted by tales of rebel crowds and the persecution that drove their parents and grandparents from the Thirteen Colonies. According to one Canadian historian, Loyalist elites had a "Vesuvian mentality" that blew up reflexively at perceived threats to their position and the legitimacy of their power.[7] Jarvis and his fellow Loyalist sons acted from the fear that Mackenzie's printed insults were the first steps toward revolution. As the threat of anarchy increased in Upper Canada, the law alone could not protect their civilization from strangers and radicals. Only Loyalist honor could hold society together.

Conservative political violence in Upper Canada in the 1820s and 1830s adopted methods that resembled the Loyalists' own persecution in the American Revolution. In addition to smashing presses, the next generation of Loyalists targeted the homes of their political opponents, burned effigies, and even tarred and feathered one reformer.[8] Fifty years after the Loyalists' political death, these symbols and rituals retained their power. The irony was not lost on the Loyalists, but whether in the hands of Whigs or Tories, such signs, symbols, and ritual violence could be employed to silence opposing political ideas by dishonoring the men who expressed them. If any group would remember the power of humiliation and emasculation, it was the Loyalists.

Historians have described loyalism as an "intractable historical problem" and the Loyalists as people who "bedevil the study of the American Revolution." In 1974 Bernard Bailyn argued that historians had not made it "clear why any sensible, well-informed, right-minded American with a modicum of imagination and common sense could possibly have opposed the Revolution."[9] Fifty years later, arguments continue over whether the Loyalists were driven by intellectual ideas shared throughout the British Atlantic or by localized self-interest. The pieces of the "Loyalist puzzle,"

CONCLUSION 177

as Robert M. Calhoon refers to the problem, multiplied even more over the decades as historians explored regional variations of loyalism as well as the rationale and experiences of women Loyalists, Black Loyalists, and Britain's Indigenous allies. The vastly different situations faced by former Loyalists who sought to reintegrate into the United States and the others who sought refuge in Canada, in the Caribbean, in Britain, and in Africa add to the bewildering complexity. The Loyalists continue to perplex historians because, as Kacy Dowd Tillman writes, there were "loyalisms, not Loyalism."[10]

This book has reexamined an important piece of the puzzle that, for generations, was regarded as the only piece: the Loyalist gentleman. For many historians, literate middling and elite white Loyalists revealed their intentions, motivations, and worldview through intellectual articulations of their political positions in newspapers and pamphlets. These histories provide essential insights into loyalism, but explaining Loyalist actions through the writings of white clergymen and newspaper editors cannot provide the full picture. For all the intellectual energy men like Thomas Bradbury Chandler, Samuel Seabury, and other Loyalist spokesmen put into their pamphlets, most Loyalists, argues Calhoon, "expressed their opposition to the Revolution in more elemental ways" than these Tory writers.[11] By adopting a cultural history approach, this book has revealed those "elemental" responses Calhoon hinted at and has explained the central importance of honor culture in the civil war between Loyalists and Patriots—and in the construction of gendered, racialized, and class-based hegemonic power in revolutionary North America.

The Patriots defeated white landowning Loyalists in the American Revolution not by killing them but by dishonoring them. They employed violence calibrated to strip formerly respected men of their status by attacking the symbols of gentility, privilege, virtue, and refined masculinity. Revolutionary crowds insulted Loyalists and attacked their homes with impunity. The Patriot press spread tales of Tory debauchery and broadcast their alliances with Indigenous warriors, Scottish Jacobites, and Black Americans to reveal the Loyalists' racial degeneracy. Across the United States, courts annulled the Loyalists' fundamental rights to own property and govern a household. Whatever privileges and respect the Loyalists had before the

178 DISHONORED AMERICANS

revolutionary crisis, Patriots argued, they had earned through deceit. Patriots tore away the Loyalists' honorable masks and transformed them into politically dead Tories.

Patriots and Loyalists held different political ideologies, but they shared a culture that prized deeply gendered and racialized notions of honor. Their conflict is preserved in dramatic scenes that demonstrate the ways people thought and expressed themselves with things. Patriots articulated their revolutionary ideas in snatched wigs and stolen stockings, in vandalized doors and toppled fences, and in shackles and branding irons. Honor and dishonor were communicated through these mutually understood symbols that built the cultural world of Revolutionary America. Shaming rituals, whether tarring and feathering or simply beating out the Rogue's March as a Tory walked by, inverted the signs and rituals of respect that once ordered society. They also provided an opportunity for people to demonstrate their open commitment to the Revolution while marking their enemies and limiting the spread of loyalism. By dishonoring Loyalists in these ways, Patriots sought to elevate their own right to respect.

Political death was at the heart of the revolutionary experience for white propertied Loyalists. Whether they joined the royal standard for intellectual reasons, out of emotional attachment to their king, from a sense of duty to their prewar oaths, or for personal gain, they were all united by the experience of dishonor. Lorenzo Sabine, one of the first American historians of the Loyalists, argued that most supporters of the Crown started on their path not because they were "monarchy-men" but because they sought to "preserve public order" and protect private property and individual rights. The revolutionaries' violent insults drove such men "beyond all hope of recall." "What Tory turned Whig," Sabine asked, "because Saltonsall was mobbed, and Oliver plundered, and Leonard shot at in his own house?" This nineteenth-century historian grasped the fundamental role that honor played, observing that "persecution made half the king's friends."[12] If a gentleman could be insulted with impunity, he was either no gentleman or, as many Loyalists told themselves and each other, their former neighbors and friends had totally lost their senses.

Men like John Peters, Joel Stone, Amos Botsford, and James Moody did not mount strong intellectual arguments against the Revolution or in favor of the Loyalist cause. They expressed their allegiance through simple yet emotionally charged expressions of outrage at the indignities they and their friends endured at the hands of the Patriots. The Loyalist identity explored in this book was formed from visceral experience, not intellectual argument. Patriot violations of the cultural norms that protected genteel bodies and household dignity provided the Loyalists with the moral certainty that their adversaries were in the wrong. The destruction of their social standing and economic livelihoods furnished the dire necessity to act. Each Loyalist gentleman had to measure his response within the limits of honor culture. For some, this gave them license to break parole given to rebels and seek violent revenge. For others, the honorable path lay in enduring loss and praying for a restoration of justice through British victory.

Bertram Wyatt-Brown called honor "the missing element in the historian's grasp" of the American Revolution. This is as true for the Loyalists as it is for the Patriots. Men in the eighteenth century invoked their honor so often and spoke of it in such expansive terms that its ubiquity, combined with its apparent pliancy, can wrongly lead scholars to conclude that it was nothing more than rhetoric. In fact, honor culture structured the imaginations and behavior of eighteenth-century people in profound ways that shaped the conflict. As demonstrated throughout this book, honor culture provided Patriot crowds with the ritual language and moral force to punish Loyalists and drive them away, and honor also justified the Loyalists' violent revenge. Honor could be a rigid force that regulated racial, gendered, and class-based hierarchies, but it could also order and restrain the conduct of gentlemen at war. Even as some Loyalists broke parole and Patriot militiamen disregarded the rules of war, genteel captors' individual evaluations of their prisoners' personal honor continued to provide concrete privileges and freedoms. The same power helped Loyalists reconcile with their enemies after the war and repair the wounds caused by political death. Though dishonor was deeply traumatic, for many Loyalist gentlemen it was not permanent. Once tempers cooled and peace treaties were signed, white male householders restored their power—if not in their homelands, then elsewhere in the British Empire. In either case they were supported by their families, dependents, the state, and even by former enemies who chose to acknowledge the Loyalists' right to respect.

180 DISHONORED AMERICANS

Honor remains a word in our language, but it has lost the weight it had in the eighteenth century. It is all too easy for historians to assume that people two and a half centuries ago thought with the same rational concepts that we do.[13] The Loyalist experience underscores how men and women regarded honor as both a matter of conscience and a highly prized set of virtues that, when publicly acknowledged, bestowed concrete privileges and freedoms to some and obligations and unfreedom on others. For the privileged few, this was a self-serving myth that justified exploitation, but people believed in it nonetheless. Honor was not simply a matter of esteem. In a world built on racial slavery and degradation, honor was power. To be dishonored, as white Loyalist householders were in the Revolution, was to lose everything that set a gentleman above other people. That was political death.

Time and cultural difference present significant challenges for historians attempting to put together the Loyalist puzzle, but so too does the mountain of myth and memory that buries the Loyalists in the United States and Canada. This, too, is a lasting consequence of the Loyalists' political death. The Tories who appear in popular American memory match almost precisely the dishonorable tropes first laid down in the revolutionary press. Effete assassins and cowardly aristocrats populate historical fiction from Hawthorne to Disney. The Patriot narrator in Harold Frederic's 1890 novel *In the Valley* perhaps best sums up the Tory stock character who was "affable, honorable, generous, and likeable among his equals [and] cold, selfish, haughty, and harsh to his inferiors." The Loyalist was ruined by "the cursed obligation to act like a 'gentleman.'" The hollowness of Tory gentility was matched by their "wanton baseness and beast-like bloodthirstiness." Similarly, Walter D. Edmonds's *Drums along the Mohawk* (1936) describes the genteel Walter Butler's "whittled attorney's face" that was transformed "with a passion of contempt." His obsession for revenge against the Patriots gave him "a bitter power" that led to the horrors of Cherry Valley. Walter Butler and another frontier Loyalist, Simon Girty, even sit on the accursed jury in Stephen Vincent Benét's "The Devil and Daniel Webster."[14] In American fiction and history, the Loyalists were the worst enemies of the Revolution: guilty of treason to their country and

CONCLUSION   181

their race, and perhaps even their God. Patriot writers and propagandists of the American Revolution created a lasting figure that evoked equal parts derision, revulsion, and fear.

Loyalist descendants in Canada were often incensed at the depiction of their ancestors as bloodthirsty villains. Nineteenth- and twentieth-century writers constructed an alternate version of the American Revolution, with the Loyalists cast in the heroic leading role. In 1869, the Canadian writer William Canniff dismissed accusations of Loyalist violence as lies intended to deflect attention from the "the deeds of atrocity enacted by the villainous 'Liberty Men.'" To Caniff, American histories were pure propaganda filled with "over-weening vanity." "The self-applauding writers of the revolutionary war," he writes, "found it convenient to forget the doings of the 'Sons of Liberty' . . . while they laid to the charge of Butler's Rangers and the Indians, acts of inhumanity." Canniff assured his readers that the violence of the revolutionaries had "not been forgotten by the United Empire Loyalists, but [has] been handed down to us, to place on record against the cruel actors."[15]

Like its American counterpart, the Canadian Loyalist myth depicted the refugees as gentlemen, but as Egerton Ryerson lamented, such men were "strangely misrepresented" by American historians. According to Ryerson, the genteel founders of Canada were in fact "the most wealthy and intelligent . . . inhabitants of the colonies."[16] James Henry Coyne, a Canadian lawyer and historian, wrote in 1898 that "the Loyalists, to a considerable extent, were the very cream of the population of the Thirteen Colonies. They represented in very large measure the learning, the piety, the gentle birth, the wealth and good citizenship of the British race in America."[17] The mythic Loyalists were Anglican in religion, conservative in politics, and gentlemen by nature.

These Canadian authors regarded Loyalists as men like themselves. They did not appreciate how much their concept of gentlemanly honor differed from that of their ancestors just a few generations before. The honor culture of Samuel Peters Jarvis, who grew up in a family of slavers, who dueled, and who engaged in open acts of political violence is not part of the Loyalist myth. Instead, according to Canniff, the gentlemen refugees of Upper Canada were pious, thrifty, and hardworking pioneers. Any aristocratic fop who refused to believe that "agriculture and gentility may go together" and was unwilling to fell the forests with his own hands starved in Upper Canada. Such unnamed men dreamed of restoring their families to prominence, but "alas," writes Canniff, "how rarely was the dream realized!"[18] Writers in Canada could not imagine that the aggressive masculine honor of the eighteenth century was embraced by the elite refugees. That form of honor had faded from culture and memory under the weight of industrialization, capitalism, evangelical Christianity, abolitionism, and representative democracy. Eventually, according to Alexander Welsh, the mechanized warfare of the First World War "opened a mass grave for honour."[19]

The gentlemen examined in this book, and the honor culture in which they lived, represent important pieces of the Loyalist puzzle, but they are only a tiny minority within a minority. Nonetheless, they hold an oversized place in the historical record. Their descendants in Canada donated their papers to archives, named streets and towns after them, and, for good or ill, Loyalist gentlemen played a significant role in shaping the politics of the new British colonies. The same men were reviled as traitors and bloodthirsty villains in the popular memory and history of the United States, infamous for their resistance to the Revolution, the public shaming they suffered, and the cautionary example they provided.

Whether they were championing the cause of republicanism or defending the British Crown, Patriots and Loyalists defended their political choices and attacked their enemies in the gendered and racialized language of honor. The Loyalists were routinely humiliated, emasculated, and dishonored by their more numerous enemies, and yet they continued to cling to ideas of honor, transforming failure and indignity into sacrifice and martyrdom. Generations of mythmaking and nationalistic interpretations cloud the history of the Loyalists in the American Revolution, and Tory stereotypes from the War of Independence live on more than two and half centuries later. The Loyalists have a unique legacy in North American history. They were regarded by some as legendary founding fathers of English Canada—and by others as dishonored Americans.

NOTES

Prologue

1. Joseph Johnson, *Traditions and Reminiscences; Chiefly of the American Revolution in the South* (Charleston, SC: Walker & James, 1851), 45–47.

2. J. Johnson, *Traditions*, 46; *South Carolina Gazette*, Nov. 7, 1771; Richard Barry, *Mr. Rutledge of South Carolina* (New York: Duell, Sloan and Pearce, 1942), 134–43.

3. Donna Andrew, "The Code of Honour and Its Critics," *Social History* 5, no. 3 (1980): 409–34; V. G. Kiernan, *The Duel in European History: Honour and the Reign of Aristocracy* (Oxford: Oxford University Press, 1988); Markku Peltonen, *The Duel in Early Modern England: Civility, Politeness, and Honour* (Cambridge: Cambridge University Press, 2003); James Kelly, *"That Damn'd Thing Called Honour": Duelling in Ireland, 1570–1860* (Cork, Ireland: Cork University Press, 1995); Jennifer Low, *Manhood and the Duel: Masculinity in Early Modern Drama and Culture* (New York: Palgrave Macmillan, 2003); Joanne B. Freeman, *Affairs of Honor: National Politics in the New Republic* (New Haven, CT: Yale University Press, 2001), 167–70.

4. *South Carolina Gazette*, Nov. 7, 1771; South Carolina Court of General Sessions Journal, 1769–1776, 154–55, South Carolina Department of Archives and History, Columbia, SC. The pardon is the only extant reference to the case in the South Carolina court records. *New Hampshire Gazette*, Dec. 6, 1771; J. Johnson, *Traditions*, 46–47.

5. David Ramsay to Benjamin Rush, July 27, 1776, quoted in Joseph Ioor Waring, *A History of Medicine in South Carolina, 1670–1825* (Columbia, SC: South Carolina Medical Association, 1964), 241.

6. *Pennsylvania Chronicle*, Sept. 9, 1771, *New Hampshire Gazette*, Oct. 4, 1771, and *Connecticut Gazette*, Sept. 27, 1771; proclamation from William Bull, governor of South Carolina, *South Carolina Gazette*, Aug. 22, 1771.

7. Peter Manigault to Ralph Izard, Aug. 24, 1771, in Maurice A. Crouse, ed., "The Letterbook of Peter Manigault, 1763–1773," *South Carolina Historical Magazine* 70, no. 3 (1969): 189–90.

8. For a discussion on the utility of the duel, see Bertram Wyatt-Brown, *Southern Honor: Ethics and Behavior in the Old South* (New York: Oxford University Press, 1983), 352–53.

9. Carl von Clausewitz, *On War* (1832; London: Oxford University Press, 2007), 13.

{183}

184   NOTES TO PAGES 7–11

Introduction

1. *Boston Gazette,* July 3, 1775; Jonathan Boucher, *Reminiscences of an American Loyalist* (Port Washington, NY: Kennikat Press, 1967), 118, 120–23.

2. Boucher, *Reminiscences,* 123; Anne Y. Zimmer, *Jonathan Boucher: Loyalist in Exile* (Detroit: Wayne State University Press, 1978), 174–76.

3. Jonathan Boucher to George Washington, Aug. 6, 1775, in *Letters of Jonathan Boucher to George Washington,* ed. Worthington Chauncey Ford (Brooklyn, NY: Historical Printing Club, 1899), 47–49.

4. George Washington to Thomas Gage, Aug. 20, 1775, from George Washington Papers, Library of Congress, Washington, DC (hereafter Washington Papers), 4th ser., General Correspondence.

5. Craig Bruce Smith, *American Honor: The Creation of the Nation's Ideals during the Revolutionary Era* (Chapel Hill: University of North Carolina Press, 2018).

6. *Spooner's Vermont Journal,* June 7, 1785.

7. *Connecticut Gazette,* Oct. 25, 1776. This mock funeral is also described in Winthrop D. Jordan, "Familial Politics: Thomas Paine and the Killing of the King, 1776," *Journal of American History* 60, no. 2 (1973): 294–308; *New-York Journal,* Oct. 19, 1775.

8. Joel Stone, "The Narrative of Joel Stone," in *Loyalist Narratives from Upper Canada,* ed. J. J. Talman (Toronto: Champlain Society, 1946), 326.

9. Stone, "Narrative of Joel Stone," 325–26; *Connecticut Journal,* June 23, 1779.

10. Francis Hopkinson, *The Miscellaneous Essays and Occasional Writings of Francis Hopkinson, Esq.,* vol. 1 (Philadelphia: Dobson, 1791).

11. Lisa Steffen, *Defining a British State: Treason and National Identity, 1608–1820* (New York: Palgrave, 2001), 1, 11, 59.

12. Brett Palfreyman, "The Loyalists and the Federal Constitution: The Origins of the Bill of Attainder Clause," *Journal of the Early Republic* 35, no. 3 (2015): 451–73; Tom Cutterham, *Gentlemen Revolutionaries: Power and Justice in the New American Republic* (Princeton, NJ: Princeton University Press, 2017), 66–74. For a specific discussion of "political death" as a legal term in Connecticut, see Ephraim Kirby, *Reports of Cases Adjudged in the Superior Court of Connecticut, 1785–1788* (Litchfield, CT: Collier and Adam, 1789), 229.

13. Joseph Galloway, *A Candid Examination of the Mutual Claims of Great-Britain, and the Colonies . . .* (New York: Rivington, 1775), 1.

14. Eileen Ka-May Cheng, "American Historical Writers and the Loyalists, 1788–1856: Dissent, Consensus, and American Nationality," *Journal of the Early Republic* 23, no. 4 (2003): 491–519; Donald G. Darnell, "'Visions of Hereditary Rank': The Loyalist in the Fiction of Hawthorne, Cooper, and Frederic," *South Atlantic Bulletin* 42, no. 2 (1977): 45–54; Nathaniel Hawthorne, "Legends of the Province House," chap. 2, "Edward Randolph's Portrait," in *Twice-Told Tales,* vol. 2 (Boston: Ticknor and Fields, 1864).

15. See R. O. MacFarlane, "The Loyalist Migrations: A Social and Economic Movement," in *The United Empire Loyalists: Men and Myths,* ed. L. F. S. Upton (Toronto: Copp Clark Publishing, 1967), 158–61; William H. Nelson, *The American Tory* (1961; Boston:

Northeastern University Press, 1992), 86, 91; Norman Knowles, *Inventing the Loyalists: The Ontario Loyalist Tradition and the Creation of Usable Pasts* (Toronto: University of Toronto Press, 1997), 14–25; Jerry Bannister and Liam Riordan, "Loyalism and the British Atlantic, 1660–1840," in *The Loyal Atlantic: Remaking the British Atlantic in the Revolutionary Era*, ed. Bannister and Riordan (Toronto: University of Toronto Press, 2012), 5; Maya Jasanoff, *Liberty's Exiles: American Loyalists in the Revolutionary World* (New York: Knopf, 2011); Christopher Minty, "Reexamining Loyalist Identity during the American Revolution," in *The Consequences of Loyalism: Essays in Honor of Robert M. Calhoon*, ed. Rebecca Brannon and Joseph S. Moore (Columbia: University of South Carolina Press, 2019), 33–47.

16. Woody Holton, "Rebel against Rebel: Enslaved Virginians and the Coming of the American Revolution," *Virginia Magazine of History and Biography* 105, no. 2 (1997): 185.

17. Philip Mason, *The English Gentleman: The Rise and Fall of an Ideal* (London: André Deutsch, 1982); Michal J. Rozbicki, *The Complete Colonial Gentleman: Cultural Legitimacy in Plantation America* (Charlottesville: University of Virginia Press, 1998); Cutterham, *Gentlemen Revolutionaries*, 1–2.

18. Michael Zuckerman, "Tocqueville, Turner, and Turds: Four Stories of Manners in Early America," *Journal of American History* 85, no. 1 (1998): 13–42.

19. Boucher, *Reminiscences*, 117–18.

20. Nicole Eustace, "The Sentimental Paradox: Humanity and Violence on the Pennsylvania Frontier," *William and Mary Quarterly*, 3rd ser., 65, no. 1 (2008): 29–64; William Guthrie Sayen, "George Washington's 'Unmannerly' Behavior: The Clash between Civility and Honor," *Virginia Magazine of History and Biography* 107, no. 1 (1999): 2–36; Philip Carter, *Men and the Emergence of Polite Society, 1660–1800* (London: Pearson Education, 2001), 2; Sarah Knott, *Sensibility and the American Revolution* (Chapel Hill: University of North Carolina Press for the Omohundro Institute, 2009); Wyatt-Brown, *Southern Honor*, 34.

21. Richard L. Bushman, *The Refinement of America: Persons, Houses, Cities* (New York: Knopf, 1992), xii, xix, 25; Rozbicki, *Complete Colonial Gentleman*, 16–24.

22. Caroline Cox, *A Proper Sense of Honor: Service and Sacrifice in George Washington's Army* (Chapel Hill: University of North Carolina Press, 2004), 38; Judith L. Van Buskirk, *Generous Enemies: Patriots and Loyalists in Revolutionary New York* (Philadelphia: University of Pennsylvania Press, 2002), 73–90.

23. Toby L. Ditz, "What's Love Got to Do with It? The History of Men, the History of Gender in the 1990s," *Reviews in American History* 28, no. 2 (2000): 168.

24. Bertram Wyatt-Brown, *The Shaping of Southern Culture: Honor, Grace, and War, 1760s–1890s* (Chapel Hill: University of North Carolina Press, 2001), xiii, 142; Orlando Patterson, *Slavery and Social Death: A Comparative Study* (Cambridge, MA: Harvard University Press, 1982), 79, 96; Elizabeth Fox-Genovese and Eugene D. Genovese, *The Mind of the Master Class: History and Faith in the Southern Slaveholder's World View* (Cambridge: Cambridge University Press, 2005), 507–8; Philip D. Morgan, *Slave Counterpoint: Black Culture in the Eighteenth-Century Chesapeake and Lowcountry* (Chapel Hill: University of North Carolina Press, 1998), 379–80, 385.

186 NOTES TO PAGES 14–19

25. Patterson, *Slavery and Social Death,* 94.

26. "Letter from Gen. Burgoyne to Gen. Gates, August 30, 1777," *New York Gazette and Weekly Mercury,* Oct. 6, 1777.

27. For example, see John Smail, "Credit, Risk, and Honor in Eighteenth-Century Commerce," *Journal of British Studies* 44 (July 2005): 450–51; Arthur N. Gilbert, "Law and Honour among Eighteenth-Century British Army Officers," *Historical Journal* 19, no. 1 (1976): 75–87; Carolyn Podruchny, *Making the Voyageur World: Travelers and Traders in the North American Fur Trade* (Lincoln: University of Nebraska Press, 2006), 13–14. For concepts of honor held by enslaved people, see the discussion in C. Smith, *American Honor,* 4–6, 99–101.

28. Keith Thomas, *The Ends of Life: Roads to Fulfillment in Early Modern England* (Oxford: Oxford University Press, 2009), 148; Courtney Erin Thomas, *If I Love My Honour I Love Myself: Honour among the Early Modern English Elite* (Toronto: University of Toronto Press, 2017), 4–6.

29. Alexis de Tocqueville, *Democracy in America,* trans. Henry Reeve (1835; New York: Bantam, 2000), 775.

30. K. Thomas, *Ends of Life,* 148, 186; Samuel Johnson, *A Dictionary of the English Language* (London: W. Strahan, 1755), 106; Frank Henderson Stewart, *Honor* (Chicago: University of Chicago Press, 1994), 21; J. G. Peristiany and Julian Pitt-Rivers, eds., *Honor and Grace in Anthropology* (New York: Cambridge University Press, 1992), 5.

31. Wyatt-Brown, *Shaping of Southern Culture,* 32; C. Smith, *American Honor,* 8–9.

32. Robert G. Parkinson, *The Common Cause: Creating Race and Nation in the American Revolution* (Chapel Hill: University of North Carolina Press, 2015), 18.

33. Toby L. Ditz, "The New Men's History and the Peculiar Absence of Gendered Power: Some Remedies from Early American Gender History," *Gender and History* 16, no. 1 (2004): 17. These arguments are also informed by the idea of hegemonic masculinity. R. W. Connell, *Masculinities* (Berkeley: University of California Press, 1995), 76–81; R. W. Connell and James W. Messerschmidt, "Hegemonic Masculinity: Rethinking the Concept," *Gender and Society* 19, no. 6 (2005): 829–59.

34. Bernard Bailyn, *Ideological Origins of the American Revolution* (1967; Cambridge, MA: Belknap Press of Harvard University Press, 1992), 312; Wyatt-Brown, *Shaping of Southern Culture,* 33.

35. Peter Burke, *What Is Cultural History?* (Cambridge: Polity Press, 2004); Robert Darnton, *The Great Cat Massacre and Other Episodes in French Cultural History* (New York: Vintage Books, 1984); Darnton, *George Washington's False Teeth: An Unconventional Guide to the Eighteenth Century* (New York: Norton, 2003); Simon P. Newman, *Embodied History: The Lives of the Poor in Early Philadelphia* (Philadelphia: University of Pennsylvania Press, 2003).

36. Thomas N. Ingersoll, *The Loyalist Problem in Revolutionary New England* (New York: Cambridge University Press, 2016), 2, 193–94; Holger Hoock, *Scars of Independence: America's Violent Birth* (New York: Crown, 2017), 50–51.

37. Adam Smith, *The Theory of Moral Sentiments* (London: A. Millar, 1761), 106.

38. Patterson, *Slavery and Social Death,* 38–45.

NOTES TO PAGES 19–24   187

39. Claude Halstead Van Tyne, *The Loyalists in the American Revolution* (1902; Bowie, MD: Heritage Books, 1989), 237; John Peters, "The Narrative of John Peters," John Peters Papers, New-York Historical Society (hereafter NYHS); *Essex Gazette,* Nov. 22, 1774; Lorenzo Sabine, *Biographical Sketches of Loyalists of the American Revolution, with an Historical Essay* (Boston: Little, Brown, 1864), 265.

40. Rebecca Brannon, *From Revolution to Reunion: The Reintegration of the South Carolina Loyalists* (Columbia: University of South Carolina Press, 2016). The Connecticut Supreme Court even declared Loyalist political death to be in error, since that effectively made them free of prewar debts; see the case of *Marks v. Johnson* in Kirby, *Reports of Cases Adjudged,* 228–29.

41. Kacy Dowd Tillman, *Stripped and Script: Loyalist Women Writers of the American Revolution* (Amherst: University of Massachusetts Press, 2019); Linda Kerber, *Women of the Republic: Intellect and Ideology in Revolutionary America* (Chapel Hill: University of North Carolina Press, 1980), 119–20.

42. Van Buskirk, *Generous Enemies,* especially chap. 2, "The Web of Family," 44–72.

43. Joy Day Buel and Richard Buel, *The Way of Duty* (New York: Norton, 1984), 134; Payne Kilbourn, *Sketches and Chronicles of the Town of Litchfield* (Hartford, CT: Press of Case, Lockwood, 1859), 116.

44. Brad A. Jones, *Resisting Independence: Popular Loyalism in the Revolutionary British Atlantic* (Ithaca, NY: Cornell University Press, 2021), 227; Robert M. Calhoon, *The Loyalists in Revolutionary America, 1760–1781* (New York: Harcourt Brace Jovanovich, 1973), 505; Janice Potter, *The Liberty We Seek: Loyalist Ideology in Colonial New York and Massachusetts* (Cambridge, MA: Harvard University Press, 1983); William A. Benton, *Whig-Loyalism: An Aspect of Political Ideology in the American Revolution* (Rutherford, NJ: Fairleigh Dickinson University Press, 1969); Gregg L. Frazer, *God against the Revolution: The Loyalist Clergy's Case against the American Revolution* (Lawrence: University of Kansas Press, 2018).

45. Ruma Chopra, "Enduring Patterns of Loyalist Study: Definitions and Contours," *History Compass* 11, no. 11 (2013): 985.

1. Dishonor

1. Nina Moore Tiffany, ed., *Letters of James Murray, Loyalist* (Boston, 1901), 160–62; *Boston Evening-Post,* Sept. 25, 1769 (original emphasis).

2. Thomas Jones, *History of New York during the Revolutionary War,* vol. 1 (New York: New York Historical Society, 1879), 77; Journal of Cadwallader Colden II (hereafter referred to as Colden's Journal), 130, University of New Brunswick Loyalist Collection, Fredericton, NB (hereafter UNBLC), HIL-MICL FC LFR.C6C3J6.

3. Ann M. Little, "'Shoot that Rogue, for He Hath an Englishman's Coat On!': Cultural Cross-Dressing on the New England Frontier, 1620–1760," *New England Quarterly* 74, no. 2 (2001): 238–73; Kathleen M. Brown, *Foul Bodies: Cleanliness in Early America* (New Haven, CT: Yale University Press, 2009), 42–51; Newman, *Embodied History,* 97–103.

4. Parkinson, *Common Cause,* 579, 629.

188   NOTES TO PAGES 24-27

5. Benjamin H. Irvin, "Tar, Feathers, and the Enemies of American Liberties, 1768–1776," *New England Quarterly* 76, no. 2 (2003): 197–238; Paul Gilje, *The Road to Mobocracy: Popular Disorder in New York City, 1763–1834* (Chapel Hill: University of North Carolina Press, 1987), 5–23; Peter Shaw, *American Patriots and the Rituals of Revolution* (Cambridge, MA: Harvard University Press, 1981), 177–231.

6. Charles P. Flynn, *Insult and Society: Patterns of Comparative Insult* (Port Washington, NY: Kennikat Press, 1977), 21–28; F. Stewart, *Honor*, 64–65, 67–68, 84; Gordon S. Wood, *The Radicalism of the American Revolution* (New York: Vintage Books, 1993), 41.

7. F. Stewart, *Honor*, 145; Erin Mackie, *Rakes, Highwaymen, and Pirates: The Making of the Modern Gentleman in the Eighteenth Century* (Baltimore: Johns Hopkins University Press, 2009); Ruth H. Bloch, "The Gendered Meanings of Virtue in Revolutionary America," *Signs* 13, no. 1 (1987): 37–58. For the effeminate vices of men, see Anne Lombard, *Making Manhood: Growing Up Male in Colonial New England* (Cambridge, MA: Harvard University Press, 2003), 10–11, 70, 164.

8. Benjamin Irvin, "Of Eloquence 'Manly' and 'Monstrous': The Henpecked Husband in Revolutionary Political Debate, 1774–1775," in *New Men: Manliness in Early America*, ed. Thomas A. Foster (New York: New York University Press, 2011), 195–216. For cuckoldry, see Foster, *Sex and the Eighteenth-Century Man: Massachusetts and the History of Sexuality in America* (Boston: Beacon Press, 2006), 45–49; Toby L. Ditz, "Shipwrecked; or, Masculinity Imperiled: Mercantile Representations of Failure and the Gendered Self in Eighteenth-Century Philadelphia," *Journal of American History* 81, no. 1 (1994): 64–65.

9. Excerpt from the Journal of Ambrose Serle, Thursday, Sept. 5, 1776, reprinted in *The American Revolution: Writings from the War of Independence*, ed. John Rhodehamel (New York: Penguin Putnam, 2001), 208; Hannah Lawrence Schieffelin, "Narrative of Events . . . during a Journey through Canada" (unpublished manuscript, ca. 1780), 11, Schieffelin Family Papers, New York Public Library (hereafter NYPL), box 7.

10. Karen Harvey, "The History of Masculinity, circa 1650–1800," *Journal of British Studies* 44, no. 2 (2005): 303; Robert B. Shoemaker, "The Decline of Public Insult in London, 1660–1800," *Past and Present*, no. 169 (Nov. 2000): 97–131, and Shoemaker, "The Taming of the Duel: Masculinity, Honor and Ritual Violence in London, 1660–1800," *Historical Journal* 45, no. 3 (2002): 525–45; Michèle Cohen, *Fashioning Masculinity: National Identity and Language in the Eighteenth Century* (New York: Routledge, 1996); Peltonen, *Duel in Early Modern England*, 52.

11. Charles Royster, *A Revolutionary People at War: The Continental Army and American Character, 1775–1783* (Chapel Hill: University of North Carolina Press, 1979), 88, 210.

12. Freeman, *Affairs of Honor*, 6–7, 168–70, 177; Linda Pollock, "Honor, Gender, and Reconciliation in Elite Culture, 1570–1700," *Journal of British Studies* 46, no. 1 (2007): 8–9. For a brief historiography of early modern English honor culture, see Brendan Kane, *The Politics and Culture of Honour in Britain and Ireland, 1541–1641* (Cambridge: Cambridge University Press, 2010), 5–7.

13. "Description Jany 27th 1774 in Consequence of a Meeting of the trading People" and "Memorandum of what past Between Major Basset & all the trading People at Detroit . . . ," Jan. 27, 1774, John Porteous Papers, UNBLC.

NOTES TO PAGES 27–30 189

14. Bushman, *Refinement of America*, 31; J. M. Toner, ed., *Washington's Rules of Civility and Decent Behaviour in Company and Conversation* (Washington, DC: W. H. Morrison, 1888), 20.

15. Alfred F. Young, *The Shoemaker and the Tea Party: Memory and the American Revolution* (Boston: Beacon Press, 1999), 46–51; Ann Hulton to Mrs. Lightbody, Jan. 31, 1774, in *Letters of a Loyalist Lady: Being the Letters of Ann Hulton, Sister of Henry Hulton, Commissioner of Customs at Boston, 1767–1776*, ed. E. Rhys Jones (Cambridge, MA: Harvard University Press, 1927), 69–72; *Boston Post-Boy*, Jan. 24, 1774.

16. Robert Blair St. George, *Conversing by Signs: Poetics of Implication in Colonial New England Culture* (Chapel Hill: University of North Carolina Press, 1998), 287.

17. Pauline Maier, "Popular Uprisings and Civil Authority in Eighteenth-Century America," *William and Mary Quarterly*, 3rd ser., 27, no. 1 (1970): 3–35; Gilje, *Road to Mobocracy*, 3–68. An alternative to the "consensus" idea of crowd action can be seen in Thomas P. Slaughter, "Crowds in Eighteenth-Century America: Reflections and New Directions," *Pennsylvania Magazine of History and Biography* 115, no. 1 (1991): 3–34.

18. Recantation of Stephen Baxter, Dec. 12, 1775, and recantation of James Miller, Dec. 12, 1775, in *American Archives* (hereafter *AA*), ed. Peter Force, 4th ser., 4:247; Massachusetts Committee of Safety, May 4, 1775, broadside (Cambridge, 1775); Catherine S. Crary, *The Price of Loyalty: Tory Writings from the Revolutionary Era* (New York: McGraw-Hill, 1973), 64–66.

19. Tiffany, *Letters of James Murray*, 161–62.

20. *Connecticut Courant*, Oct. 2, 1775.

21. *Connecticut Journal*, Feb. 8, 1775.

22. Such insults are very similar to those recorded in England. Laura Gowing, "Gender and the Language of Insult in Early Modern London," *History Workshop*, no. 35 (Spring 1993): 1–21; Shoemaker, "Decline of Public Insult."

23. Edwin G. Burrows, *Forgotten Patriots: The Untold Story of American Prisoners during the Revolutionary War* (New York: Basic Books, 2008), 10, 138.

24. For criminal punishments of adultery in colonial America, see Mary Beth Norton, *Founding Mothers and Fathers: Gendered Power and the Forming of American Society* (New York: Vintage Books, 1996), 74, 342–43; Lisa Wilson, *Ye Heart of a Man: The Domestic Life of Men in Colonial New England* (New Haven, CT: Yale University Press, 1999), 92–93; Jennifer Panek, "'A Wittall Cannot Be a Cuckold': Reading the Contented Cuckold in Early Modern English Drama and Culture," *Journal of Early Modern Cultural Studies* 1, no. 2 (2001): 66–92.

25. "Battle of the Kegs," *Pennsylvania Evening Post*, July 18, 1778.

26. Anonymous letter, New York, Jan. 25, 1778, in *Historical Anecdotes, Civil and Military: In a Series of Letters, Written from America in the Years 1777 and 1778 . . .* (London: J. Bew, 1779), 40, 48.

27. Faramerz Dabhoiwala, "The Construction of Honour, Reputation and Status in Late Seventeenth- and Early Eighteenth-Century England," *Transactions of the Royal Historical Society*, 6th ser., 6 (1996): 211.

190   NOTES TO PAGES 30–34

28. *Copy of letters sent to Great-Britain, by His Excellency Thomas Hutchinson, the Hon. Andrew Oliver, and several other persons . . .* (Boston, MA: Edes and Gill, 1773), 3–5, 6, 16. Also see Thomas C. Leonard, "News for a Revolution: The Exposé in America, 1768–1773," *Journal of American History* 67, no. 1 (1980): 26.

29. *Boston Gazette*, Jan. 10, 1774; *Essex Gazette*, Jan. 18, 1774.

30. Peters, "Narrative"; Israel Williams deposition, no date (but likely late spring 1777), Hatfield Committee of Safety, Israel Chapin, Chairman, to Massachusetts General Court, Sept. 1779, Israel Williams Papers, UNBLC.

31. T. H. Breen, *The Marketplace of Revolution: How Consumer Politics Shaped American Independence* (New York: Oxford University Press, 2004), 23–24, 129.

32. Letter from "Britannicus," *New-York Journal*, Mar. 2, 1775; T. H. Breen, *Tobacco Culture: The Mentality of the Great Tidewater Planters on the Eve of Revolution* (Princeton, NJ: Princeton University Press, 1985), 161–62.

33. Thomas Paine, *The Crisis*, no. 2 (Philadelphia: Styner and Cist, 1777), 21.

34. *Connecticut Courant*, Aug. 5, 1776.

35. Alexander Hamilton, *A Full Vindication of the Measures of Congress from the Calumnies of Their Enemies in Answer to a Letter Under the Signature A. W. Farmer* (New York: James Rivington, 1774), 3, 6, 22.

36. Markman Ellis, "Suffering Things: Lapdogs, Slaves, and Counter Sensibility," in *The Secret Life of Things: Animals, Objects, and It-Narratives in Eighteenth-Century England*, ed. Mark Blackwell (Lewisburg, PA: Bucknell University Press, 2007), 94, 97.

37. Thomas Paine, *Common Sense* (Philadelphia: Robert Bell, 1776), 66, 24; Lisbeth Chapin, "Shelley's Great Chain of Being: From 'Blind Worms' to 'New-Fledged Eagles,'" in *Humans and Other Animals in Eighteenth-Century British Culture: Representation, Hybridity, Ethics*, ed. Frank Palmeri (Aldershot, UK: Ashgate, 2006), 153–68. Also see Robert Darnton's discussion of the relationship of animals to insults in *Great Cat Massacre*, 89–90, 193.

38. Ann Hulton to Mrs. Adam Lightbody, June 30, 1768, in E. R. Jones, *Letters of a Loyalist Lady*, 11.

39. Gilje, *Road to Mobocracy*, 5–35; David Hackett Fischer, *Albion's Seed: Four British Folkways in America* (New York: Oxford University Press, 1989), 121, 188, 195, 397, 540; Toni M. Massaro, "Shame, Culture, and American Criminal Law," *Michigan Law Review* 89, no. 7 (1991): 1912–15.

40. *Connecticut Gazette*, Sept. 29, 1775.

41. James Allen, "Diary of James Allen, Esq. of Philadelphia, Counsellor-at-Law, 1770–1778," *Pennsylvania Magazine of History and Biography* 9, no. 2 (1885): 196 (entry for Jan. 25, 1777); "The Diary of Benjamin Marston," Sept. 22, 1776, Winslow Papers, UNBLC.

42. Hugh Edward Egerton, ed., *The Royal Commission on the Losses and Services of the American Loyalists, 1783–1785* (Oxford, 1915), xxix, 282, 322, 173, 234, and passim; Newman, *Embodied History*, 1–15; Bushman, *Refinement of America*, 63–72; Michael Meranze, "A Criminal Is Being Beaten: The Politics of Punishment and the History of the Body," in *Possible Pasts: Becoming Colonial in Early America*, ed. Robert Blair St. George (Ithaca, NY: Cornell University Press, 2000), 302–23; Cox, *Proper Sense of Honor*, xi.

NOTES TO PAGES 34–38   191

43. Peter Oliver, *Peter Oliver's "Origin and Progress of the American Rebellion,"* ed. Douglass Adair and John Schutz (Stanford, CA: Stanford University Press, 1967), 152–57; *Boston Weekly News-Letter,* Feb. 23, 1775; Justin Winsor, *History of the Town of Duxbury, Massachusetts, with Genealogical Registers* (Boston: Crosby & Nichols, 1849), 139–40.

44. *Boston Gazette,* May 5, 1783.

45. William Woodford to the Virginia Convention, Dec. 12, 1775, in Force, *AA,* 4th ser., 4:245; T. Cole Jones, *Captives of Liberty: Prisoners of War and the Politics of Vengeance in the American Revolution* (Philadelphia: University of Pennsylvania Press, 2020), 111.

46. "Evidence on the Claim of Peter Guire late of Connecticut," Jan. 18, 1787, Loyalist Claims Commission Records, Archives of Ontario, Toronto, AO 12.1, 204; *New Jersey Gazette,* Jan. 29, 1783; M. E., *Essays on the Injustice and Impolicy of Inflicting Capital Punishment . . .* (Philadelphia: Democratic Press, 1809), 37.

47. Irvin, "Tar, Feathers," 199–200; *Boston Evening-Post,* Nov. 6, 1769.

48. Oliver, *"Origin and Progress,"* 157; *Connecticut Gazette,* Feb. 10, Sept. 22, and Oct. 22, 1775; Calhoon, *Loyalists in Revolutionary America,* 282.

49. Irvin, "Tar, Feathers," 215; Oliver, *"Origin and Progress,"* 152–53.

50. William Aitchison to James Parker, Nov. 14, 1774, in Crary, *Price of Loyalty,* 58–59.

51. Henry Glassie, *Material Culture* (Bloomington: Indiana University Press, 1999), 325, 345; Robert Blair St. George, "Reading Spaces in Eighteenth-Century New England," in *Gender, Taste, and Material Culture in Britain and North America, 1700–1830,* ed. John Styles and Amanda Vickery (New Haven: Yale Center for British Art/Yale University Press, 2006), 81–105.

52. Amanda Vickery, "An Englishman's Home Is His Castle? Thresholds, Boundaries and Privacies in the Eighteenth-Century London House," *Past and Present,* no. 199 (May 2008): 152–54; Karen Harvey, *The Little Republic: Masculinity and Domestic Authority in Eighteenth-Century Britain* (Oxford: Oxford University Press, 2012), 11.

53. Wallace Brown, *The Good Americans: The Loyalists in the American Revolution* (New York: William Morrow, 1969), 132; Brown, *The King's Friends: The Composition and Motives of the American Loyalist Claimants* (Providence, RI: Brown University Press, 1965), 34–35.

54. Oliver, *"Origin and Progress,"* 152.

55. Van Tyne, *Loyalists in the American Revolution,* 213, 216; Elizabeth Fenn, *Pox Americana: The Great Smallpox Epidemic of 1775–1782* (New York: Hill and Wang, 2002), 29–31.

56. Alfred F. Young, "English Plebeian Culture and Eighteenth-Century Radicalism," in *The Origins of Anglo-American Radicalism,* ed. Margaret Jacob and James Jacob (London: Allen & Unwin, 1984), 185–212; Steven J. Stewart, "Skimmington in the Middle and Northern Colonies," in *Riot and Revelry in Early America,* ed. William Pencak, Matthew Dennis, and Simon P. Newman (University Park: Pennsylvania State University Press, 2002), 41–86; E. P. Thompson, "Rough Music Reconsidered," *Folklore* 103, no. 1 (1992): 3–26.

57. St. George, *Conversing by Signs,* 286–87, 294.

58. Edmund S. Morgan, *The Stamp Act Crisis: Prologue to Revolution* (Chapel Hill: University of North Carolina Press), 165–69; Bernard Bailyn, *The Ordeal of Thomas Hutchinson* (Cambridge, MA: Belknap Press of Harvard University Press, 1974), 35–36.

192   NOTES TO PAGES 39–43

59. Oliver, *"Origin and Progress,"* 152; Stone, "Narrative of Joel Stone," 325–26; Diary of Dothe Stone Cutler, Joel Stone Family Fonds, Archives of Ontario, reel 1.

60. Sharon Block, *Rape and Sexual Power in Early America* (Chapel Hill: University of North Carolina Press, 2006), 230–38; Block, "Rape without Women: Print Culture and the Politicization of Rape, 1765–1815," *Journal of American History* 89, no. 3 (2002): 849–68.

61. Tillman, *Stripped and Script,* 62, 31–33.

62. Block, *Rape and Sexual Power,* 210.

63. T. Jones, *History of New York,* 77; Tillman, *Stripped and Script,* 110.

64. W. Brown, *King's Friends,* 35; Tillman, *Stripped and Script,* 1, 60; Hulton in E. R. Jones, *Letters from a Loyalist Lady,* 85.

65. Egerton, *Royal Commission,* 116–17; *Pennsylvania Ledger,* Dec. 13, 1777.

66. Janice Potter-MacKinnon, *While the Women Only Wept: Loyalist Refugee Women* (Montreal and Kingston: McGill-Queen's University Press, 1993), 53.

67. Crary, *Price of Loyalty,* 78–80; Philip J. Schuyler to Mary Johnson, May 14, 1776, Washington Papers, 4th ser.

68. Kerber, *Women of the Republic,* 123, 50–51. That British and Revolutionary authorities also convicted women of spying shows the popular acceptance of women's political agency in other areas as well. For women's role as spies, see Mary Beth Norton, *Liberty's Daughters: The Revolutionary Experience of American Women, 1750–1800* (Toronto: Little, Brown, 1980), 174–75; Carol Berkin, *Revolutionary Mothers: Women in the Struggle for America's Independence* (New York: Knopf Doubleday, 2007), 135–47.

69. Kerber, *Women of the Republic,* 119–20, 123–24; Tillman, *Stripped and Script,* 31.

70. Egerton, *Royal Commission,* 71. This would have been allowed under "Ordinances passed at a general convention of delegates and representatives . . ." from May 6, 1776 (Williamsburg: Alexander Purdie, 1776), 25.

71. W. Brown, *Good Americans,* 127.

72. *Almon's Remembrancer,* Dec. 17, 1782, quoted in Van Tyne, *Loyalists in the American Revolution,* 280–81.

73. Robert Livingston to Benjamin Franklin, Jan. 2, 1782, in *The Works of Benjamin Franklin,* vol. 9, ed. Jared Sparks (Boston: Hilliard, Gray, 1840), 139.

74. James Allen, "Diary of James Allen, Esq. of Philadelphia, Counsellor-at-Law, 1770–1778," *Pennsylvania Magazine of History and Biography* 9, no. 3 (1885): 288, 285 (entry for Sept. 5, 1777).

75. W. Brown, *King's Friends,* 115, 7; Jasanoff, *Liberty's Exiles,* 68.

76. J. R. Lander, "Attainder and Forfeiture, 1453–1509," *Historical Journal* 4, no. 2 (1961): 119.

77. *Pennsylvania Packet,* Oct. 22, 1776.

78. Henry Cruger Van Schaak, *The Life of Peter Van Schaak, LL.D.: Embracing Selections from His Correspondence and Other Writings during the American Revolution, and His Exile in England* (New York: D. Appleton, 1842), 114–15; Van Tyne, *Loyalists in the American Revolution,* 281.

NOTES TO PAGES 43–49   193

79. *Independent Ledger,* Apr. 9, 1778, and Oct. 4, 1779; *Pennsylvania Packet,* Apr. 24, 1779; Statement of Enos Mitchell, Nov. 14, 1781, Loyalist Claims Commission Records, Archives of Ontario, Toronto, series 1, AO 12.

80. Calhoon, *Loyalists in Revolutionary America,* 317; *Boston Weekly News-Letter,* Feb. 23, 1775. The same story was repeated verbatim in Peter Oliver, *"Origin and Progress,"* 153.

81. W. Brown, *Good Americans,* 132; Nathaniel Whitworth Jr. to N. Whitworth Sr., Dec. 1775, Gideon White Papers, UNBLC.

82. Benjamin H. Irvin, *Clothed in Robes of Sovereignty: The Continental Congress and the People Out of Doors* (New York: Oxford University Press, 2011), 12–13, 49–50.

83. C. Smith, *American Honor,* 80; T. C. Jones, *Captives of Liberty,* 110; Irvin, *Clothed in Robes,* 151; Van Buskirk, *Generous Enemies,* 73–105.

84. Colden's Journal, 130–31, UNBLC.

85. William Roberts to Charles Mifflin, New York, Sept. 9, 1781, Schieffelin Family Papers, NYPL, box 1.

86. "The Minutes of the Commissioners for Detecting and Defeating Conspiracies in the State of New York, Dec. 11, 1776 to Sept. 23, 1778," 9 (bound documents), NYHS.

87. Hoock, *Scars of Independence,* 38, 55.

88. Letter from A. D. Spalding to John Peters, no date, John Peters Papers, NYHS.

89. Egerton, *Royal Commission,* 191.

90. William Bayard to unnamed recipient, Nov. 12, 1778; similar details are recorded in the undated "Schedule of Loss, No. 4," Bayard, Campbell, Pearsall Collection, NYPL.

91. Jane Byrne to William Bayard, New York, Sept. 27, 1785, Bayard, Campbell, Pearsall Collection, NYPL; Henry Onderdonk, *Queen's County in Olden Times, Being a Supplement to the Several Histories . . .* (Jamaica, NY: Charles Welling, 1865), 44.

92. Jasanoff, *Liberty's Exiles,* 7; Stone, "Narrative of Joel Stone," 326.

93. Crary, *Price of Loyalty,* 125.

94. W. Brown, *King's Friends,* 65.

95. Samuel Peters to Amos Botsford, Feb. 10, 1788, Botsford Family Papers, UNBLC. The story of the Tower of Siloam can be found in Luke 13:1–5 (KJV).

96. William Bayard to Elizabeth Cornell, Sept. 20, 1783, Bayard, William Sr., Misc. Mss., NYHS; Nicole Eustace, *Passion Is the Gale: Emotion, Power, and the Coming of the American Revolution* (Chapel Hill: University of North Carolina Press, 2008), 286.

2. Captivity

1. Philip Livingston, John Jay, and Gouverneur Morris to George Washington, June 21, 1776, in Force, *AA,* 4th ser., 6:1158; *Minutes of a Conspiracy against the Liberties of America* (1786; New York: Arno Press, 1969); Carl Van Doren, *Secret History of the American Revolution: An Account of the Conspiracies of Benedict Arnold and Numerous Others, Drawn from the Secret Service Papers of the British Headquarters in North America* (New York: Viking Press, 1941), 14–15; Jonathan Trumbull to Ezekiel Williams, Aug. 1, 1776,

194   NOTES TO PAGES 50–54

in *Letters and Documents of Ezekiel Williams of Wethersfield, Connecticut*, ed. John C. Parsons (Hartford, CT: Acorn Club, 1976), 44–45; Cox, *Proper Sense of Honor*, 201–7; Van Buskirk, *Generous Enemies*, 75–81, 92–104.

2. David Mathews to Gouverneur Morris, July 2, 1776, in Force, *AA*, 4th ser., 6:1215; Jonathan Trumbull to Moses Seymour, Aug. 22, 1776, Woodruff Collection, Litchfield Historical Society, Litchfield, CT; Kilbourn, *Sketches and Chronicles*, 112–13; Richard Buel, *Dear Liberty: Connecticut's Mobilization for the Revolutionary War* (Middletown, CT: Wesleyan University Press, 1980), 93–94.

3. Testimonial of David Mathews, Feb. 12, 1784, American Loyalist Claims, National Archives, Kew, UK, AO 13/42, Joel Stone, 560–61; *Connecticut Journal*, Nov. 27, 1776; Egerton, *Royal Commission*, 168.

4. Historians have attempted to categorize Loyalists to explain the varied Patriot treatment, but these models do not account for the inconsistencies. Van Tyne, *Loyalists in the American Revolution*, 213, 216, 227, 231–32; Charles Metzger, *The Prisoner in the American Revolution* (Chicago: Loyola University Press, 1971), 4–5.

5. An example of this sort of treason act was Connecticut's Act for the Punishment of High Treason and Other Atrocious Crimes against the State, though every state had some version of this. See Charles J. Hoadly, ed., *The Public Records of the State of Connecticut from October, 1776 to February, 1778, Inclusive* (Hartford, CT: Case, Lockwood & Brainard, 1894), 4–5. The Continental Congress also supported the extradition of captured Loyalist soldiers to their home counties or states, but this was applied inconsistently. See, for example, *Journals of the Continental Congress, from January 1st, 1780 to January 1st, 1781* (Philadelphia: David Claypoole, 1781), 374.

6. John Ferdinand Smyth to unnamed recipient, Nov. 24, 1775, in Force, *AA*, 4th ser., 4:615–16; Charles Lucas, *The Political Works of C. Lucas*, vol. 3 (Dublin: Henry Holmes, 1785), 470.

7. Burrows, *Forgotten Patriots*, xi, 161–93; see also Philip Ranlet, "Tory David Sproat of Pennsylvania and the Death of American Prisoners of War," *Pennsylvania History* 61, no. 2 (1994): 185–205; Cox, *Proper Sense of Honor*, 199–236.

8. Ethan Allen, *A Narrative of Colonel Ethan Allen's Captivity* (Philadelphia: Bell, 1779), 29–31.

9. Philip Freneau, *The British Prison-Ship: A Poem* (Philadelphia: Bailey, 1781), 16; Burrows, *Forgotten Patriots*, 174. For more on the debate surrounding the treatment of American prisoners, see Philip Davidson, *Propaganda and the American Revolution, 1763–1783* (Chapel Hill: University of North Carolina Press, 1941), 369–71; Metzger, *Prisoner*, 151–52; Larry G. Bowman, *Captive Americans: Prisoners during the American Revolution* (Athens: Ohio University Press, 1976), 5; Burrows, *Forgotten Patriots*, xi.

10. William Franklin to Lord Germaine, Nov. 10, 1778, in *Documents of the American Revolution, 1770–1783*, Colonial Office Series, vol. 15, ed. K. G. Davies (Dublin: Irish University Press, 1976), 241–47.

11. Metzger, *Prisoner*, 241–80; Richard Sampson, *Escape in America: The British Convention Prisoners, 1777–1783* (Chippenham, UK: Picton Publishing, 1995); Daniel Krebs, *A Generous and Merciful Enemy: Life for German Prisoners of War during the American War of Independence* (Norman: University of Oklahoma Press, 2013), chap. 9. For the local

NOTES TO PAGES 54–58   195

impact of British prisoners, see Laura L. Becker, "Prisoners of War in the American Revolution: A Community Perspective," *Military Affairs* 46, no. 4 (1982): 169–73; Ken Miller, *Dangerous Guests: Enemy Captives and Revolutionary Communities during the War for Independence* (Ithaca, NY: Cornell University Press, 2014).

12. T. C. Jones, *Captives of Liberty*, 8; John E. Ferling, *Almost a Miracle: The American Victory in the War of Independence* (New York: Oxford University Press, 2007), 432.

13. Entry of Sept. 3, 1776, in Ambrose Serle, *The American Journal of Ambrose Serle* (New York: Arno Press, 1969), 90.

14. Richard Phelps, *A History of Newgate of Connecticut* (1860; New York: Arno Press, 1969), 76; T. C. Jones, *Captives of Liberty*, 115.

15. *Royal Gazette*, June 9, 1781; Calhoon, *Loyalists in Revolutionary America*, 311.

16. George Washington to the Committee of Symsbury, Dec. 11, 1775, and Philip Schuyler to John Hancock, Feb. 10, 1776, in Force, *AA*, 4th ser., 4:235–36, 990; Hoock, *Scars of Independence*, 44–49.

17. T. C. Jones, *Captives of Liberty*, 119–23.

18. Major General William Phillips on behalf of John Peters, "Burgoyne's official order or permission," John Peters Papers, NYHS; Peters, "Narrative," 7, John Peters Papers, NYHS; Sampson, *Escape in America*, 39; Anthony Allaire, *The Diary of Anthony Allaire* (New York: Arno Press, 1968), entry for Saturday, Oct. 14, 1780, 32.

19. Letter from Gen. Burgoyne to Gen. Gates, Aug. 30, 1777, published in the *New York Gazette and Weekly Mercury*, Oct. 6, 1777; Cornwallis to Smallwood, Nov. 10, 1780, and General Orders, Colonel William Campbell, Oct. 11, 1780, King's Mountain Papers, Draper Manuscripts, D. B. Weldon Library, University of Western Ontario, series DD, reel 83; Robert Scott Davis, "The Loyalist Trials at Ninety Six in 1779," *South Carolina Historical Magazine* 80, no. 2 (1979): 177; Thomas Shaw to Ezekiel Williams, June 13, 1778, Williams Family Papers, Connecticut Historical Society (hereafter CHS).

20. Burrows, *Forgotten Patriots*, 30; Van Buskirk, *Generous Enemies*, 76.

21. Lord Germain to William Howe, Feb. 1, 1776, in Force, *AA*, 4th ser., 5:903; Cox, *Proper Sense of Honor*, 214; Bowman, *Captive Americans*, 81, 110–15; Cox, *Proper Sense of Honor*, 216; Burrows, *Forgotten Patriots*, 77, 49.

22. Van Buskirk, *Generous Enemies*, 81; Burrows, *Forgotten Patriots*, 99.

23. George Washington to Matthias Ogden, Apr. 13, 1778, Washington Papers, 4th ser., General Correspondence.

24. Burrows, *Forgotten Patriots*, 110; Van Buskirk, *Generous Enemies*, 73–105.

25. Major General David Wooster to Captain David Dimon, July 10, 1775, Ezekiel Williams Papers, CHS, MS 82827; John Hancock to Ezekiel Williams, July 6, 1775, Williams Family Papers, CHS; "In Congress, May 21, 1776," handbill detailing prisoner treatment and parole conditions (Philadelphia, 1776).

26. George Washington to Jonathan Trumbull, Aug. 11, 1776, Washington Papers, 2nd ser., Letterbook 10, July 15–Oct. 26, 1776.

27. George Washington to Suffolk, New York Safety Committee, May 16, 1776, Washington Papers, 2nd ser., Letterbook 8; George Washington to Joseph Kirkbride, Apr. 20, 1778, Washington Papers, 4th ser., General Correspondence.

196 NOTES TO PAGES 58–66

28. George Washington to William Heath, July 3, 1779, Washington Papers, 4th ser., General Correspondence.

29. Gen. Philip Schuyler to Jonathan Trumbull, Dec. 12, 1775, in Force, *AA*, 4th ser., 5:248.

30. *Pennsylvania Evening Post,* July 27, 1776.

31. Colden's Journal, 102, UNBLC.

32. Diary of Thomas Gilpin, Oct. 7, 1777, NYHS.

33. "The Diary of Major Christopher French," Saturday, June 22, 1776, American Revolution Collection, CHS, Micro. 79956, copy UNBLC, HIL-MICL FC LSC .U5C6A4; T. Jones, *History of New York,* 268.

34. Samuel McKay to George Washington, Apr. 9, 1776, and George Washington to Samuel McKay, Apr. 11, 1776, Washington Papers, 4th ser., General Correspondence; "Diary of Major Christopher French," May 22 and 23, 1776, UNBLC; *Connecticut Journal,* May 29, 1776.

35. Elias Boudinot to Ezekiel Williams, Dec. 4, 1777, in Parsons, *Letters and Documents of Ezekiel Williams,* 11.

36. Copy of letter to Sir Henry Clinton, Jan. 13, 1779, Colden's Journal, 199, UNBLC.

37. *Minutes of the Committee and of the First Commission for Detecting and Defeating Conspiracies in the State of New York,* vol. 1 (New York: New York Historical Society, 1924), 14–16; Petition to Committee, Dec. 26, 1776, Colden's Journal, 5–7, 10, UNBLC; E. R. Fingerhut, *Survivor: Cadwallader Colden II in Revolutionary America* (Washington, DC: University Press of America, 1983), 58.

38. Colden's Journal, 17, 28–29, 39, UNBLC.

39. Fingerhut, *Survivor,* 52–53, 81; Colden's Journal, 130–31, UNBLC.

40. Copy of a letter from Cadwallader Colden II to James Livingston, Jan. 23, 1777, Colden's Journal, 41, UNBLC.

41. Colden's Journal, 47, 57, UNBLC.

42. Colden's Journal, 67, 71, 83, 89, 91, 98, UNBLC; Fingerhut, *Survivor,* 75.

43. Colden's Journal, 111–12, 114, UNBLC.

44. Fingerhut, *Survivor,* 94–97; Colden's Journal, 182, UNBLC.

45. Colden's Journal, 198–200, UNBLC.

46. George Washington to Essex County, New Jersey, Committee, June 30, 1776, Washington Papers, 2nd ser., Letterbook 8, 201–3; Sheila L. Skemp, *William Franklin: Son a Patriot, Servant of a King* (New York: Oxford University Press, 1990), 214.

47. Skemp, *William Franklin,* 215.

48. Skemp, *William Franklin,* 220–21; William Franklin to Lord Germaine, Nov. 10, 1778, in Davies, *Documents of the American Revolution,* 243.

49. Entry for July 28, 1777, *Journals of the Continental Congress,* vol. 8 (Washington, DC: Government Printing Office, 1907), 584.

50. *Connecticut Gazette,* July 18, 1777.

51. Skemp, *William Franklin,* 222, 225.

52. "Diary of Major Christopher French," UNBLC. A transcribed version of the diary is used for ease of citation: Sheldon S. Cohen, ed., "The Connecticut Captivity

of Major Christopher French," *Connecticut Historical Society Bulletin* 55, nos. 3–4 (1990): 125, 151.

53. S. Cohen, "Connecticut Captivity," 182.

54. S. Cohen, "Connecticut Captivity," 141–45 (Mar. 9 to May 9, 1776); Oscar Zeichner, *Connecticut's Years of Controversy, 1750–1776* (1949; Archon Books, 1970), 206; Robert A. East, *Connecticut's Loyalists* (Chester, CT: Pequot Press, 1974); David H. Villiers, "King Mob and the Rule of Law: Revolutionary Justice and the Suppression of Loyalism in Connecticut, 1774–1783," in *Loyalists and Community in North America,* ed. Robert M. Calhoon, Timothy M. Barnes, and George A. Rawlyk (Westport, CT: Greenwood Press, 1994), 17–30. The election of Skene's slave as a governor was part of a festival in the region variously referred to as Election Day or Pinkster. See Shane White, "'It Was a Proud Day': African Americans, Festivals, and Parades in the North, 1741–1834," *Journal of American History* 81, no. 1 (1994): 13–50.

55. S. Cohen, "Connecticut Captivity," 146–47 (May 21, 1776).

56. S. Cohen, "Connecticut Captivity," 156, 197, 213.

57. S. Cohen, "Connecticut Captivity," 179, 184, 186, 220.

58. *Connecticut Courant,* Nov. 4, 1776.

59. S. Cohen, "Connecticut Captivity," 201.

60. S. Cohen, "Connecticut Captivity," 203–4, 206, 223. There is no mention of this episode or French's disguise in the Patriot press, even though it could have been used to show the ludicrous emasculation of an archenemy. The failure to capitalize on this may owe to the fact that David Mathews had escaped the same week, and Patriot authorities were reluctant to expose their inability to retain high-value prisoners.

61. *Connecticut Gazette,* Feb. 28, 1777.

62. George Washington to Thomas Gage, Aug. 11, 1775, Washington Papers, 4th ser., General Correspondence.

63. James Moody, *Lieutenant James Moody's Narrative of His Exertions and Sufferings* (London: Richardson and Urquhart, 1783); Susan Burgess Shenstone, *So Obstinately Loyal: James Moody, 1744–1809* (Montreal and Kingston: McGill-Queen's University Press, 2000), 9.

64. Robert Pollard, "Lieutenant Moody" (London: R, Pollard, 1785), LOC, https://lccn.loc .gov/2004670176; Shenstone, *So Obstinately Loyal,* 162–63.

65. *New Jersey Gazette,* Aug. 9, 1780; Shenstone, *So Obstinately Loyal,* 81–82.

66. Van Buskirk, *Generous Enemies,* 92, 96–97.

67. Shenstone, *So Obstinately Loyal,* 81–82.

68. Moody, *Narrative,* 24–31; George Washington to William Livingston, Aug. 17, 1780, Washington Papers, 3rd ser., Varick Transcripts, subseries C, Letterbook 3, 362–64.

69. John Graves Simcoe, *A Journal of the Operations of the Queen's Rangers* (Exeter, 1789), appendix, 191–92.

70. Bernard W. Sheehan, "'The Famous Hair Buyer General': Henry Hamilton, George Rogers Clark, and the American Indian," *Indiana Magazine of History* 79, no. 1 (1983): 2; Colin G. Calloway, *The American Revolution in Indian Country: Crisis and Diversity*

198 NOTES TO PAGES 72–79

in Native American Communities (New York: Cambridge University Press, 1995), 40–41, 56.

71. Major Joseph Bowman, "Bowman's Journal," in *Col. George Rogers Clark's Sketch of His Campaign in the Illinois,* by George Rogers Clark (Cincinnati: Robert Clarke, 1907), 90.

72. *Royal Gazette,* July 15, 1780; Gerald O. Haffner, "A British Prisoner of War in the American Revolution: The Experiences of Jacob Schieffelin from Vincennes to Williamsburg, 1779–1780," *Virginia Magazine of History and Biography* 86, no. 1 (1978): 17–25, 20.

73. *Pennsylvania Packet,* June 29, 1779; *Pennsylvania Evening Post,* July 3, 1779; *Independent Chronicle,* July 8, 1779; *Connecticut Courant,* July 13, 1779.

74. George Washington to Thomas Jefferson, July 10, 1779, Washington Papers, 4th ser., General Correspondence.

75. *Royal Gazette,* July 15, 1780.

76. "In Council, June 16, 1779 . . ." broadside (Williamsburg, VA: Dixon & Nicolson, 1779); *Pennsylvania Evening Post,* July 3, 1779; *Continental Journal,* Dec. 30, 1779.

77. *Continental Journal,* Jan. 18, 1781. Also see Clark, *Col. George Rogers Clark's Sketch,* 65; George Washington to Thomas Jefferson, Aug. 6, 1779, Washington Papers, 4th ser., General Correspondence.

3. Revenge

1. *The Royal Gazette,* July 14, 1779; Association of Loyal Refugees, *Declaration and Address of His Majesty's Loyal Associated Refugees* (New York: Rivington, 1779); James Clarke, "Association of Loyal Refugees, Newport, Rhode Island," Mar. 30, 1779, broadside (Newport, RI, 1779).

2. "The Frigate Restoration" handbill (New York: Rivington, 1779).

3. Alan S. Brown, "James Simpson's Reports of the Carolina Loyalists, 1779–1780," *Journal of Southern History* 21, no. 4 (1955): 519; Wayne E. Lee, *Barbarians and Brothers: Anglo-American Warfare, 1500–1865* (New York: Oxford University Press, 2014), 223; Wyatt-Brown, *Southern Honor,* 34; F. Stewart, *Honor,* 64–71.

4. David Ramsay, *The History of the American Revolution,* vol. 2 (Philadelphia: R. Aitken & Son, 1789), 240.

5. *Boston Evening-Post,* Apr. 26, 1783.

6. Thomas Paine, *The Crisis,* no. 1 (Norwich: Trumbull, 1776), 5.

7. Lorenzo Sabine, *The American Loyalists, Or Biographical Sketches of the Loyalists of the American Revolution* (Boston: Thurston, Torry, 1847), 21–22.

8. Van Tyne, *Loyalists in the American Revolution,* 166–67, 173–74.

9. W. Nelson, *American Tory,* 85; Robert M. Calhoon, *The Loyalist Perception and Other Essays* (Columbia: University of South Carolina Press, 1989), 147–48, 154; Calhoon, *Loyalists in Revolutionary America,* 504. Also see Royster, *Revolutionary People at War,* 277.

10. John Shy, *A People Numerous and Armed: Reflections on the Military Struggle for American Independence* (New York: Oxford University Press, 1976), 213, 206; Shy, "American Society and Its War for Independence," in *Reconsiderations on the Revolutionary War: Selected Essays*, ed. Don Higginbotham (Westport, CT: Greenwood Press, 1978), 81.

11. Harry M. Ward, *Between the Lines: Banditti of the American Revolution* (Westport, CT: Praeger, 2002), x.

12. T. C. Jones, *Captives of Liberty*, 75, 91, 241.

13. Wolfgang Schivelbusch, *The Culture of Defeat: On National Trauma, Mourning, and Recovery*, trans. Jefferson Chase (New York: Henry Holt, 2001), 23; Lee, *Barbarians and Brothers*, 223; A. Brown, "James Simpson's Reports," 519; Charles Stewart to Joseph Galloway, Dec. 1, 1778, quoted in Edward H. Tebbenhoff, "The Associated Loyalists: An Aspect of Militant Loyalism," *New York Historical Quarterly* 63 (Apr. 1979): 118; W. Brown, *Good Americans*, 254; John Blackburn to Christian Daniel Claus, July 30, 1776, Claus Family Papers, UNBLC; "The Diary of Henry Nase," 3, UNBLC; Thomas Brewer Vincent, "Keeping the Faith: The Poetic Development of Jacob Bailey, Loyalist," *Early American Literature* 14, no. 1 (1979): 8.

14. Eustace, *Passion Is the Gale*, 159–60.

15. *Pennsylvania Gazette*, Feb. 26, 1754.

16. John Perkins, "Thoughts on Agency" (New Haven, CT: B. Mecom, 1765), 32.

17. Harold Skulsky, "Revenge, Honor, and Conscience in 'Hamlet,'" *PMLA* 85, no. 1 (1970): 78–87. Thomas Kyd, *The Spanish Tragedy* (1582–89?), John Marston, *Antonio's Revenge* (1599–1600), and Thomas Middleton, *The Revenger's Tragedy* (1606) are just three examples that share many of the themes of protagonists undone and killed by their quest for vengeance.

18. Edward Young, *The Revenge: A Tragedy* (1721; London: R. Butters, ca. 1780).

19. Carl Lefevre, "Lord Byron's Fiery Convert of Revenge," *Studies in Philology* 49, no. 3 (1952): 468–87; Lord Byron, *The Siege of Corinth: A Poem* (London: T. Davidson, 1816); James Fenimore Cooper, *The Last of the Mohicans: A Narrative of 1757* (London: John Miller, 1826); John Richardson, *Wacousta; or the Prophecy: A Tale of the Canadas* (London: T. Cadell, Strand and W. Blackwood, 1832). For a discussion of Indigenous attitudes toward revenge, see Wayne E. Lee, "Peace Chiefs and Blood Revenge: Patterns of Restraint in Native American Warfare, 1500–1800," *Journal of Military History* 71, no. 3 (2007): 701–41.

20. Wyatt-Brown, *Southern Honor*, 34. For the Scotch-Irish culture of revenge, see Fischer, *Albion's Seed*, 663, 668, 756, 767.

21. Samuel Johnson, *The Rambler*, vol. 4 (London: T. Longman et al., 1793), 135, originally printed as no. 185, Dec. 24, 1751; F. Stewart, *Honor*, 64–71; Bernard Mandeville, *The Fable of the Bees* (London: J. Tonson, 1732), 245; Alexander Welsh, *What Is Honor? A Question of Moral Imperatives* (New Haven, CT: Yale University Press, 2008), 91.

22. Samuel Seabury, *A Discourse on Brotherly Love* (New York: Hugh Gaine, 1777), 13, 9, 12.

23. Charles Inglis, *The Christian Soldier's Duty* (New York: Hugh Gaine, 1777), 2, 21.

24. Simeon Baxter, *Tyrannicide Proved Lawful* . . . (London: S. Bladon, 1782), 8–13, 25–27.

25. Jonathan Odell, "Song for St. George's Day" (New York, 1777).

200   NOTES TO PAGES 85–89

26. "The Speech of the Honourable Henry Temple Luttrell," *Norwich Packet*, June 1, 1775.

27. Calhoon, *Loyalists in Revolutionary America*, 480–83.

28. Jonathan Odell, "The Congratulation," in *The Loyal Verses of Joseph Stansbury and Doctor Jonathan Odell*, ed. Winthrop Sargent (Albany: J. Munsell, 1860), 45–50; *Royal Gazette*, Nov. 6, 1779.

29. *Royal Pennsylvania Gazette*, Mar. 20, 1778.

30. Association of Loyal Refugees, "To Further in Some Degree . . . ," Mar. 30, 1779 (Newport, RI); *Royal Gazette*, July 14, 1779.

31. Shenstone, *So Obstinately Loyal*, 308.

32. Moody, *Narrative*, 44.

33. John Ferdinand Dalziel Smyth, *Narrative or Journal of Capt. John Ferdinand Dalziel Smith* (New York: Hugh Gaine, 1778), 1.

34. Andrew Elliot to the Earl of Carlisle, Feb. 1, 1779, quoted in Tebbenhoff, "Associated Loyalists," 121–22; John Shy, "The Loyalist Problem in the Lower Hudson Valley: The British Perspective," in *The Loyalist Americans: A Focus on Greater New York*, ed. Robert A. East and Jacob Judd (Tarrytown, NY: Sleepy Hollow Restorations, 1975), 9.

35. George Washington to Thomas Gage, Aug. 11, 1775, George Washington Papers, 4th ser., General Correspondence.

36. Charles Inglis, *The Duty of Honouring the King* (New York: Hugh Gaine, 1780), 23.

37. *Providence Gazette and Country Journal*, June 10, 1775.

38. Ruma Chopra, *Unnatural Rebellion: Loyalists in New York City during the Revolution* (Charlottesville: University of Virginia Press, 2011), 110–12.

39. James Parker quoted in Keith Mason, "The American Loyalist Problem of Identity in the Revolutionary Atlantic World," in Bannister and Riordan, *Loyal Atlantic*, 59.

40. Joseph Stansbury, "A Pasquinade," in Sargent, *Loyal Verses*, 67–68.

41. Chopra, *Unnatural Rebellion*, 109–10.

42. Paul H. Smith, *Loyalists and Redcoats: A Study in British Revolutionary Policy* (Chapel Hill: University of North Carolina Press, 1964), ix, 72–73.

43. Shy, "Loyalist Problem," 7.

44. Lee, *Barbarians and Brothers*, 2.

45. Royster, *Revolutionary People at War*, 277.

46. Edward J. Cashin, *The King's Ranger: Thomas Brown and the American Revolution on the Southern Frontier* (Athens: University of Georgia Press, 1989), 28, 219; Gary D. Olson, "Dr. David Ramsay and Lt. Colonel Thomas Brown: Patriot Historian and Loyalist Critic," *South Carolina Historical Magazine* 77, no. 4 (1976): 257–67; Ramsay, *History of the American Revolution*, 2:237, 240–41; Hugh McCall, *The History of Georgia: Containing Brief Sketches of the Most Remarkable Events* (1811; Atlanta: A. B. Caldwell, 1909), 523.

47. *Connecticut Gazette*, July 28, 1775; *Pennsylvania Ledger*, Nov. 11, 1775.

48. *Essex Journal*, Jan. 23, 1777.

49. *Connecticut Courant*, Oct. 2, 1775; *Connecticut Journal*, Dec. 20, 1775.

50. For the idea of Scottish savagery and the Jacobite Rebellion, see Geoffrey Plank, *Rebellion and Savagery: The Jacobite Rising of 1745 and the British Empire* (Philadelphia:

University of Pennsylvania Press, 2006). For the Scots in Virginia, see Adele Hast, *Loyalism in Revolutionary Virginia: The Norfolk Area and the Eastern Shore* (Ann Arbor, MI: UMI Research Press, 1982), 11.

51. Simon Schama, *Rough Crossings: Britain, the Slaves, and the American Revolution* (Toronto: Viking Canada, 2005), 75–76; Woody Holton, *Forced Founders: Indians, Debtors, Slaves and the Making of the American Revolution in Virginia* (Chapel Hill: University of North Carolina Press, 1999), 133–63; Holton, "Rebel against Rebel: Enslaved Virginians and the Coming of the American Revolution," *Virginia Magazine of History and Biography* 105, no. 2 (1997): 157–92; Cassandra Pybus, *Epic Journeys of Freedom: Runaway Slaves of the American Revolution and Their Global Quest for Liberty* (Boston: Beacon Press, 2006), chapters 1–3. "Negro Thief" found in *Constitutional Gazette*, Jan. 20, 1776.

52. *Pennsylvania Evening Post*, Dec. 5 and 12, 1775.

53. Holton, "Rebel against Rebel," 189–92.

54. William Woodford to the Virginia Convention, Dec. 12, 1775, in Force, *AA*, 4th ser., 5:245; *Pennsylvania Evening Post*, Apr. 6, 1776; *Pennsylvania Packet*, Mar. 24, 1776; *Pennsylvania Ledger*, Dec. 30, 1775; Schama, *Rough Crossings*, 79–82.

55. *Pennsylvania Evening Post*, Mar. 23, 1776; Duane Meyer, *The Highland Scots of North Carolina, 1732–1776* (Chapel Hill: University of North Carolina Press, 1987), 159–61.

56. P. Smith, *Loyalists and Redcoats*, 58–59.

57. W. Brown, *Good Americans*, 64–65; Chopra, *Unnatural Rebellion*, 119; P. Smith, *Loyalists and Redcoats*, 70–71.

58. P. Smith, *Loyalists and Redcoats*, 71–75.

59. P. Smith, *Loyalists and Redcoats*, 48–49, 63–65.

60. *Royal Pennsylvania Gazette*, Apr. 3, 1778.

61. *New York Gazette*, Sept. 21, 1778.

62. Ward, *Between the Lines*, 17–32.

63. Catherine S. Crary, "Guerrilla Activities of James DeLancey's Cowboys in Westchester County: Conventional Warfare or Self-Interested Freebooting?," in East and Judd, *Loyalist Americans*, 19–20.

64. *New York Gazette*, May 29, 1780.

65. *Connecticut Gazette*, June 9, 1780.

66. Crary, "Guerrilla Activities," 16, 20, 22, 24.

67. Michael C. Scoggins, *The Day It Rained Militia: Huck's Defeat and the Revolution in the South Carolina Backcountry, May–July 1780* (Charleston, SC: History Press, 2005), 44–46.

68. *New York Gazette*, June 19, 1780.

69. David Ramsay, *The History of the Revolution in South-Carolina, from a British Province to an Independent State* (Trenton, NJ: Isaac Collins, 1785), 110; Jim Piecuch, "Massacre or Myth? Banastre Tarleton at the Waxhaws, May 29, 1780," *Southern Campaigns of the American Revolution* 1, no. 2 (2004): 4–19; J. Tracy Power, "'The Virtue of Humanity Was Totally Forgot': Buford's Massacre, May 29, 1780," *South Carolina Historical Magazine* 93, no. 1 (1992): 9.

202   NOTES TO PAGES 93–99

70. Jim Piecuch, *Three Peoples, One King: Loyalists, Indians, and Slaves in the Revolutionary South, 1775–1782* (Columbia: University of South Carolina Press, 2008). Chapters 5 and 6 contain a thorough account of the cycle of violence in the South.

71. Jim Piecuch, *The Blood Be upon Your Head: Tarleton and the Myth of Buford's Massacre, the Battle of the Waxhaws, May 29, 1780* (Lugoff, SC: Southern Campaigns of the American Revolution Press, 2010).

72. Colin G. Calloway, "Simon Girty: Interpreter and Intermediary," in *Being and Becoming Indian: Biographical Studies of North American Frontiers,* ed. James A. Clifton (Chicago: Dorsey Press, 1989), 39.

73. Peter Silver, *Our Savage Neighbors: How Indian War Transformed Early America* (New York: Norton, 2008), xviii–xx, 240–42; *Connecticut Courant,* July 21, 1778.

74. Thomas S. Abler, *Cornplanter: Chief Warrior of the Allegany Senecas* (Syracuse, NY: Syracuse University Press, 2007), 2, 45–46; Lee, *Barbarians and Brothers,* 217–19; Obadiah Gore Jr. to Nathaniel Gallup, Mar. 17, 1779 (copy), Mss 84460, Obadiah Gore Folder, CHS.

75. *Connecticut Courant,* July 21, 1778; *New Jersey Gazette,* July 22, 1778 (also see reports of a "Painted Tory" in Lee, *Barbarians and Brothers,* 213); *Connecticut Courant,* July 28, 1778. For a description of the Battle of Wyoming Valley, see Barbara Graymont, *The Iroquois in the American Revolution* (Syracuse, NY: Syracuse University Press, 1972), 168–74.

76. Calloway, *American Revolution in Indian Country,* 124–25; Alan Taylor, *The Divided Ground: Indians, Settlers, and the Northern Borderland of the American Revolution* (New York: Vintage, 2007), 93–94.

77. Taylor, *Divided Ground,* 93–94.

78. *Connecticut Journal,* Dec. 3, 1778.

79. Graymont, *Iroquois in the American Revolution,* 161–62.

80. Quoted in George M. Wrong, *The Chronicles of Canada,* vol. 4 (Toronto: Fireship Press, 2009), 119.

81. Frederick Haldimand to John Peters, July 25, 1778, John Peters Papers, NYHS.

82. Sir John Johnson to Daniel Claus, July 16, 1778, Claus Family Papers, UNBLC, reel 8.

83. *Independent Chronicle and the Universal Advertiser,* Dec. 24, 1778.

84. Hannah Lawrence Shieffelin, "Narrative of Events . . . during a Journey through Canada," 16–18, Schieffelin Family Papers, NYPL.

85. *New Jersey Gazette,* Nov. 14, 1781.

86. Taylor, *Divided Ground,* 84–85.

87. James Parker to Charles Steuart, June 1, 1778, quoted in K. Mason, "American Loyalist Problem," 60.

88. Taylor, *Divided Ground,* 100.

89. Daniel Claus to F. Haldimand, Oct. 26, 1778, Claus Family Papers, UNBLC, reel 8.

90. Oliver, *"Origin and Progress,"* 132–34.

91. Marquis de Chastellux, *Travels in North America in the Years 1780, 1781, and 1782,* vol. 2 (London: G. G. J. and J. Robinson, 1787), 5–6.

92. *Connecticut Courant*, July 27, 1779; *Pennsylvania Packet*, Aug. 7, 1779; *New Jersey Gazette*, Aug. 18, 1779.

93. Priscilla Lothrop Burr, Aug. 10, 1779, American Revolution Papers, CHS, box 1.

94. Paul David Nelson, *William Tryon and the Course of Empire: A Life in British Imperial Service* (Chapel Hill: University of North Carolina Press, 1990), 169–74. The *Independent Ledger*, Aug. 9, 1779, also picked up on the controversy among the British commanders and printed a mocking poem in which even Henry Clinton refused to "own poor Tryon as a brother."

95. Richard Pougher argues that the primary motivation of Loyalist privateers was "public virtue." See "'Averse . . . to Remaining Idle Spectators': The Emergence of Loyalist Privateering during the American Revolution, 1775–1778" (PhD diss., University of Maine, 2002), 1:43–47, 52, 85; "Frigate Restoration" handbill.

96. Petition of Evert Bancker Jr., undated, Bancker Family Papers, NYPL.

97. Pougher, "'Averse . . . to Remaining Idle Spectators,'" 2; John Richardson to John Porteous, Mar. 15, 1779, Porteous Papers, UNBLC; *Royal Gazette*, Jan. 6, 1779. The *Fair American* is also mentioned in Van Tyne, *Loyalists in the American Revolution*, 178.

98. Stone, "Narrative of Joel Stone," 331–32.

99. John Richardson to John Porteous, Aug. 22, 1780, Porteous Papers, UNBLC.

100. James Simpson to Claims Commission, quoted in W. Brown, *King's Friends*, 278–79.

101. *American Journal and General Advertiser*, Aug. 25, 1781; *Independent Chronicle*, Dec. 24, 1778.

102. *American Journal*, Apr. 15, 1779.

103. *Providence Gazette*, Apr. 21, 1781.

104. The last reference found was in the *Independent Gazetteer*, May 31, 1783, which reported an incident from March of the same year.

105. *Royal Gazette*, Feb. 7, 1781.

106. *New Jersey Gazette*, Apr. 24, 1782.

107. *Royal Gazette*, Apr. 17, 1779; Crary, *Price of Loyalty*, 194–95.

108. George Washington to Continental Congress, Apr. 20, 1782, Washington Papers, ser. 3a, Varick Transcripts, Letterbook 6, 221.

109. For a concise rendition of the Asgill Affair, see T. C. Jones, *Captives of Liberty*, 231–35.

110. Address of Richard Lippincott to the Court, June 17, 1782, transcribed in *Sources of American Independence: Selected Manuscripts from the Collections of the William L. Clements Library*, ed. Howard H. Peckham, vol. 2 (Chicago: University of Chicago Press, 1978), 558–62; Skemp, *William Franklin*, 256–66.

111. Henry Clinton to William Franklin, Apr. 20, 1782, George Washington Papers, LOC, 4th ser., General Correspondence; Tebbenhoff, "Associated Loyalists," 143.

112. Marquis de Chastellux, *Travels in North America*, 1:337.

113. Lawrence Labree, *Rebels and Tories; Or, The Blood of the Mohawks! A Tale of the American Revolution* (New York: Dewitt & Davenport, 1851), 32. Also see depictions of the Loyalists in John Pendleton Kennedy, *Horse-Shoe Robinson: A Tale of the Tory Ascendency* (London: Richard Bentley, 1835), 1:228.

114. Harold Frederic, *In the Valley* (New York: Charles Scribner's Sons, 1890), 328, 207.

4. Loyalist Honor

1. Peters, "Narrative," 11 (Aug. 1785), John Peters Papers, NYHS; Claim of Col. John Peters, Loyalist Claims Commission Records, Archives of Ontario, Toronto, AO 12.30, 276–88.

2. Jasanoff, *Liberty's Exiles*, 351–58; Philip Ranlet, "How Many American Loyalists Left the United States?," *The Historian* 76, no. 2 (2014): 291–306.

3. For a discussion on the problems of Loyalist identity, see K. Mason, "American Loyalist Problem." On allegiance and ideology, see Jasanoff, *Liberty's Exiles*, 8–9; Jasanoff, "The Other Side of the Revolution: Loyalists in the British Empire," *William and Mary Quarterly*, 3rd ser., 65, no. 2 (2008): 222–27.

4. Gregory T. Knouff, "Masculinity, Race, and Citizenship: Soldiers' Memories of the American Revolution," in *Gender, War and Politics: Transatlantic Perspectives, 1775–1830*, ed. Karen Hagemann, Gisela Mettele, and Jane Rendall (New York: Palgrave Macmillan, 2010), 325.

5. John Peters, "Defence of the Provincials and Indians against Burgoyne's Charges. Dated 9 Dec. 1779," John Peters Papers, NYHS.

6. F. Stewart, *Honor*, 21–22.

7. Schivelbusch, *Culture of Defeat*, 10.

8. Joseph Galloway, *Historical and Political Reflections on the Rise and Progress of the American Rebellion* . . . (London, 1780), 94–95, 107.

9. Schivelbusch, *Culture of Defeat*, 6; Galloway, *Historical and Political Reflections*, 108.

10. Jasanoff, *Liberty's Exiles*, 58. A comprehensive history of the peace negotiations can be found in Andrew Stockley, *Britain and France at the Birth of America: The European Powers and the Peace Negotiations of 1782–1783* (Exeter, UK: University of Exeter Press, 2001).

11. Treaty of Paris, 1783, National Archives and Records Administration, https://www .archives.gov/milestone-documents/treaty-of-paris.

12. *Connecticut Journal*, Apr. 10, 1783.

13. *South Carolina Gazette and General Advertiser*, Apr. 5, 1783.

14. *Connecticut Courant*, Apr. 22, 1783.

15. *South Carolina Weekly Gazette*, June 28, 1783. For the British cession of Loyalist Florida to Spain, see Carole Troxler, "Loyalist Refugees and the British Evacuation of East Florida, 1783–1785," *Florida Historical Quarterly* 60, no. 1 (1981): 1–28; Troxler, "Refuge, Resistance, and Reward: The Southern Loyalists' Claim on East Florida," *Journal of Southern History* 55, no. 4 (1989): 563–96.

16. Stone, "Narrative of Joel Stone," 336; Jasanoff, *Liberty's Exiles*, 99.

17. Mather Byles Jr. to Kitty Byles, Halifax, Oct. 28, 1783, Byles Papers, UNBLC.

18. Joshua Chandler to Charles Chauncey, London, Apr. 13, 1784, reprinted in *The Descendants of William and Annis Chandler, Who Settled in Roxbury, Mass. 1637*, ed. George Chandler (Worcester, MA: Press of Charles Hamilton, 1883), 255–56.

19. Galloway, *Historical and Political Reflections*; Alexander Hewatt, *An Historical Account of the Rise and Progress of the Colonies of South Carolina and Georgia*, vol. 2 (London, 1779).

NOTES TO PAGES 112–118   205

Peter Oliver's *Origin and Progress of the American Rebellion* was written around 1781 but was not published until the twentieth century. Samuel Peters, *A General History of Connecticut from Its First Settlement . . .* , 2nd ed. (London, 1782), published anonymously; Jonathan Boucher, *A View of the Causes and Consequences of the American Revolution in Thirteen Discourses* (1797; New York: Russell & Russell, 1967).

20. An excellent summation of the Loyalist histories can be found in Mary Beth Norton, *The British-Americans: The Loyalist Exiles in England, 1774–1789* (Toronto: Little, Brown, 1972), 130–54; for the Loyalist consensus that there was little cause for upheaval, see 134.

21. Peters, *General History*, 317, 304, 307–12, 321.

22. Galloway, *Historical and Political Reflections*, 110.

23. Boucher, *View of the Causes*, xxxiv–xxxv, xxxvii; Norton, *British-Americans*, 134.

24. Oliver, *"Origin and Progress,"* 39–41, 79, 83; Edward Larkin, "Seeing through Language: Narrative, Portraiture, and Character in Peter Oliver's 'The Origin & Progress of the American Rebellion,'" *Early American Literature* 36, no. 3 (2001): 427–54; K. Mason, "American Loyalist Problem," 46–47.

25. Peters, "Narrative" (manuscript copy), no date, John Peters Papers, NYHS.

26. Galloway, *Observations on the Fifth Article of the Treaty with America and on the Necessity of Appointing a Judicial Enquiry into the Merits and Losses of the American Loyalists* (London, 1783), 10–12.

27. Norton, *British-Americans*, 191–92; Jasanoff, *Liberty's Exiles*, 121.

28. Jasanoff, *Liberty's Exiles*, 120–23, 142; Norton, *British-Americans*, 185–222.

29. Galloway, *Observations on the Fifth Article*, 10–11.

30. Jasanoff, *Liberty's Exiles*, 120–23, 142; Galloway, *Observations on the Fifth Article*, 11.

31. Mary Beth Norton, "Eighteenth-Century American Women in Peace and War: The Case of the Loyalists," *William and Mary Quarterly*, 3rd ser., 33, no. 3 (1976): 389–90. Jasanoff, *Liberty's Exiles*, 131, 134–35. Jasanoff reports that of the 3,225 claims, 468 were submitted by women, and 47 were submitted by African Americans. Most Black Loyalists who claimed to have owned property prior to the war were dismissed as liars.

32. Jasanoff, *Liberty's Exiles*, 130–31; James Stuart, "Further Intelligence Communicated to the commissioners . . . ," Loyalist Claims Commission Records, Archives of Ontario, Toronto, AO 12/107, 45; Mary Beth Norton, *British-Americans*, 194.

33. L. F. S. Upton, "The Claims: The Mission of John Anstey," in *Red, White, and True Blue: The Loyalists in the Revolution*, ed. Esmond Wright (New York: AMS Press, 1976), 135–47; Norton, *British-Americans*, 198–99; Jasanoff, *Liberty's Exiles*, 134.

34. Jasanoff, *Liberty's Exiles*, 132–33; Norton, *British-Americans*, 201, 209, 212, 216, 219; Joseph Galloway, *The Claim of the American Loyalists Reviewed and Maintained Upon Incontrovertible Principles of Law and Justice* (London, 1788), v, vii.

35. Peter Oliver, July 1784, quoted in Egerton, *Royal Commission*, 31.

36. K. Mason, "American Loyalist Problem," 45.

37. Stone, "Narrative of Joel Stone," 323–32; Moody, *Narrative*; John Connolly, *A Narrative of the Transactions, Imprisonment, and Sufferings of John Connolly, An American Loyalist . . .* (London, 1783). John Peters's narrative, already cited, can be found in

206 NOTES TO PAGES 119–125

the John Peters Papers, NYHS. Egerton, *Royal Commission*, 133–34; Shenstone, *So Obstinately Loyal*, 149–52.

38. "A Loyalist," *Directions to the American Loyalists in order to Enable them to State their Cases . . . to the Honourable Commissioners . . .* (London, 1783), 23; Jasanoff, *Liberty's Exiles*, 132–33.

39. Connolly, *Narrative of the Transactions*, 1–2; Moody, *Narrative*, 1–2, 4; Peters, "Narrative," 1, John Peters Papers, NYHS.

40. Norton, *British-Americans*, 198, 130–54.

41. Moody, *Narrative*, 2; Stone, "Narrative of Joel Stone," 323–24.

42. Connolly, *Narrative of the Transactions*, 2–8; Peters, "Narrative," 2, John Peters Papers, NYHS.

43. Amos Botsford Claim, Loyalist Claims Commission Records, Archives of Ontario, Toronto, AO 12.1, 61–62.

44. Charles Wattles to Edward Thorp, July 24, 1783, Loyalist Claims Commission Records, Archives of Ontario, Toronto, AO 13.42, 300–301.

45. Stone, "Narrative of Joel Stone," 324; Connolly, *Narrative of the Transactions*, 10; Moody, *Narrative*, 3; "The Memorial of Amos Botsford," Loyalist Claims Commission Records, Archives of Ontario, Toronto, AO 12.1, 54.

46. Munson Jarvis, Loyalist Claims Commission Records, Archives of Ontario, Toronto, AO 12.2, 41; Timothy Hierlihy, Loyalist Claims Commission Records, Archives of Ontario, Toronto, AO 12.1, 28; "Memorial of Lieut. Hugh Fraser," in Egerton, *Royal Commission*, 32.

47. "Memorial of Edward Jessup," London, 29 Mar. 1785, Edward Jessup Papers, UNBLC, FC LFR. J4E3P3, reel 1.

48. Isaac Moseley, Loyalist Claims Commission Records, Archives of Ontario, Toronto, AO 12.2, 65–73.

49. See Zimmer, *Jonathan Boucher*, 196; Bailyn, *Ordeal of Thomas Hutchinson*, 274–330.

50. A good example is that of Frederick Haldimand's attestation of Major Edward Jessup, wherein he "certifies" that the Loyalist "acquitted Himself until His Corps was disbanded, in every respect, to my entire Satisfaction. I beg leave therefore to recommend Him as worthy the Protection of Government, not only as a Loyalist who has forfeited considerable Property by His early & steady Attachment to the Royal Cause, but as a Zealous, Active, and deserving Officer." No particulars were needed in this case and many others like it. Attestation of Frederick Haldimand, Mar. 20, 1785, Jessup Papers, UNBLC.

51. Peters, "Narrative," 3, 6, John Peters Papers, NYHS; Connolly, *Narrative of the Transactions*, 15–17.

52. Moody, *Narrative*, 16–17.

53. Joseph Galloway, *Letters to a Nobleman on the Conduct of the War in the Middle Colonies* (London, 1779), v–vi; John E. Ferling, *The Loyalist Mind: Joseph Galloway and the American Revolution* (University Park: Pennsylvania State University Press, 1977), 42–44, 49.

54. Galloway, *Letters to a Nobleman*, 2–6.

55. Galloway, *Letters to a Nobleman*, 33–36. For the most recent analysis of William Howe's conduct in the Philadelphia Campaign, see Andrew Jackson O'Shaughnessy, *The Men Who Lost America: British Leadership, the American Revolution, and the Fate of Empire* (New Haven, CT: Yale University Press, 2013), 83–122, 114.

56. Galloway, *Letters to a Nobleman*, 36–43, 44–93, quotations on 57, 89.

57. O'Shaughnessy, *Men Who Lost America*, 120–21.

58. Sir William Howe, *The Narrative of Lieut. Gen. Sir William Howe, in a Committee of the House of Commons* (London: H. Baldwin, 1781), 42, 46, 59–60.

59. Howe, *Narrative*, 40–41, 43–44, 55, 56.

60. Joseph Galloway, *A Reply to the Observations of Lieut. Gen. Sir William Howe, on a Pamphlet, Entitled Letters to a Nobleman* (London, 1780), 13.

61. Joseph Galloway, *A Short History of the War in America, During the Command of Sir William Howe . . .* (Philadelphia: Enoch Story, 1788), 89–90.

62. O'Shaughnessy, *Men Who Lost America*, 121–22.

63. Ferling, *Loyalist Mind*, 64.

64. Max M. Mintz, *The Generals of Saratoga: John Burgoyne and Horatio Gates* (New Haven, CT: Yale University Press, 1990); O'Shaunessy, *Men Who Lost America*, 123–64.

65. John Peters to unnamed recipient, with title added in a different hand: "Defence of the Provincials and Indians against Burgoyne's Charges. Dated 9 Dec. 1779," John Peters Papers, NYHS. Around two hundred were killed and seven hundred captured. Mintz, *Generals of Saratoga*, 168–74.

66. John Peters to unnamed recipient, Dec. 9, 1779, John Peters Papers, NYHS.

67. Peters, "Narrative," 7, and Major General William Phillips on behalf of John Peters, "Burgoyne's official order or permission," John Peters Papers, NYHS.

68. John Burgoyne, *A State of the Expedition from Canada, as Laid before the House of Commons, by Lieutenant-General Burgoyne, and Verified by Evidence* (London: J. Almon, 1780), 74, 88.

69. Burgoyne, *State of the Expedition*, 102.

70. Burgoyne, *State of the Expedition*, 102. In an important footnote to this passage, Burgoyne adds that some provincials "were sincere in their loyalty" and commends "Mr. Fistar [Francis Pfister], who fell at Bennington, and Capt. Sherwood, who was forward in every service of danger to the end of the campaign." Captain Justus Sherwood served under John Peters. Again, this must have struck Peters as a personal slight.

71. John Peters to Sir Guy Carleton, July 10, 1786, John Peters Papers, NYHS.

72. Jonathan Odell, "Lord Dorchester and General Carleton," excerpt dated Sept. 6, 1804, but it is likely that the passage was composed earlier. See Jonathan Odell Papers, 1784–1803, UNBLC, MIC-Loyalist FC LFR. O3F3P3, page marked "22," reel 1; Paul David Nelson, *General Sir Guy Carleton, Lord Dorchester: Soldier-Statesman of Early British Canada* (London: Associated University Presses, 2000).

73. John Peters to Sir Guy Carleton, July 10, 1786, John Peters Papers, NYHS.

74. John Peters to Sir Guy Carleton, July 10, 1786, John Peters Papers, NYHS.

208   NOTES TO PAGES 133-140

75. John Peters to Sir Guy Carleton, July 10, 1786, John Peters Papers, NYHS.

76. Peters, "Narrative," 9–11 (Aug. 1785), John Peters Papers, NYHS.

77. Claim of Col. John Peters, Loyalist Claims Commission Records, Archives of Ontario, Toronto, AO 12.30, 276–88. Rev. Samuel Peters, John Peters's uncle, submitted an official posthumous claim in 1788 on behalf of the Peters family relocated to Cape Breton.

78. For background on Mariana Starke, see Jeanne Moskal, "Politics and the Occupation of a Nurse in Mariana Starke's *Letters from Italy*," in *Romantic Geographies: Discourses of Travel, 1775–1844*, ed. Amanda Gilroy (Manchester: Manchester University Press, 2000), 150–64.

79. Mariana Starke, *The Poor Soldier; An American Tale: Founded on a Recent Fact* (London: J. Walter, 1789), 2–4.

80. Starke, *Poor Soldier*, 9, 11, 18–19, 24, 33–34.

81. Boucher, *View of the Causes*, xx.

5. Political Rebirth

1. Joel Stone to Leman Stone, Nov. 19, 1782, Stone Papers, Archives of Ontario, MS519, reel 1.

2. Stone, "Narrative of Joel Stone," 333–34; "List of Debts owed to Bacon and Stone of Woodbury in Connecticut Dec. 25, 1776," Joel Stone's Claim, Loyalist Claims, AO 13/42, 530–32.

3. Amos Botsford Claim, Loyalist Claims Commission Records, Archives of Ontario, Toronto, AO 12.1, 60; Sally E. Hadden, "Lawyering for Loyalists in the Post-Revolutionary World," in Brannon and Moore, *Consequences of Loyalism*, 138–39; Mather Byles Jr. to Mather Byles Sr., Oct. 7, 1786, Byles Family Papers, UNBLC.

4. Diary of Dothe Stone Cutler, Oct. 15, 1789, Joel Stone Family Fonds, Archives of Ontario; George Ramsay, *The Dalhousie Journals*, ed. Marjory Whitelaw (Toronto: Oberon Press, 1978), 127–28.

5. William Whitney Cone and George Allen Root, *Record of the Descendants of John Bishop, One of the Founders of Guilford, Connecticut in 1639* (Nyack, NY: John Guy Bishop, 1951), 18; newspaper article from unpublished scrapbook, "Litchfield County Celebration, 1851," 45, acc. no. 1978-23-116, Litchfield Historical Society.

6. For detailed histories on Loyalist settlement and culture in Canada, see Neil MacKinnon, *This Unfriendly Soil: The Loyalist Experience in Nova Scotia, 1783–1791* (Montreal and Kingston: McGill-Queen's University Press, 1988); Ann Gorman Condon, *The Envy of the American States: The Loyalist Dream for New Brunswick* (Fredericton, NB: New Ireland, 1984); Jane Errington, *The Lion, the Eagle, and Upper Canada: A Developing Colonial Ideology* (Montreal and Kingston: McGill-Queen's University Press, 1987); G. M. Craig, *Upper Canada: The Formative Years, 1784–1841* (Toronto: McClelland & Stewart, 1963).

7. Brannon, *From Revolution to Reunion*; Aaron Nathan Coleman, "Justice and Moderation? The Reintegration of the American Loyalists as an Episode of Transitional

NOTES TO PAGES 140–148 209

Justice," and Rebecca Brannon, "America's Revolutionary Experience with Transitional Justice," in Brannon and Moore, *Consequences of Loyalism,* 177–89, 190–207; Ingersoll, *Loyalist Problem,* chap. 9; Oscar Zeichner, "The Rehabilitation of Loyalists in Connecticut," *New England Quarterly* 11, no. 2 (1938): 308–30; David E. Maas, *The Return of the Massachusetts Loyalists* (New York: Garland, 1989); Robert M. Calhoon, "The Reintegration of the Loyalists and Disaffected," in Calhoon, *Loyalist Perception,* 195–215; Roberta Tansman Jacobs, "The Treaty and the Tories: The Ideological Reaction to the Return of the Tories, 1783–1787" (PhD diss., Cornell University, 1974); Valerie H. McKito, *From Loyalists to Loyal Citizens: The DePeyster Family of New York* (Potsdam, NY: SUNY Press, 2016).

8. Brannon, *From Revolution to Reunion,* 78.

9. Wyatt-Brown, *Shaping of Southern Culture,* 34.

10. David E. Maas, "The Massachusetts Loyalists and the Problem of Amnesty, 1775–90," in Calhoon, Barnes, and Raylwk, *Loyalists and Community,* 69; *Essex Gazette,* Nov. 22, 1774; Ingersoll, *Loyalist Problem,* 283.

11. David Gagan, *The Denison Family of Toronto, 1792–1925* (Toronto: University of Toronto Press, 1973), 14.

12. Ernest Cruickshank, *The Story of Butler's Rangers and the Settlement of Niagara* (Welland, ON: Tribune Printing House, 1893), 112; *New York Daily Gazette,* Aug. 13, 1792.

13. *Pennsylvania Packet or General Advertiser,* June 26, 1783.

14. *Boston Evening-Post,* Apr. 26, 1783; "Evidence on the Claim of Peter Guire late of Connecticut," Jan. 18, 1787, Loyalist Claims Commission Records, Archives of Ontario, Toronto, AO 12.1, 204.

15. Zeichner, "Rehabilitation of Loyalists," 321–22.

16. *Connecticut Journal,* Apr. 17, 1783.

17. Stephen Jarvis, "The Narrative of Colonel Stephen Jarvis," in Talman, *Loyalist Narratives,* 217–19.

18. Jarvis, "Narrative," 219.

19. Jarvis, "Narrative," 221; personal memorial contained in Stephen Jarvis to Ward Chipman, Oct. 11, 1784; W. O. Raymond, ed., *Winslow Papers, 1776–1826* (Saint John, NB: Sun Printing, 1901), 240–41. Jarvis later settled in New Brunswick before moving to York, Upper Canada, just prior to the War of 1812.

20. S. Stewart, "Skimmington," 43; Jarvis, "Narrative," 149–50.

21. Coleman, "Justice and Moderation?," 181–82; Brannon, "America's Revolutionary Experience," 197; Maas, *Return of the Massachusetts Loyalists,* 444–48; Henry Laurens to William Manning, Dec. 4, 1782, in David R. Chestnutt and C. James Taylor, eds., *The Papers of Henry Laurens,* vol. 16 (Columbia: University of South Carolina Press, 2003), 67–68.

22. Brannon, *From Revolution to Reunion,* 105, and Brannon, "America's Revolutionary Experience," 202; Cutterham, *Gentlemen Revolutionaries,* 79; Calhoon, *Loyalist Perspective,* 207; Palfreyman, "Loyalists and the Federal Constitution."

23. Alexander Hamilton, "A Letter from Phocion to the Considerate Citizens of New York," in *The Papers of Alexander Hamilton,* vol. 3, ed. Harold C. Syrett (New York:

210   NOTES TO PAGES 148–157

Columbia University Press, 1962), 483–97; Eliga H. Gould, *Among the Powers of the Earth: The American Revolution and the Making of New World Empire* (Cambridge, MA: Harvard University Press, 2012), 127–29; Cutterham, *Gentlemen Revolutionaries,* 79–84; Coleman, "Justice and Moderation?," 184.

24. Brannon, *From Revolution to Reunion,* 91–92.

25. Brannon, "America's Revolutionary Experience," 203.

26. Ingersoll, *Loyalist Problem,* 276; Joseph S. Tiedemann, "Patriots, Loyalists, and Conflict Resolution in New York, 1783–1787," in Calhoon, Barnes, and Rawlyk, *Loyalists and Community,* 78.

27. Van Buskirk, *Generous Enemies,* 185–88; Ranlet, *The New York Loyalists* (Knoxville: University of Tennessee Press, 1986), 170–74; McKito, *From Loyalists to Loyal Citizen,* 57.

28. Brannon, *From Revolution to Reunion,* 120–26, 130; Wyatt-Brown, *Southern Honor,* 12, 364.

29. Wyatt-Brown, *Southern Honor,* 28–29; Brannon, *From Revolution to Reunion,* 76–85, 88; Maas, "Massachusetts Loyalists," 67; Henry Laurens to John Owen, Aug. 9, 1783, in Chestnutt and Taylor, *Papers of Henry Laurens,* vol. 16, 260.

30. Maas, "Massachusetts Loyalists," 72; Ingersoll, *Loyalist Problem,* 286–88; Rachel N. Klein, *Unification of a Slave State: The Rise of the Planter Class in the South Carolina Backcountry, 1760–1808* (Chapel Hill: University of North Carolina Press, 1999), 120–23; Patricia West, *Domesticating History: The Political Origins of America's House Museums* (Washington, DC: Smithsonian Institution Press, 1999), 6.

31. Alan Taylor, "'The Art of Hook and Snivey': Political Culture in Upstate New York during the 1790s," *Journal of American History* 79, no. 4 (1993): 1383; Jacob Griswold to John Porteous, Mar. 31, 1795, John Porteous Papers, UNBLC; Maas, "Massachusetts Loyalists," 73.

32. Pollock, "Honor, Gender, and Reconciliation," 8–9, 14–17; Brannon, *From Revolution to Reunion,* chap. 5.

33. *Royal Gazette,* July 21, 1802; Condon, *Envy of the American States,* 203.

34. *Royal Gazette,* Sept. 8, 1802.

35. K. Mason, "American Loyalist Problem," 65.

36. David Mills, *The Idea of Loyalty in Upper Canada, 1784–1850* (Montreal and Kingston: McGill-Queen's University Press, 1988), 5–7.

37. Edward Winslow to Ward Chipman, Apr. 26, 1784, in Raymond, *Winslow Papers,* 192.

38. MacKinnon, *This Unfriendly Soil,* 87; *Vindication of Governor Parr and His Council* (London, 1784), 8–10.

39. *Vindication of Governor Parr,* 30–33; John Viator (Samuel Peters), *An Answer to Dr. Inglis's Defence of His Character* (London: John Stockdale, 1785), 2.

40. MacKinnon, *This Unfriendly Soil,* 86; Charles Inglis, *Remarks on a Late Pamphlet* (London: John Stockdale, 1784), 10, 14; Edward Winslow to Ward Chipman, Apr. 26, 1784, in Raymond, *Winslow Papers,* 188; Condon, *Envy of the American States,* 98.

41. Condon, *Envy of the American States,* 180–83.

42. MacKinnon, *This Unfriendly Soil*, 119; Condon, *Envy of the American States*, 92; petition of Joseph Barton, Joseph Hatfield, Richard Hill, Richard Williams, and Thomas Marjoribanks, undated, Amos Botsford Papers, UNBLC. See Amos Botsford's entry in the *Dictionary of Canadian Biography*, vol. 5 (Toronto: University of Toronto Press, 1983), 94.

43. Condon, *Envy of the American States*, 180.

44. Mather Byles Jr. to Kitty Byles, Oct. 7, 1786, Byles Family Papers, UNBLC; MacKinnon, *This Unfriendly Soil*, 75; unaddressed letter from Mather Byles Jr., Mar. 1789, Byles Family Papers, UNBLC. For an explanation of party politics in Nova Scotia, see MacKinnon, *This Unfriendly Soil*, 118–36; Judith Fingard, *The Anglican Design in Loyalist Nova Scotia, 1783–1816* (London: Published for the Church Historical Society [by] S.P.C.K., 1972), 91, 176–77.

45. Craig, *Upper Canada*, 11–14, 49.

46. Kenneth Donovan, "'Taking Leave of an Ungrateful Country': The Loyalist Exile of Joel Stone," *Dalhousie Review* 60, no. 4 (1984): 123–45; Joel Stone to Stephen Stone, Jan. 25, 1788, McDonald, Stone, Baker Family Fonds, Library and Archives Canada (hereafter LAC), Ottawa, Ontario; Joel Stone to unnamed recipient, Jan. 19, 1790, Joel Stone Papers, UNBLC.

47. Elizabeth Posthuma Simcoe, *The Diary of Mrs. John Graves Simcoe*, ed. J. Ross Robertson (Toronto: William Briggs, 1911; repr., Toronto: Coles Publishing, 1973), 252.

48. "Deposition of Joel Stone," 1787, McDonald, Stone, Baker Family Fonds, LAC.

49. Sir John Johnson to Joel Stone, Oct. 30, 1790; Joel Stone to Sir John Johnson, Nov. 13, 1790, McDonald, Stone, Baker Family Fonds, LAC; Donovan, "'Taking Leave,'" 140; W. L. Smith, *The Pioneers of Old Ontario* (Toronto: George N. Morang, 1923), 71.

50. Condon, *Envy of the American States*, 137–38; Condon, "The Family in Exile: Loyalist Social Values after the Revolution," in *Intimate Relations: Family and Community in Planter Nova Scotia, 1759–1800*, ed. Margaret Conrad (Fredericton, NB: Acadiensis Press, 1995), 47.

51. Jay Fliegelman, *Prodigals and Pilgrims: The American Revolution against Patriarchal Authority, 1750–1800* (New York: Cambridge University Press, 1982), 3–4; Melvin Yazawa, *From Colonies to Commonwealth: Familial Ideology and the Beginnings of the American Republic* (Baltimore: Johns Hopkins University Press, 1985), 195; Nancy L. Rhoden, "Patriarchal Authority in Revolutionary Virginia: Connecting Familial Relations and Revolutionary Crises," in *English Atlantics Revisited: Essays Honouring Professor Ian K. Steele*, ed. Rhoden (Montreal and Kingston: McGill-Queen's University Press, 2007), 410–49.

52. Kerber, *Women of the Republic*, 123–34; Carole Shammas, *A History of Household Government in America* (Charlottesville: University of Virginia Press, 2002), 79.

53. Mark E. Kann, *A Republic of Men: The American Founders, Gendered Language, and Patriarchal Politics* (New York: New York University Press, 1998), 155, 143. Kann's ideas about bachelors have been challenged by John Gilbert McCurdy, *Citizen Bachelors: Manhood and the Creation of the United States* (Ithaca, NY: Cornell University Press, 2009); Lombard, *Making Manhood*, 146–47.

212   NOTES TO PAGES 161–165

54. Potter-MacKinnon, *While the Women Only Wept,* 142, 144–46, 160; Nancy Christie, "'He Is the Master of His House': Families and Political Authority in Counterrevolutionary Montreal," *William and Mary Quarterly* 70, no. 2 (2013): 341–70; Kathleen Wilson, "Rethinking the Colonial State: Family, Gender, and Governmentality in Eighteenth-Century British Frontiers," *American Historical Review* 116, no. 5 (2011): 1294–322.

55. Bonnie Huskins, "'Shelburnian Manners': Gentility and the Loyalists of Shelburne, Nova Scotia," *Early American Studies* 13, no. 1 (2015): 151–88.

56. Thomas F. McIlwraith, *Looking for Old Ontario: Two Centuries of Landscape Change* (Toronto: University of Toronto Press, 1999), 39, 108–10; Condon, *Envy of the American States,* 175–80; Katherine McKenna, *A Life of Propriety: Anne Murray Powell and Her Family, 1755–1849* (Montreal and Kingston: McGill-Queen's University Press, 1994); D. H. Akenson, *The Irish in Ontario: A Study in Rural History* (Montreal and Kingston: McGill-Queen's University Press, 1984), 72.

57. Catherine M. A. Cottreau-Robins, "Exploring the Landscape of Slavery in Loyalist Era Nova Scotia," in *The Consequences of Loyalism: Essays in Honor of Robert M. Calhoon,* ed. Rebecca Brannon and Joseph S. Moore (Columbia: University of South Carolina Press, 2019), 122–32.

58. See Henry Lewis to William Jarvis, May 3, 1798, William Jarvis Papers, UNBLC; Harvey Amani Whitfield, *North to Bondage: Loyalist Slavery in the Maritimes* (Vancouver: University of British Columbia Press, 2016), 66, 68–71.

59. Whitfield, *North to Bondage,* 71, 119–20.

60. Whitfield, *North to Bondage,* 63–64, 13, 52–53, 80–84, and chap. 5, "Ending Slavery." For the history of Black Loyalists, see John W. Pulis, ed., *Moving On: Black Loyalists in the Afro-American World* (New York: Garland, 1999); Pybus, *Epic Journeys of Freedom;* James W. St. G. Walker, *The Black Loyalists: The Search for a Promised Land in Nova Scotia and Sierra Leone, 1783–1870* (New York: Dalhousie University Press/Holmes and Meier, 1976; repr., Toronto: University of Toronto Press, 1992).

61. Sarah Botsford to Amos Botsford, July 11, 1788, and Amos Botsford to William Botsford, Jan. 2, 1789, Amos Botsford Papers, UNBLC.

62. Mather Byles to Kitty Byles, June 10, 1783; Mather Byles Jr. to Mather Byles Sr., Mar. 15, 1787; Mather Byles Jr. to his sisters, Sept. 4, 1788, Byles Family Papers, UNBLC.

63. Leman Stone to Joel Stone, June 14, 1789, McDonald, Stone, Baker Family Fonds, LAC; Diary of Dothe Stone Cutler, Oct. 15, 1789, Joel Stone Family Fonds, Archives of Ontario.

64. Josiah Pomeroy to Joel Stone, June 8, 1789, McDonald, Stone, Baker Family Fonds, LAC.

65. Notice dated June 15, 1789, Joel Stone Family Fonds, Archives of Ontario.

66. *The Daily Advertiser,* July 4, 1789; Court of Common Pleas, TL 16 S2, Bos 124, Joel Stone v. Leah Stone, Aug. 15, 1791, City of Montreal Archives.

67. Constance Backhouse, *Petticoats and Prejudice: Women and Law in Nineteenth-Century Canada* (Toronto: Osgoode Society, 1991), 167–68, 332.

NOTES TO PAGES 165–168   213

68. Potter-MacKinnon, *While the Women Only Wept*, 134; Condon, "Family in Exile," 43–45, 49; Kathleen M. Brown, *Good Wives, Nasty Wenches, and Anxious Patriarchs: Gender, Race, and Power in Colonial Virginia* (Chapel Hill: University of North Carolina Press, 1996), 249. For a discussion of the impact of the revolutionary ideology on divorce, see Nancy F. Cott, *Public Vows: A History of Marriage and the Nation* (Cambridge, MA: Harvard University Press, 2009), 47–50; and Cott, "Divorce and the Changing Status of Women in Eighteenth-Century Massachusetts," *William and Mary Quarterly* 33, no. 4 (1976): 592–95. Fliegelman, *Prodigals and Pilgrims*, 123–27.

69. G. Patrick O'Brien, "'Gilded Misery': The Robie Women in Loyalist Exile and Repatriation, 1775–1790," *Acadiensis* 49, no. 1 (2020): 39–68.

70. Errington, *The Lion, the Eagle*, 35–54, 39, 46; G. A. Rawlyk, "The Federalist-Loyalist Alliance in New Brunswick, 1784–1815," *Humanities Association Review* 27 (1976): 142–60.

71. *Royal Gazette*, July 21, 1802.

72. Luther Bishop and Dan Throop to Joel Stone, Feb. 9, 1789, Gananoque Museum Collection (copied from McDonald, Stone, Baker Family Fonds, LAC); Luther Bishop to Joel Stone, undated, Sheldon Family Papers, Litchfield Historical Society.

73. Warrant Against Libeous Armstrong, Nov. 27, 1813, McDonald, Stone, Baker Family Fonds, LAC; Memoranda, July 8, 1816, Hawke, "Joel Stone," 76. For a succinct discussion of late Loyalists and the Upper Canadian government, see Alan Taylor, "The Late Loyalists: Northern Reflections of the Early American Republic," *Journal of the Early American Republic* 27, no. 1 (2007): 1–34.

74. Condon, "Family in Exile," 49–50.

75. Mather Byles to Kitty Byles, Oct. 7, 1786, and May 14, 1787, Byles Family Papers, UNBLC.

76. Charles Inglis, address, no date, Charles Inglis Correspondence, UNBLC, reel 1.

77. Craig, *Upper Canada*, 25; Condon, *Envy of the American States*, 174; Anthony Di Mascio, "Educational Discourse and the Making of Educational Legislation in Early Upper Canada," *History of Education Quarterly* 50, no. 1 (2010): 34–54. Katherine McKenna also explores the predicament of finding a genteel education for both boys and girls in Upper Canada in *Life of Propriety*, 155–71.

78. Joel Stone to Rev. Jeremiah Leaming, Apr. 27, 1791, Joel Stone Family Fonds, Archives of Ontario.

79. Edmund S. Morgan, *The Puritan Family: Religion and Domestic Relationships in Seventeenth-Century New England* (New York: Harper Collins, 1966), 77; Fischer, *Albion's Seed*, 101.

80. William Stone to Joel Stone, July 15, 1792, and Dothe Cutler to Joel Stone, Dec. 17, 1794, McDonald, Stone, Baker Family Fonds, LAC.

81. Rene Stone Hopkins to Joel Stone, Dec. 13, 1794, Joel Stone Papers, Queen's University Archives.

82. William Stone to Joel Stone, Feb. 18, 1803, McDonald, Stone, Baker Family Fonds, LAC.

83. H. William Hawke, "Joel Stone of Gananoque: His Life and Letters" (unpublished manuscript, Gananoque Public Library, 1966), 59–60.

214   NOTES TO PAGES 168–177

84. Amos Botsford to William Botsford, Feb. 1, 1788, and Mar. 12, 1788, Amos Botsford Papers, UNBLC.

85. Amos Botsford to William Botsford, May 5, 1790, Amos Botsford Papers, UNBLC; Jeffrey A. Mullins, "Honorable Violence: Youth Culture, Masculinity, and Contested Authority in Liberal Education in the Early Republic," *American Transcendental Quarterly* 17, no. 3 (2003): 161–79; Lori Glover, *Southern Sons: Becoming Men in the New Nation* (Baltimore: Johns Hopkins University Press, 2007), 64–82.

86. Amos Botsford to William Botsford, May 5, 1790, Amos Botsford Papers, UNBLC.

87. Amos Botsford to William Botsford, May 12, 1792, Amos Botsford Papers, UNBLC.

88. "William Botsford," *Dictionary of Canadian Biography,* vol. 9 (Toronto: University of Toronto Press, 1976), 62–63.

89. Condon, *Envy of the American States,* 206.

Conclusion

1. *Colonial Advocate,* May 4, 1826. For a succinct biography, see David Flint, *William Lyon Mackenzie: Rebel against Authority* (Toronto: Oxford University Press, 1971).

2. Jeffrey L. McNairn, *The Capacity to Judge: Public Opinion and Deliberative Democracy in Upper Canada, 1791–1854* (Toronto: University of Toronto Press, 2000), 18, 35; David W. L. Earl, *The Family Compact: Aristocracy or Oligarchy?* (Toronto: Copp Clark Publishing, 1967), 12–15.

3. For an articulation of these principles, see Samuel Peters Jarvis, *Statement of Facts, Relating to the Trespass on the Printing Press in the Possession of Mr. William Lyon Mackenzie, in June 1826* (Ancaster, Upper Canada: George Gurnett, 1828), 7.

4. Jarvis, *Statement of Facts,* 13; *Colonial Advocate,* May 18 and June 1, 1826; Sheldon S. Cohen, *Connecticut's Loyalist Gadfly: The Reverend Samuel Andrew Peters* (Hartford, CT: American Revolution Bicentennial Commission of Connecticut, 1971).

5. William Lyon Mackenzie, *The History of the Destruction of the Colonial Advocate Press* (York: W. L. Mackenzie, 1827); Carol Wilton, "'Lawless Law': Conservative Political Violence in Upper Canada, 1818–41," *Law and History Review* 13, no. 1 (1995): 111–36.

6. Jarvis, *Statement of Facts,* 12–14, 21–24, 29; Peristiany and Pitt-Rivers, *Honor and Grace,* 5.

7. S. F. Wise, *God's Peculiar Peoples: Essays on Political Culture in Nineteenth-Century Canada* (Ottawa: Carleton University Press, 1993), 60.

8. Wilton, "'Lawless Law,'" 117–20.

9. Calhoon, *Loyalist Perception,* 3; Calhoon, Barnes, and Rawlyk, *Loyalists and Community,* 1; Bailyn, *Ordeal of Thomas Hutchinson,* x.

10. B. Jones, *Resisting Independence,* 11; Calhoon, *Loyalist Perception,* 3; Kacy Dowd Tillman, "Constructing Female Loyalism(s) in the Delaware Valley: Quaker Women Writers of the American Revolution," in Brannon and Moore, *Consequences of Loyalism,* 50.

11. Potter, *Liberty We Seek;* B. Jones, *Resisting Independence;* Calhoon, *Loyalist Perception,* 11.

12. Sabine, *American Loyalists*, 66, 75–76.

13. Burke, *What Is Cultural History?*, 2, 99.

14. Nancy L. Rhoden, "Patriots, Villains, and the Quest for Liberty: How American Film Has Depicted the American Revolution," *Canadian Review of American Studies* 37, no. 2 (2007): 214–20; Frederic, *In the Valley*, 328; Walter D. Edmonds, *Drums along the Mohawk* (1936; Syracuse, NY: Syracuse University Press, 1997), 247, 424–28; Stephen Vincent Benét, *The Devil and Daniel Webster* (New York: Farrar & Rinehart, 1937).

15. William Canniff, *History of the Settlement of Upper Canada, with Special Reference to the Bay of Quinte* (Toronto: Dudley and Burns, 1869), 56–57, 76–78.

16. Egerton Ryerson, *The Loyalists of America and Their Times, from 1620–1816* (Montreal: Dawson Bros., 1880), 1:507.

17. James Henry Coyne, "Memorial to the U.E. Loyalists," in Upton, *United Empire Loyalists*, 138.

18. Canniff, *History of the Settlement*, 582.

19. Welsh, *What Is Honor?*, x.

BIBLIOGRAPHY

Manuscript Sources

Archives of Ontario, Toronto

Loyalist Claims Commission Records, AO 12 and AO 13 (microfilm)
Joel Stone Family Fonds

City of Montreal Archives

Court of Common Pleas

Connecticut Historical Society, Hartford, CT (CHS)

American Revolution Collection
Obadiah Gore Folder
Ezekiel Williams Papers
Williams Family Papers

D. B. Weldon Library, University of Western Ontario

Draper Manuscripts (microfilm)
Public Records of Great Britain, North America (microfilm)

Gananoque Museum Collections, Gananoque, Ontario

Joel Stone Papers

Library and Archives Canada, Ottawa, Ontario (LAC)

McDonald, Stone, Baker Family Fonds

{217}

218   BIBLIOGRAPHY

Library of Congress, Washington, DC (LOC)

"The Bostonian's paying the excise-man, or tarring & feathering" (London: Sayer and Bennett, 1774), Prints and Photographs Division, cph 3a11950
George Washington Papers, Digital Collections, https://www.loc.gov/collections/george-washington-papers/about-this-collection/

Litchfield Historical Society, Litchfield, CT

Litchfield County American Revolutionary War-Era Court Records, 1774–1781
Sheldon Family Papers
Woodruff Collection

National Archives, Kew, UK

American Loyalist Claims, AO 12 and AO 13

New-York Historical Society, New York, NY (NYHS)

Bayard, William Sr., Misc. Mss.
Diary of Thomas Gilpin
John Peters Papers

New York Public Library, New York, NY (NYPL)

Bancker Family Papers
Bayard, Campbell, Pearsall Collection
Schieffelin Family Papers

Queen's University Archives, Kingston, Ontario

Joel Stone Papers

South Carolina Department of Archives and History, Columbia, SC

South Carolina Court of General Sessions Journal, 1769–1776

University of New Brunswick Loyalist Collection, Fredericton, New Brunswick (Microfilm Collection) (UNBLC)

Amos Botsford Papers
Byles Family Papers
Claus Family Papers

"The Diary of Henry Nase"
"Diary of Major Christopher French"
Charles Inglis Correspondence
William Jarvis Papers
Edward Jessup Papers
Journal of Cadwallader Colden II
New Brunswick Museum Archives Collection
Jonathan Odell Papers, 1784–1803
John Porteous Papers
Joel Stone Papers (Toronto Public Library Collection)
Gideon White Papers
Israel Williams Papers
Edward Winslow Papers

Newspapers

The American Journal and General Advertiser
Boston Chronicle
Boston Evening-Post
The Boston Gazette and Country Journal
Boston News-Letter
Boston Post-Boy
Boston Weekly News-Letter
The Colonial Advocate (York, Upper Canada)
The Connecticut Courant
The Connecticut Gazette
Connecticut Journal
The Constitutional Gazette
The Daily Advertiser (New York City)
Essex Gazette
Essex Journal
The Independent Chronicle and the Universal Advertiser
The Independent Gazetteer
The Independent Ledger
Massachusetts Gazette
The Massachusetts Spy
Middlesex Gazetteer
The New Hampshire Gazette
The New-Hampshire Mercury
New Jersey Gazette
The New York Gazette
The New York Gazette and Weekly Mercury
New-York Journal
The New York Mercury

The Norwich Packet
The Pennsylvania Chronicle
Pennsylvania Evening Herald
The Pennsylvania Evening Post
The Pennsylvania Ledger
Pennsylvania Mercury
The Pennsylvania Packet
The Providence Gazette
The Royal Gazette (New York)
The Royal Gazette (New Brunswick)
The Royal Pennsylvania Gazette
Salem Mercury
The South Carolina Gazette
The South Carolina Weekly Gazette
Spooner's Vermont Journal

Printed Primary Sources

Addison, Joseph. *The Works of the Late Right Honourable Joseph Addison*. Vol. 1. London: Tonson, 1730.

"An Address to the Inhabitants of Pennsylvania." Philadelphia: Bell, 1777.

Allaire, Anthony. *The Diary of Anthony Allaire*. New York: Arno Press, 1968.

Allen, Ethan. *A Narrative of Colonel Ethan Allen's Captivity*. Philadelphia: Bell, 1779.

Allen, James. "Diary of James Allen, Esq. of Philadelphia, Counsellor-at-Law, 1770–1778." *Pennsylvania Magazine of History and Biography* 9, no. 2 (1885): 176–96.

Association of Loyal Refugees. *Declaration and Address of His Majesty's Loyal Associated Refugees*. New York: Rivington, 1779.

———. "To Further in Some Degree. . . ." Newport, RI, March 30, 1779.

Baxter, Simeon. *Tyrannicide Proved Lawful. . . .* London: S. Bladon, 1782.

Boucher, Jonathan. *Reminiscences of an American Loyalist*. Port Washington, NY: Kennikat Press, 1967.

———. *A View of the Causes and Consequences of the American Revolution in Thirteen Discourses*. 1797. New York: Russell & Russell, 1967.

Burgoyne, John. *A State of the Expedition from Canada, as Laid before the House of Commons, by Lieutenant-General Burgoyne, and Verified by Evidence*. London: J. Almon, 1780.

Byron, Lord. *The Siege of Corinth: A Poem*. London: T. Davidson, 1816.

Chastellux, Marquis de. *Travels in North America in the Years 1780, 1781, and 1782*. Vol. 2. London: G. G. J. and J. Robinson, 1787.

Chestnutt, David R., and C. James Taylor, eds. *The Papers of Henry Laurens*. Vol. 16. Columbia: University of South Carolina Press, 2003.

Clark, George Rogers. *Col. George Rogers Clark's Sketch of His Campaign in the Illinois*. Cincinnati: Robert Clarke, 1907.

Clausewitz, Carl von. *On War*. 1832. London: Oxford University Press, 2007.

Cohen, Sheldon S., ed. "The Connecticut Captivity of Major Christopher French." *Connecticut Historical Society Bulletin* 55, nos. 3–4 (1990): 125–232.

Connolly, John. *The Last of the Mohicans: A Narrative of 1757.* London: John Miller, 1826.

———. *A Narrative of the Transactions, Imprisonment, and Sufferings of John Connolly, An American Loyalist.* London, 1783.

Copy of letters sent to Great-Britain, by His Excellency Thomas Hutchinson, the Hon. Andrew Oliver, and several other persons. . . . Boston, MA: Edes and Gill, 1773.

Crary, Catherine S. *The Price of Loyalty: Tory Writings from the Revolutionary Era.* New York: McGraw-Hill, 1973.

Crouse, Maurice A., ed. "The Letterbook of Peter Manigault, 1763–1773." *South Carolina Historical Magazine* 70, no. 3 (1969): 177–95.

Davies, K. G., ed. *Documents of the American Revolution, 1770–1783.* Vol. 15. Dublin: Irish University Press, 1976.

Defoe, Daniel. *The Compleat English Gentleman.* Edited by Karl Daniel Bülbring. London: Ballantyne, Hanson, 1890.

"Diary of James Allen, Esq. of Philadelphia, Counsellor-at-Law, 1770–1778 (Continued)." *Pennsylvania Magazine of History and Biography* 9, no. 3 (1885): 278–96.

"Diary of James Allen, Esq. of Philadelphia, Counsellor-at-Law, 1770–1778 (Concluded)." *Pennsylvania Magazine of History and Biography* 9, no. 4 (1886): 424–41.

Dyche, Thomas, and William Pardon. *A New and General Dictionary.* London, 1771.

Edmonds, Walter D. *Drums along the Mohawk.* Syracuse, NY: Syracuse University Press, 1997.

Egerton, Hugh Edward, ed. *The Royal Commission on the Losses and Services of the American Loyalists, 1783–1785.* Oxford, 1915.

Force, Peter, ed. *American Archives.* 3rd through 5th ser. Washington: M. St. Claire and Peter Force, 1843–53.

Ford, Worthington Chauncey, ed. *Letters of Jonathan Boucher to George Washington.* Brooklyn, NY: Historical Printing Club, 1899.

Frederic, Harold. *In the Valley.* New York: Charles Scribner's Sons, 1890.

Freneau, Philip. *The British Prison-Ship: A Poem.* Philadelphia: Bailey, 1781.

"The Frigate Restoration." New York: Rivington, 1779. Early American Imprints 49318.

Galloway, Grace. *The Diary of Grace Growden Galloway.* New York: Arno Press, 1971.

Galloway, Joseph. *A Candid Examination of the Mutual Claims of Great-Britain, and the Colonies. . . .* New York: Rivington, 1775.

———. *The Claim of the American Loyalists Reviewed and Maintained Upon Incontrovertible Principles of Law and Justice.* London, 1788.

———. *Historical and Political Reflections on the Rise and Progress of the American Rebellion. . . .* London, 1780.

———. *Letters to a Nobleman on the Conduct of the War in the Middle Colonies.* London, 1779.

———. *Observations on the Fifth Article of the Treaty with America and on the Necessity of Appointing a Judicial Enquiry into the Merits and Losses of the American Loyalists.* London, 1783.

———. *A Reply to the Observations of Lieut. Gen. Sir William Howe, on a Pamphlet, Entitled Letters to a Nobleman. . . .* London, 1780.

———. *A Short History of the War in America, During the Command of Sir William Howe. . . .* Philadelphia: Enoch Story, 1788.

BIBLIOGRAPHY

Haffner, Gerald O., ed. "A British Prisoner of War in the American Revolution: The Experiences of Jacob Schieffelin from Vincennes to Williamsburg, 1779–1780." *Virginia Magazine of History and Biography* 86, no. 1 (1978): 17–25.

Hamilton, Alexander. *A Full Vindication of the Measures of Congress from the Calumnies of Their Enemies in Answer to a Letter Under the Signature A. W. Farmer.* New York: James Rivington, 1774.

Hawthorne, Nathaniel. *Twice-Told Tales.* Vol. 2. Boston: Ticknor and Fields, 1864.

Hewatt, Alexander. *An Historical Account of the Rise and Progress of the Colonies of South Carolina and Georgia.* Vol. 2. London, 1779.

Historical Anecdotes, Civil and Military: In a Series of Letters, Written from America in the Years 1777 and 1778. . . . London: J. Bew, 1779.

Hoadly, Charles J., ed. *The Public Records of the State of Connecticut from October, 1776 to February, 1778, Inclusive.* Hartford: Case, Lockwood & Brainard, 1894.

Hopkinson, Francis. *The Miscellaneous Essays and Occasional Writings of Francis Hopkinson, Esq.* Vol. 1. Philadelphia: Dobson, 1791.

Howe, Sir William. *The Narrative of Lieut. Gen. Sir William Howe, in a Committee of the House of Commons.* London: H. Baldwin, 1781.

Inglis, Charles. *The Christian Soldier's Duty.* New York: Hugh Gaine, 1777.

———. *Remarks on a Late Pamphlet.* London: John Stockdale, 1784.

"Instructions given by Peter DeLancey, Esquire, His Majesty's deputy post-master general of the southern district of North-America. . . ." Charleston, SC, 1766.

Jarvis, Samuel Peters. *Statement of Facts, Relating to the Trespass on the Printing Press in the Possession of Mr. William Lyon Mackenzie, in June 1826.* Ancaster, Upper Canada [Ontario]: George Gurnett, 1828.

Johnson, Samuel. *A Dictionary of the English Language.* London: W. Strahan, 1755.

———. *The Rambler.* Vol. 4. London: T. Longman et al., 1793.

Jones, E. Rhys, ed. *Letters of a Loyalist Lady: Being the Letters of Ann Hulton, Sister of Henry Hulton, Commissioner of Customs at Boston, 1767–1776.* Cambridge, MA: Harvard University Press, 1927.

Journals of the Continental Congress, from January 1st, 1780 to January 1st, 1781. Philadelphia: David Claypoole, 1781.

Journals of the Continental Congress, 1774–1789. Vol. 8. Washington, DC: Government Printing Office, 1907.

Journals of the Continental Congress, 1774–1789. Vol. 10. Washington, DC: Government Printing Office, 1908.

Kennedy, John Pendleton. *Horse-Shoe Robinson: A Tale of the Tory Ascendency.* London: Richard Bentley, 1835.

Kirby, Ephraim. *Reports of Cases Adjudged in the Superior Court of Connecticut, 1785–1788.* Litchfield, CT: Collier and Adam, 1789.

Labree, Lawrence. *Rebels and Tories; Or, The Blood of the Mohawks! A Tale of the American Revolution.* New York: Dewitt & Davenport, 1851.

["A Loyalist."] *Directions to the American Loyalists in order to Enable them to State their Cases . . . to the Honourable Commissioners. . . .* London, 1783.

Lucas, Charles. *The Political Works of C. Lucas.* Vol. 3. Dublin: Henry Holmes, 1785.

Mackenzie, William Lyon. *The History of the Destruction of the Colonial Advocate Press*. York: W. L. Mackenzie, 1827.

Mandeville, Bernard. *The Fable of the Bees*. London: J. Tonson, 1732.

McCall, Hugh. *The History of Georgia: Containing Brief Sketches of the Most Remarkable Events*. 1811. Atlanta: A. B. Caldwell, 1909.

[M. E.]. *Essays on the Injustice and Impolicy of Inflicting Capital Punishment*. . . . Philadelphia: Democratic Press, 1809.

Minutes of a Conspiracy against the Liberties of America. 1786. New York: Arno Press, 1969.

Moody, James. *Lieutenant James Moody's Narrative of His Exertions and Sufferings*. London: Richardson and Urquhart, 1783.

Odell, Jonathan. "Song for St. George's Day." New York, 1777.

Oliver, Peter. *Peter Oliver's "Origin and Progress of the American Rebellion."* Edited by Douglass Adair and John Schutz. Stanford, CA: Stanford University Press, 1967.

"Ordinances passed at a general convention." May 6, 1776. Williamsburg: Alexander Purdie, 1776.

Paine, Thomas. *Common Sense*. Philadelphia: Robert Bell, 1776.

———. *The Crisis*. No. 1. Norwich: Trumbull, 1776.

———. *The Crisis*. No. 2. Philadelphia: Styner and Cist, 1777.

Parsons, John C., ed. *Letters and Documents of Ezekiel Williams of Wethersfield, Connecticut*. Hartford, CT: Acorn Club, 1976.

Perkins, John. "Thoughts on Agency; wherein, the article of motive. . . ." New Haven, CT: B. Mecom, 1765.

Peters, Samuel. *An Answer to Dr. Inglis's Defence of His Character*. London: John Stockdale, 1785.

———. *A General History of Connecticut from Its First Settlement*. . . . 2nd ed. London, 1782.

Ramsay, David. *The History of the American Revolution*. Vol. 2. Philadelphia: R. Aitken & Son, 1789.

———. *The History of the Revolution in South-Carolina, from a British Province to an Independent State*. Trenton, NJ: Isaac Collins, 1785.

Ramsay, George. *The Dalhousie Journals*. Edited by Marjory Whitelaw. Toronto: Oberon Press, 1978.

Raymond, W. O., ed. *Winslow Papers, 1776–1826*. Saint John, NB: Sun Printing, 1901.

Rhodehamel, John, ed. *The American Revolution: Writings from the War of Independence*. New York: Penguin Putnam, 2001.

Richardson, John. *Wacousta; or the Prophecy: A Tale of the Canadas*. London: T. Cadell, Strand and W. Blackwood, 1832.

Sargent, Winthrop, ed. *The Loyal Verses of Joseph Stansbury and Doctor Jonathan Odell*. Albany: J. Munsell, 1860.

Seabury, Samuel. *A Discourse on Brotherly Love*. New York: Hugh Gaine, 1777.

Serle, Ambrose. *The American Journal of Ambrose Serle*. New York: Arno Press, 1969.

Simcoe, Elizabeth Posthuma. *The Diary of Mrs. John Graves Simcoe*. Edited by J. Ross Robertson. Toronto: William Briggs, 1911. Reprint, Toronto: Coles Publishing, 1973.

Simcoe, John Graves. *A Journal of the Operations of the Queen's Rangers*. Exeter, 1789.

Smith, Adam. *The Theory of Moral Sentiments*. London: A. Millar, 1761.

224 BIBLIOGRAPHY

Smyth, John Ferdinand Dalziel. *Narrative or Journal of Capt. John Ferdinand Dalziel Smith.* New York: Hugh Gaine, 1778.

Sparks, Jared, ed. *The Works of Benjamin Franklin.* Vol. 9. Boston: Hilliard, Gray, 1840.

Starke, Mariana. *The Poor Soldier; An American Tale: Founded on a Recent Fact.* London: J. Walter, 1789.

Syrett, Harold C., ed. *The Papers of Alexander Hamilton.* Vol. 3. New York: Columbia University Press, 1962.

Talman, J. J., ed. *Loyalist Narratives from Upper Canada.* Toronto: Champlain Society, 1946.

Tiffany, Nina Moore, ed. *Letters of James Murray, Loyalist.* Boston, 1901.

Tocqueville, Alexis de. *Democracy in America.* Translated by Henry Reeve. 1835. New York: Bantam, 2000.

"To all Adherents to the British Government. . . ." New York: Morton & Horner, August 15, 1783.

Toner, J. M., ed. *Washington's Rules of Civility and Decent Behaviour in Company and Conversation.* Washington, DC: W. H. Morrison, 1888.

"To the People of America, Stop Him! Stop Him!" New London, CT, May 4, 1775. [Broadside.]

Vindication of Governor Parr and His Council. London, 1784.

"The votes and proceedings of the Assembly of the state of New-York, at their second session, begun and holden in the Assembly chamber, at Poughkeepsie, in Duchess County, on Thursday, the first day of October, 1778." Poughkeepsie, NY: John Holt, 1778.

"Votes and Proceedings of the Senate of the State of New-York, at their first session, held at Kingston, in Ulster County, commencing September 9th, 1777." Kingston, NY: John Holt, 1779.

Young, Edward. *The Revenge: A Tragedy.* London: R. Butters, ca. 1780.

Secondary Sources

Abler, Thomas S. *Cornplanter: Chief Warrior of the Allegany Senecas.* Syracuse, NY: Syracuse University Press, 2007.

Adair, Douglass. *Fame and the Founding Fathers.* New York: Norton, 1974.

Akenson, D. H. *The Irish in Ontario: A Study in Rural History.* Montreal and Kingston: McGill-Queen's University Press, 1984.

Andrew, Donna. "The Code of Honour and Its Critics." *Social History* 5, no. 3 (1980): 409–34.

Backhouse, Constance. *Petticoats and Prejudice: Women and Law in Nineteenth-Century Canada.* Toronto: Osgoode Society, 1991.

Bailyn, Bernard. *Ideological Origins of the American Revolution.* Cambridge, MA: Belknap Press of Harvard University Press, 1992.

———. *The Ordeal of Thomas Hutchinson.* Cambridge, MA: Belknap Press of Harvard University Press, 1974.

Bannister, Jerry, and Liam Riordan, eds. *The Loyal Atlantic: Remaking the British Atlantic in the Revolutionary Era.* Toronto: University of Toronto Press, 2012.

Barry, Richard. *Mr. Rutledge of South Carolina.* New York: Duell, Sloan and Pearce, 1942.

Becker, Laura L. "Prisoners of War in the American Revolution: A Community Perspective." *Military Affairs* 46, no. 4 (1982): 169–73.

Benton, William A. *Whig-Loyalism: An Aspect of Political Ideology in the American Revolution.* Rutherford, NJ: Fairleigh Dickinson University Press, 1969.

Berkin, Carol. *Jonathan Sewall: Odyssey of an American Loyalist.* New York: Columbia University Press, 1974.

———. *Revolutionary Mothers: Women in the Struggle for America's Independence.* New York: Knopf Doubleday, 2007.

Bloch, Ruth H. "The Gendered Meanings of Virtue in Revolutionary America." *Signs* 13, no. 1 (1987): 37–58.

Block, Sharon. *Rape and Sexual Power in Early America.* Chapel Hill: University of North Carolina Press, 2006.

———. "Rape without Women: Print Culture and the Politicization of Rape, 1765–1815." *Journal of American History* 89, no. 3 (2002): 849–68.

Bowman, Larry G. *Captive Americans: Prisoners during the American Revolution.* Athens: Ohio University Press, 1976.

Brannon, Rebecca. *From Revolution to Reunion: The Reintegration of the South Carolina Loyalists.* Columbia: University of South Carolina Press, 2016.

Brannon, Rebecca, and Joseph S. Moore, eds. *The Consequences of Loyalism: Essays in Honor of Robert M. Calhoon.* Columbia: University of South Carolina Press, 2019.

Breen, T. H. *The Marketplace of Revolution: How Consumer Politics Shaped American Independence.* New York: Oxford University Press, 2004.

———. *Tobacco Culture: The Mentality of the Great Tidewater Planters on the Eve of Revolution.* Princeton, NJ: Princeton University Press, 1985.

Brown, Alan S. "James Simpson's Reports of the Carolina Loyalists, 1779–1780." *Journal of Southern History* 21, no. 4 (1955): 513–19.

Brown, Kathleen M. *Foul Bodies: Cleanliness in Early America.* New Haven, CT: Yale University Press, 2009.

———. *Good Wives, Nasty Wenches, and Anxious Patriarchs: Gender, Race, and Power in Colonial Virginia.* Chapel Hill: University of North Carolina Press, 1996.

Brown, Wallace. *The Good Americans: The Loyalists in the American Revolution.* New York: William Morrow, 1969.

———. *The King's Friends: The Composition and Motives of the American Loyalist Claimants.* Providence, RI: Brown University Press, 1965.

Buel, Joy Day, and Richard Buel. *The Way of Duty.* New York: Norton, 1984.

Buel, Richard. *Dear Liberty: Connecticut's Mobilization for the Revolutionary War.* Middletown, CT: Wesleyan University Press, 1980.

Burke, Peter. *What Is Cultural History?* Cambridge: Polity Press, 2004.

Burrows, Edwin. *Forgotten Patriots: The Untold Story of American Prisoners during the Revolutionary War.* New York: Basic Books, 2008.

Bushman, Richard L. *The Refinement of America: Persons, Houses, Cities.* New York: Knopf, 1992.

Calhoon, Robert M. *The Loyalist Perception and Other Essays.* Columbia: University of South Carolina Press, 1989.

———. *The Loyalists in Revolutionary America, 1760–1781.* New York: Harcourt Brace Jovanovich, 1973.

Calhoon, Robert M., Timothy M. Barnes, and George A. Rawlyk, eds. *Loyalists and Community in North America.* Westport, CT: Greenwood Press, 1994.

BIBLIOGRAPHY

Calloway, Colin G. *The American Revolution in Indian Country: Crisis and Diversity in Native American Communities*. New York: Cambridge University Press, 1995.

———. "Simon Girty: Interpreter and Intermediary." In *Being and Becoming Indian: Biographical Studies of North American Frontiers*, edited by James A. Clifton, 38–58. Chicago: Dorsey Press, 1989.

Canniff, William. *History of the Settlement of Upper Canada, with Special Reference to the Bay of Quinte*. Toronto: Dudley and Burns, 1869.

Carter, Philip. *Men and the Emergence of Polite Society, 1660–1800*. London: Pearson Education, 2001.

Cashin, Edward J. *The King's Ranger: Thomas Brown and the American Revolution on the Southern Frontier*. Athens: University of Georgia Press, 1989.

Chandler, George, ed. *The Descendants of William and Annis Chandler, Who Settled in Roxbury, Mass. 1637*. Worcester, MA: Press of Charles Hamilton, 1883.

Chapin, Lisbeth. "Shelley's Great Chain of Being: From 'Blind Worms' to 'New-Fledged Eagles.'" In *Humans and Other Animals in Eighteenth-Century British Culture: Representation, Hybridity, Ethics*, edited by Frank Palmeri, 153–68. Aldershot, UK: Ashgate, 2006.

Cheng, Eileen Ka-May. "American Historical Writers and the Loyalists, 1788–1856: Dissent, Consensus, and American Nationality." *Journal of the Early Republic* 23, no. 4 (2003): 491–519.

Chopra, Ruma. "Enduring Patterns of Loyalist Study: Definitions and Contours." *History Compass* 11, no. 11 (2013): 983–93.

———. *Unnatural Rebellion: Loyalists in New York City during the Revolution*. Charlottesville: University of Virginia Press, 2011.

Christie, Nancy. "'He Is the Master of His House': Families and Political Authority in Counterrevolutionary Montreal." *William and Mary Quarterly* 70, no. 2 (2013): 341–70.

Clark, Esther Wright. *The Loyalists of New Brunswick*. Fredericton, NB, 1955.

Cohen, Michèle. *Fashioning Masculinity: National Identity and Language in the Eighteenth Century*. New York: Routledge, 1996.

Cohen, Sheldon S. *Connecticut's Loyalist Gadfly: The Reverend Samuel Andrew Peters*. Hartford, CT: American Revolution Bicentennial Commission of Connecticut, 1971.

Condon, Ann Gorman. *The Envy of the American States: The Loyalist Dream for New Brunswick*. Fredericton, NB: New Ireland, 1984.

———. "The Family in Exile: Loyalist Social Values after the Revolution." In *Intimate Relations: Family and Community in Planter Nova Scotia, 1759–1800*, edited by Margaret Conrad, 42–53. Fredericton, NB: Acadiensis Press, 1995.

Cone, William Whitney, and George Alan Root. *Record of the Descendants of John Bishop, One of the Founders of Guilford, Connecticut in 1639*. Nyack, NY: John Guy Bishop, 1951.

Connell, R. W. *Masculinities*. Berkeley: University of California Press, 1995.

Connell, R. W., and James W. Messerchmidt. "Hegemonic Masculinity: Rethinking the Concept." *Gender and Society* 19, no. 6 (2005): 829–59.

Cott, Nancy F. "Divorce and the Changing Status of Women in Eighteenth-Century Massachusetts." *William and Mary Quarterly* 33, no. 4 (1976): 586–614.

———. *Public Vows: A History of Marriage and the Nation*. Cambridge, MA: Harvard University Press, 2009.

Cox, Caroline. *A Proper Sense of Honor: Service and Sacrifice in George Washington's Army.* Chapel Hill: University of North Carolina Press, 2004.

Craig, G. M. *Upper Canada: The Formative Years, 1784–1841.* Toronto: McClelland & Stewart, 1963.

Crary, Catherine S. "Guerrilla Activities of James DeLancey's Cowboys in Westchester County: Conventional Warfare or Self-Interested Freebooting?" In *The Loyalist Americans: A Focus on Greater New York,* edited by Robert A. East and Jacob Judd, 14–24. Tarrytown, NY: Sleepy Hollow Restorations, 1975.

Cruickshank, Ernest. *The Story of Butler's Rangers and the Settlement of Niagara.* Welland, ON: Tribune Printing House, 1893.

Cutterham, Tom. *Gentlemen Revolutionaries: Power and Justice in the New American Republic.* Princeton, NJ: Princeton University Press, 2017.

Dabhoiwala, Faramerz. "The Construction of Honour, Reputation and Status in Late Seventeenth- and Early Eighteenth-Century England." *Transactions of the Royal Historical Society,* 6th ser., 6 (1996): 201–13.

Darnell, Donald G. "'Visions of Hereditary Rank': The Loyalist in the Fiction of Hawthorne, Cooper, and Frederic." *South Atlantic Bulletin* 42, no. 2 (1977): 45–54.

Darnton, Robert. *George Washington's False Teeth: An Unconventional Guide to the Eighteenth Century.* New York: Norton, 2003.

———. *The Great Cat Massacre and Other Episodes in French Cultural History.* New York: Vintage Books, 1984.

Davidson, Philip. *Propaganda and the American Revolution, 1763–1783.* Chapel Hill: University of North Carolina Press, 1941.

Davis, Robert Scott. "The Loyalist Trials at Ninety Six in 1779." *South Carolina Historical Magazine* 80, no. 2 (1979): 172–81.

Di Mascio, Anthony. "Educational Discourse and the Making of Educational Legislation in Early Upper Canada." *History of Education Quarterly* 50, no. 1 (2010): 34–54.

Ditz, Toby L. "The New Men's History and the Peculiar Absence of Gendered Power: Some Remedies from Early American Gender History." *Gender and History* 16, no. 1 (2004): 1–35.

———. "Shipwrecked; or, Masculinity Imperiled: Mercantile Representations of Failure and the Gendered Self in Eighteenth-Century Philadelphia." *Journal of American History* 81, no. 1 (1994): 51–80.

———. "What's Love Got to Do with It? The History of Men, the History of Gender in the 1990s." *Reviews in American History* 28, no. 2 (2000): 167–80.

Donovan, Kenneth. "'Taking Leave of an Ungrateful Country': The Loyalist Exile of Joel Stone." *Dalhousie Review* 60, no. 4 (1984): 123–45.

Earl, David W. L. *The Family Compact: Aristocracy or Oligarchy?* Toronto: Copp Clark Publishing, 1967.

East, Robert A. *Connecticut's Loyalists.* Chester, CT: Pequot Press, 1974.

Edelberg, Cynthia Dubin. *Jonathan Odell: Loyalist Poet of the American Revolution.* Durham, NC: Duke University Press, 1987.

Ellis, Markman. "Suffering Things: Lapdogs, Slaves, and Counter Sensibility." In *The Secret Life of Things: Animals, Objects, and It-Narratives in Eighteenth-Century England,* ed. Mark Blackwell, 92–113. Lewisburg, PA: Bucknell University Press, 2007.

Errington, Jane. *The Lion, the Eagle, and Upper Canada: A Developing Colonial Ideology*. Montreal and Kingston: McGill-Queen's University Press, 1987.

Eustace, Nicole. *Passion Is the Gale: Emotion, Power, and the Coming of the American Revolution*. Chapel Hill: University of North Carolina Press, 2008.

———. "The Sentimental Paradox: Humanity and Violence on the Pennsylvania Frontier." *William and Mary Quarterly*, 3rd ser., 65, no. 1 (2008): 29–64.

Fenn, Elizabeth. *Pox Americana: The Great Smallpox Epidemic of 1775–1782*. New York: Hill and Wang, 2002.

Ferling, John E. *Almost a Miracle: The American Victory in the War of Independence*. New York: Oxford University Press, 2007.

———. *The Loyalist Mind: Joseph Galloway and the American Revolution*. University Park: Pennsylvania State University Press, 1977.

Fingard, Judith. *The Anglican Design in Loyalist Nova Scotia, 1783–1816*. London: Published for the Church Historical Society [by] S.P.C.K., 1972.

Fingerhut, E. R. *Survivor: Cadwallader Colden II in Revolutionary America*. Washington, DC: University Press of America, 1983.

Fischer, David Hackett. *Albion's Seed: Four British Folkways in America*. New York: Oxford University Press, 1989.

Fliegelman, Jay. *Prodigals and Pilgrims: The American Revolution against Patriarchal Authority, 1750–1800*. New York: Cambridge University Press, 1982.

Flint, David. *William Lyon Mackenzie: Rebel against Authority*. Toronto: Oxford University Press, 1971.

Flynn, Charles P. *Insult and Society: Patterns of Comparative Insult*. Port Washington, NY: Kennikat Press, 1977.

Foster, Thomas A., ed. *New Men: Manliness in Early America*. New York: New York University Press, 2011.

———. *Sex and the Eighteenth-Century Man: Massachusetts and the History of Sexuality in America*. Boston: Beacon Press, 2006.

Fox-Genovese, Elizabeth, and Eugene D. Genovese. *The Mind of the Master Class: History and Faith in the Southern Slaveholder's World View*. Cambridge: Cambridge University Press, 2005.

Frazer, Gregg L. *God against the Revolution: The Loyalist Clergy's Case against the American Revolution*. Lawrence: University of Kansas Press, 2018.

Freeman, Joanne B. *Affairs of Honor: National Politics in the New Republic*. New Haven, CT: Yale University Press, 2001.

French, Henry, and Mark Rothery. *Man's Estate: Landed Gentry Masculinities, 1660–1900*. Oxford: Oxford University Press, 2012.

Frey, Sylvia. *Water from the Rock: Black Resistance in a Revolutionary Age*. Princeton, NJ: Princeton University Press, 1991.

Fryer, Mary Beacock, and Christopher Dracott. *John Graves Simcoe, 1752–1806: A Biography*. Toronto: Dundurn Press, 1998.

———. *King's Men: The Soldier Founders of Ontario*. Toronto: Dundurn Press, 1980.

Gagan, David. *The Denison Family of Toronto, 1792–1925*. Toronto: University of Toronto Press, 1973.

Gilbert, Arthur N. "Law and Honour among Eighteenth-Century British Army Officers." *Historical Journal* 19, no. 1 (1976): 75–87.

Gilje, Paul. *The Road to Mobocracy: Popular Disorder in New York City, 1763–1834.* Chapel Hill: University of North Carolina Press, 1987.

Gilpin, Thomas. *Exiles in Virginia.* Philadelphia: C. Sherman, 1848.

Glassie, Henry. *Material Culture.* Bloomington: Indiana University Press, 1999.

Glover, Lorri. *Southern Sons: Becoming Men in the New Nation.* Baltimore: Johns Hopkins University Press, 2007.

Godbeer, Richard. *The Overflowing of Friendship: Love between Men and the Creation of the American Republic.* Baltimore: Johns Hopkins University Press, 2009.

Goring, Paul. *The Rhetoric of Sensibility in the Eighteenth Century.* New York: Cambridge University Press, 2005.

Gould, Eliga H. *Among the Powers of the Earth: The American Revolution and the Making of New World Empire.* Cambridge, MA: Harvard University Press, 2012.

Gould, Philip. "Wit and Politics in Revolutionary British America: The Case of Samuel Seabury and Alexander Hamilton." *Eighteenth-Century Studies* 41, no. 3 (2008): 383–403.

———. *Writing the Rebellion: Loyalists and the Literature of Politics in British America.* New York: Oxford University Press, 2013.

Gowing, Laura. "Gender and the Language of Insult in Early Modern London." *History Workshop,* no. 35 (Spring 1993): 1–21.

Graymont, Barbara. *The Iroquois in the American Revolution.* Syracuse, NY: Syracuse University Press, 1972.

Greene, Evarts B. "The Code of Honor in Colonial and Revolutionary Times with Special References to New England." *Publications of the Colonial Society of Massachusetts* 26 (1927): 367–88.

Greenberg, Kenneth. "The Nose, the Lie, and the Duel in the Antebellum South." *American Historical Review* 95, no. 1 (1990): 57–74.

Harvey, Karen. "The History of Masculinity, circa 1650–1800." *Journal of British Studies* 44, no. 2 (2005): 296–311.

———. *The Little Republic: Masculinity and Domestic Authority in Eighteenth-Century Britain.* Oxford: Oxford University Press, 2012.

Hast, Adele. *Loyalism in Revolutionary Virginia: The Norfolk Area and the Eastern Shore.* Ann Arbor, MI: UMI Research Press, 1982.

Hawke, H. William. "Joel Stone of Gananoque: His Life and Letters." Unpublished manuscript, Gananoque Public Library, 1966.

Hessinger, Rodney. *Seduced, Abandoned, and Reborn: Visions of Youth in Middle-Class America, 1780–1850.* Philadelphia: University of Pennsylvania Press, 2005.

Higginbotham, Don. *War and Society in Revolutionary America: The Wider Dimensions of Conflict.* Columbia: University of South Carolina Press, 1988.

Hinton, Alexander Laban. "A Head for an Eye: Revenge in the Cambodian Genocide." *American Ethnologist* 25, no. 3 (1998): 352–77.

Hitchcock, Tim, and Michèle Cohen, eds. *English Masculinities, 1660–1800.* London: Addison Wesley Longman, 1999.

Holton, Woody. *Forced Founders: Indians, Debtors, Slaves and the Making of the American Revolution in Virginia.* Chapel Hill: University of North Carolina Press, 1999.

———. "Rebel against Rebel: Enslaved Virginians and the Coming of the American Revolution." *Virginia Magazine of History and Biography* 105, no. 2 (1997): 157–92.

230 BIBLIOGRAPHY

Hoock, Holger. *Scars of Independence: America's Violent Birth*. New York: Crown, 2017.

Huskins, Bonnie. "'Shelburnian Manners': Gentility and the Loyalists of Shelburne, Nova Scotia." *Early American Studies* 13, no. 1 (2015): 151–88.

Ingersoll, Thomas N. *The Loyalist Problem in Revolutionary New England*. New York: Cambridge University Press, 2016.

Irvin, Benjamin H. *Clothed in Robes of Sovereignty: The Continental Congress and the People Out of Doors*. New York: Oxford University Press, 2011.

———. "Tar, Feathers, and the Enemies of American Liberties, 1768–1776." *New England Quarterly* 76, no. 2 (2003): 197–238.

Isaac, Rhys. *The Transformation of Virginia, 1740–1790*. Chapel Hill: Published for the Institute of Early American History and Culture, Williamsburg, VA, by the University of North Carolina Press, 1982.

Jacobs, Roberta Tansman. "The Treaty and the Tories: The Ideological Reaction to the Return of the Tories, 1783–1787." PhD diss., Cornell University, 1974.

Jasanoff, Maya. *Liberty's Exiles: American Loyalists in the Revolutionary World*. New York: Knopf, 2011.

———. "The Other Side of Revolution: Loyalists in the British Empire." *William and Mary Quarterly*, 3rd ser., 65, no. 2 (2008): 205–32.

Johnson, Joseph. *Traditions and Reminiscences; Chiefly of the American Revolution in the South*. Charleston, SC: Walker & James, 1851.

Jones, Brad A. *Resisting Independence: Popular Loyalism in the Revolutionary British Atlantic*. Ithaca, NY: Cornell University Press, 2021.

Jones, T. Cole. *Captives of Liberty: Prisoners of War and the Politics of Vengeance in the American Revolution*. Philadelphia: University of Pennsylvania Press, 2020.

Jones, Thomas. *History of New York during the Revolutionary War*. Vol. 1. New York: New York Historical Society, 1879.

Jordan, Winthrop D. "Familial Politics: Thomas Paine and the Killing of the King, 1776." *Journal of American History* 60, no. 2 (1973): 294–308.

Kammen, Michael. "The American Revolution as a Crise de Conscience: The Case of New York." In *Society, Freedom, and Conscience: The Coming of the Revolution in Virginia, Massachusetts, and New York*, edited by Richard M. Jellison, 125–89. New York: Norton, 1976.

Kane, Brendan. *The Politics and Culture of Honour in Britain and Ireland, 1541–1641*. Cambridge: Cambridge University Press, 2010.

Kann, Mark E. *A Republic of Men: The American Founders, Gendered Language, and Patriarchal Politics*. New York: New York University Press, 1998.

Kelly, James. *"That Damn'd Thing Called Honour": Duelling in Ireland, 1570–1860*. Cork, Ireland: Cork University Press, 1995.

Kerber, Linda. "The Republican Mother: Women and Enlightenment—An American Perspective." *American Quarterly* 28, no. 2 (1976): 187–205.

———. *Women of the Republic: Intellect and Ideology in Revolutionary America*. Chapel Hill: University of North Carolina Press, 1980.

Ketchum, Richard M. *Saratoga: Turning Point of America's Revolutionary War*. New York: Henry Holt, 1997.

Kiernan, V. G. *The Duel in European History: Honour and the Reign of Aristocracy*. Oxford: Oxford University Press, 1988.

BIBLIOGRAPHY 231

Kilbourn, Payne. *Sketches and Chronicles of the Town of Litchfield*. Hartford, CT: Press of Case, Lockwood, 1859.

Kimber, Stephen. *Loyalists and Layabouts: The Rapid Rise and Faster Fall of Shelburne, Nova Scotia: 1783–1792*. Toronto: Doubleday Canada, 2008.

Klein, Rachel N. *Unification of a Slave State: The Rise of the Planter Class in the South Carolina Backcountry, 1760–1808*. Chapel Hill: University of North Carolina Press, 1999.

Knott, Sarah. *Sensibility and the American Revolution*. Chapel Hill: University of North Carolina Press for the Omohundro Institute, 2009.

Knouff, Gregory T. "Masculinity, Race, and Citizenship: Soldiers' Memories of the American Revolution." In *Gender, War and Politics: Transatlantic Perspectives, 1775–1830*, edited by Karen Hagemann, Gisela Mettele, and Jane Rendall, 325–42. New York: Palgrave Macmillan, 2010.

Knowles, Norman. *Inventing the Loyalists: The Ontario Loyalist Tradition and the Creation of Usable Pasts*. Toronto: University of Toronto Press, 1997.

Krebs, Daniel. *A Generous and Merciful Enemy: Life for German Prisoners of War during the American War of Independence*. Norman: University of Oklahoma Press, 2013.

Lander, J. R. "Attainder and Forfeiture, 1453–1509." *Historical Journal* 4, no. 2 (1961): 119–51.

Larkin, Edward. "Seeing through Language: Narrative, Portraiture, and Character in Peter Oliver's 'The Origin & Progress of the American Rebellion.'" *Early American Literature* 36, no. 3 (2001): 427–54.

Lee, Wayne E. *Barbarians and Brothers: Anglo-American Warfare, 1500–1865*. New York: Oxford University Press, 2014.

————. "Peace Chiefs and Blood Revenge: Patterns of Restraint in Native American Warfare, 1500–1800." *Journal of Military History* 71, no. 3 (2007): 701–41.

Lefevre, Carl. "Lord Byron's Fiery Convert of Revenge." *Studies in Philology* 49, no. 3 (1952): 468–87.

Leonard, Thomas C. "News for a Revolution: The Exposé in America, 1768–1773." *Journal of American History* 67, no. 1 (1980): 26–40.

Little, Ann M. "'Shoot that Rogue, for He Hath an Englishman's Coat On!': Cultural Cross-Dressing on the New England Frontier, 1620–1760." *New England Quarterly* 74, no. 2 (2001): 238–73.

Lockridge, Kenneth. *On the Sources of Patriarchal Rage: The Commonplace Books of William Byrd and Thomas Jefferson and the Gendering of Power in the Eighteenth Century*. New York: New York University Press, 1992.

Lombard, Anne. *Making Manhood: Growing Up Male in Colonial New England*. Cambridge, MA: Harvard University Press, 2003.

Low, Jennifer. *Manhood and the Duel: Masculinity in Early Modern Drama and Culture*. New York: Palgrave Macmillan, 2003.

Maas, David E. "The Massachusetts Loyalists and the Problem of Amnesty, 1775–90." In *Loyalists and Community in North America*, edited by Robert M. Calhoon, Timothy M. Barnes, and George A. Rawlyk, 65–74. Westport, CT: Greenwood Press, 1994.

————. *The Return of the Massachusetts Loyalists*. New York: Garland, 1989.

Mackie, Erin. *Rakes, Highwaymen, and Pirates: The Making of the Modern Gentleman in the Eighteenth Century*. Baltimore: Johns Hopkins University Press, 2009.

MacKinnon, Neil. "The Enlightenment and Toryism: A Loyalist's Plan for Education in British North America." *Dalhousie Review*, vol. 55 (summer 1975): 307–14.

———. *This Unfriendly Soil: The Loyalist Experience in Nova Scotia, 1783–1791*. Montreal and Kingston: McGill-Queen's University Press, 1988.

MacNutt, W. S. "Our Loyalist Founders." *Humanities Association Review* 27 (Spring 1976): 120–28.

Maier, Pauline. "Popular Uprisings and Civil Authority in Eighteenth-Century America." *William and Mary Quarterly*, 3rd ser., 27, no. 1 (1970): 3–35.

Mancke, Elizabeth. "Early Modern Imperial Governance and the Origins of Canadian Political Culture." *Canadian Journal of Political Science* 32, no. 1 (1999): 3–20.

Mason, Keith. "The American Loyalist Diaspora and the Reconfiguration of the British Atlantic World." In *Empire and Nation: The American Revolution in the Atlantic World*, edited by Eliga H. Gould and Peter S. Onuf, 239–59. Baltimore: Johns Hopkins University Press, 2005.

———. "The American Loyalist Problem of Identity in the Revolutionary Atlantic World." In *The Loyal Atlantic: Remaking the British Atlantic in the Revolutionary Era*, edited by Jerry Bannister and Liam Riordan, 39–74. Toronto: University of Toronto Press, 2012.

Mason, Philip. *The English Gentleman: The Rise and Fall of an Ideal*. London: André Deutsch, 1982.

Massaro, Toni M. "Shame, Culture, and American Criminal Law." *Michigan Law Review* 89, no. 7 (1991): 1912–15.

McCalla, Douglas. *Planting the Province: The Economic History of Upper Canada, 1784–1870*. Toronto: University of Toronto Press, 1993.

McCurdy, John Gilbert. *Citizen Bachelors: Manhood and the Creation of the United States*. Ithaca, NY: Cornell University Press, 2009.

McIlwraith, Thomas F. *Looking for Old Ontario: Two Centuries of Landscape Change*. Toronto: University of Toronto Press, 1999.

McKenna, Katherine. *A Life of Propriety: Anne Murray Powell and Her Family, 1755–1849*. Montreal and Kingston: McGill-Queen's University Press, 1994.

McKito, Valerie H. *From Loyalists to Loyal Citizens: The DePeyster Family of New York*. Potsdam, NY: SUNY Press, 2016.

McNairn, Jeffrey L. *The Capacity to Judge: Public Opinion and Deliberative Democracy in Upper Canada, 1791–1854*. Toronto: University of Toronto Press, 2000.

Meranze, Michael. "A Criminal Is Being Beaten: The Politics of Punishment and the History of the Body." In *Possible Pasts: Becoming Colonial in Early America*, edited by Robert Blair St. George, 302–23. Ithaca, NY: Cornell University Press, 2000.

Metzger, Charles. *The Prisoner in the American Revolution*. Chicago: Loyola University Press, 1971.

Meyer, Duane. *The Highland Scots of North Carolina, 1732–1776*. Chapel Hill: University of North Carolina Press, 1987.

Miller, Ken. *Dangerous Guests: Enemy Captives and Revolutionary Communities during the War for Independence*. Ithaca, NY: Cornell University Press, 2014.

Mills, David. *The Idea of Loyalty in Upper Canada, 1784–1850*. Montreal and Kingston: McGill-Queen's University Press, 1988.

BIBLIOGRAPHY 233

Mintz, Max M. *The Generals of Saratoga: John Burgoyne and Horatio Gates.* New Haven, CT: Yale University Press, 1990.

Morgan, Edmund S. *The Puritan Family: Religion and Domestic Relationships in Seventeenth-Century New England.* New York: Harper Collins, 1966.

——. *The Stamp Act Crisis: Prologue to Revolution.* Chapel Hill: University of North Carolina Press, 1963.

Morgan, Philip D. *Slave Counterpoint: Black Culture in the Eighteenth-Century Chesapeake and Lowcountry.* Chapel Hill: University of North Carolina Press, 1998.

Moskal, Jeanne. "Politics and the Occupation of a Nurse in Mariana Starke's *Letters from Italy.*" In *Romantic Geographies: Discourses of Travel, 1775–1844,* edited by Amanda Gilroy, 150–64. Manchester: Manchester University Press, 2000.

Mullins, Jeffrey A. "Honorable Violence: Youth Culture, Masculinity, and Contested Authority in Liberal Education in the Early Republic." *American Transcendental Quarterly* 17, no. 3 (2003): 161–79.

Neatby, Hilda. *Quebec: The Revolutionary Age, 1760–1791.* Toronto: McLelland & Stewart, 1966.

Nelson, Paul David. *General Sir Guy Carleton, Lord Dorchester: Soldier-Statesman of Early British Canada.* London: Associated University Presses, 2000.

——. *William Tryon and the Course of Empire: A Life in British Imperial Service.* Chapel Hill: University of North Carolina Press, 1990.

Nelson, William H. *The American Tory.* 1961. Boston: Northeastern University Press, 1992.

Newman, Simon P. *Embodied History: The Lives of the Poor in Early Philadelphia.* Philadelphia: University of Pennsylvania Press, 2003.

Nicolson, Colin. "'McIntosh, Otis & Adams Are Our Demagogues': Nathaniel Coffin and the Loyalist Interpretation of the Origins of the American Revolution." *Proceedings of the Massachusetts Historical Society,* 3rd ser., 108 (1996): 72–114.

Noel, Françoise. *Family Life and Sociability in Upper and Lower Canada, 1780–1870: A View from Diaries and Family Correspondence.* Montreal and Kingston: McGill-Queen's University Press, 2003.

Noel, S. J. R. *Patrons, Clients, and Brokers: Ontario Society and Politics, 1791–1896.* Toronto: University of Toronto Press, 1990.

Norton, Mary Beth. *The British-Americans: The Loyalist Exiles in England, 1774–1789.* Boston: Little, Brown, 1972.

——. "Eighteenth-Century American Women in Peace and War: The Case of the Loyalists." *William and Mary Quarterly,* 3rd ser., 33, no. 3 (1976): 386–409.

——. *Founding Mothers and Fathers: Gendered Power and the Forming of American Society.* New York: Vintage Books, 1996.

——. *Liberty's Daughters: The Revolutionary Experience of American Women, 1750–1800.* Toronto: Little, Brown, 1980.

O'Brien, G. Patrick. "'Gilded Misery': The Robie Women in Loyalist Exile and Repatriation, 1775–1790." *Acadiensis* 49, no. 1 (2020): 39–68.

Olson, Gary D. "Dr. David Ramsay and Lt. Colonel Thomas Brown: Patriot Historian and Loyalist Critic." *South Carolina Historical Magazine* 77, no. 4 (1976): 257–67.

——. "Loyalists and the American Revolution: Thomas Brown and the South Carolina Backcountry, 1775–1776." *South Carolina Historical Magazine* 68, no. 4 (1967): 201–19.

234   BIBLIOGRAPHY

Onderdonk, Henry. *Queen's County in Olden Times, Being a Supplement to the Several Histories. . . .* Jamaica, NY: Charles Welling, 1865.

O'Shaughnessy, Andrew Jackson. *The Men Who Lost America: British Leadership, the American Revolution, and the Fate of Empire.* New Haven, CT: Yale University Press, 2013.

Palfreyman, Brett. "The Loyalists and the Federal Constitution: The Origins of the Bill of Attainder Clause." *Journal of the Early Republic* 35, no. 3 (2015): 451–73.

Palmer, Bryan. "Discordant Music: Charivaris and Whitecapping in Nineteenth Century North America." *Labour* 3 (1978): 5–62.

Panek, Jennifer. "'A Wittall Cannot Be a Cuckold': Reading the Contented Cuckold in Early Modern English Drama and Culture." *Journal of Early Modern Cultural Studies* 1, no. 2 (2001): 66–92.

Parkinson, Robert G. *The Common Cause: Creating Race and Nation in the American Revolution.* Chapel Hill: University of North Carolina Press, 2015.

Patterson, Orlando. *Slavery and Social Death: A Comparative Study.* Cambridge, MA: Harvard University Press, 1982.

Peckham, Howard H., ed. *Sources of American Independence: Selected Manuscripts from the Collections of the William L. Clements Library.* Vol. 2. Chicago: University of Chicago Press, 1978.

Peltonen, Markku. *The Duel in Early Modern England: Civility, Politeness, and Honour.* Cambridge: Cambridge University Press, 2003.

Peristiany, J. G., and Julian Pitt-Rivers, eds. *Honor and Grace in Anthropology.* New York: Cambridge University Press, 1992.

Phelps, Richard. *A History of Newgate of Connecticut.* 1860. New York: Arno Press, 1969.

Piecuch, Jim. *The Blood Be upon Your Head: Tarleton and the Myth of Buford's Massacre, the Battle of the Waxhaws, May 29, 1780.* Lugoff, SC: Southern Campaigns of the American Revolution Press, 2010.

———. "Massacre or Myth? Banastre Tarleton at the Waxhaws, May 29, 1780." *Southern Campaigns of the American Revolution* 1, no. 2 (2004): 4–19.

———. *Three Peoples, One King: Loyalists, Indians, and Slaves in the Revolutionary South, 1775–1782.* Columbia: University of South Carolina Press, 2008.

Plank, Geoffrey. *Rebellion and Savagery: The Jacobite Rising of 1745 and the British Empire.* Philadelphia: University of Pennsylvania Press, 2006.

Podruchny, Carolyn. *Making the Voyageur World: Travelers and Traders in the North American Fur Trade.* Lincoln: University of Nebraska Press, 2006.

Pollock, Linda. "Honor, Gender, and Reconciliation in Elite Culture, 1570–1700." *Journal of British Studies* 46, no. 1 (2007): 3–29.

Potter, Janice. *The Liberty We Seek: Loyalist Ideology in Colonial New York and Massachusetts.* Cambridge, MA: Harvard University Press, 1983.

Potter-MacKinnon, Janice. *While the Women Only Wept: Loyalist Refugee Women.* Montreal and Kingston: McGill-Queen's University Press, 1993.

Pougher, Richard D. "'Averse . . . to Remaining Idle Spectators': The Emergence of Loyalist Privateering During the American Revolution, 1775–1778." Vol. 1. PhD diss., University of Maine, 2002.

Power, J. Tracy. "'The Virtue of Humanity Was Totally Forgot': Buford's Massacre, May 29, 1780." *South Carolina Historical Magazine* 93, no. 1 (1992): 5–14.

Pulis, John W., ed. *Moving On: Black Loyalists in the Afro-American World.* New York: Garland, 1999.

Pybus, Cassandra. *Epic Journeys of Freedom: Runaway Slaves of the American Revolution and Their Global Quest for Liberty.* Boston: Beacon Press, 2006.

Ranlet, Philip. "How Many American Loyalists Left the United States?" *The Historian* 76, no. 2 (2014): 291–306.

———. *The New York Loyalists.* Knoxville: University of Tennessee Press, 1986.

———. "Tory David Sproat of Pennsylvania and the Death of American Prisoners of War." *Pennsylvania History* 61, no. 2 (1994): 185–205.

Ravenel, Charlotte St. Julian. *Charleston: The Place and the People.* London: Macmillan, 1906.

Rawlyk, G. A. "The Federalist-Loyalist Alliance in New Brunswick, 1784–1815." *Humanities Association Review* 27 (1976): 142–60.

Rhoden, Nancy L. "Patriarchal Authority in Revolutionary Virginia: Connecting Familial Relations and Revolutionary Crises." In *English Atlantics Revisited: Essays Honouring Professor Ian K. Steele,* edited by Nancy L. Rhoden, 410–49. Montreal and Kingston: McGill-Queen's University Press, 2007.

———. "Patriots, Villains, and the Quest for Liberty: How American Film Has Depicted the American Revolution." *Canadian Review of American Studies* 37, no. 2 (2007): 205–38.

Roberts, Julia. *In Mixed Company: Taverns and Public Life in Upper Canada.* Vancouver: University of British Columbia Press, 2009.

Royster, Charles. *A Revolutionary People at War: The Continental Army and American Character, 1775–1783.* Chapel Hill: University of North Carolina Press, 1979.

Rozbicki, Michal J. *The Complete Colonial Gentleman: Cultural Legitimacy in Plantation America.* Charlottesville: University of Virginia Press, 1998.

Ryerson, Egerton. *The Loyalists of America and Their Times, from 1620–1816.* Montreal: Dawson Bros., 1880.

Sabine, Lorenzo. *The American Loyalists, Or Biographical Sketches of the Loyalists of the American Revolution.* Boston: Thurston, Torry, 1847.

———. *Biographical Sketches of Loyalists of the American Revolution, with an Historical Essay.* Vol. 1. Boston: Little, Brown, 1864.

Sampson, Richard. *Escape in America: The British Convention Prisoners, 1777–1783.* Chippenham, UK: Picton Publishing, 1995.

Sayen, William Guthrie. "George Washington's 'Unmannerly' Behavior: The Clash between Civility and Honor." *Virginia Magazine of History and Biography* 107, no. 1 (1999): 2–36.

Schama, Simon. *Rough Crossings: Britain, the Slaves, and the American Revolution.* Toronto: Viking Canada, 2005.

Schivelbusch, Wolfgang. *The Culture of Defeat: On National Trauma, Mourning, and Recovery.* Translated by Jefferson Chase. New York: Henry Holt, 2001.

Scoggins, Michael C. *The Day It Rained Militia: Huck's Defeat and the Revolution in the South Carolina Backcountry, May–July 1780.* Charleston, SC: History Press, 2005.

Shammas, Carole. *A History of Household Government in America.* Charlottesville: University of Virginia Press, 2002.

Shaw, Peter. *American Patriots and the Rituals of Revolution.* Cambridge, MA: Harvard University Press, 1981.

Sheehan, Bernard W. "'The Famous Hair Buyer General': Henry Hamilton, George Rogers Clark, and the American Indian." *Indiana Magazine of History* 79, no. 1 (1983): 1–28.

Shenstone, Susan Burgess. *So Obstinately Loyal: James Moody, 1744–1809.* Montreal and Kingston: McGill-Queen's University Press, 2000.

Shoemaker, Robert B. "The Decline of Public Insult in London, 1660–1800." *Past and Present,* no. 169 (Nov. 2000): 97–131.

———. "The Taming of the Duel: Masculinity, Honour and Ritual Violence in London, 1660–1800." *Historical Journal* 45, no. 3 (2002): 525–45.

Shy, John. "American Society and Its War for Independence." In *Reconsiderations on the Revolutionary War: Selected Essays,* edited by Don Higginbotham, 72–82. Westport, CT: Greenwood Press, 1978.

———. "The Loyalist Problem in the Lower Hudson Valley: The British Perspective." In *The Loyalist Americans: A Focus on Greater New York,* edited by Robert A. East and Jacob Judd, 3–13. Tarrytown, NY: Sleepy Hollow Restorations, 1975.

———. *A People Numerous and Armed: Reflections on the Military Struggle for American Independence.* New York: Oxford University Press, 1976.

Silver, Peter. *Our Savage Neighbors: How Indian War Transformed Early America.* New York: Norton, 2008.

Skemp, Sheila L. *William Franklin: Son a Patriot, Servant of a King.* New York: Oxford University Press, 1990.

Skulsky, Harold. "Revenge, Honor, and Conscience in 'Hamlet.'" *PMLA* 85, no. 1 (1970): 78–87.

Slaughter, Thomas P. "Crowds in Eighteenth-Century America: Reflections and New Directions." *Pennsylvania Magazine of History and Biography* 115, no. 1 (1991): 3–34.

Smail, John. "Credit, Risk, and Honor in Eighteenth-Century Commerce." *Journal of British Studies* 44 (July 2005): 439–56.

Smith, Craig Bruce. *American Honor: The Creation of the Nation's Ideals during the Revolutionary Era.* Chapel Hill: University of North Carolina Press, 2018.

Smith, Merril, ed. *Sex and Sexuality in Early America.* New York: New York University Press, 1998.

Smith, Paul H. "The American Loyalists: Notes on their Organization and Strength." *The William and Mary Quarterly,* 3rd ser., 25, no. 2 (1968): 259–77.

———. *Loyalists and Redcoats: A Study in British Revolutionary Policy.* Chapel Hill: University of North Carolina Press, 1964.

Smith, W. L. *The Pioneers of Old Ontario.* Toronto: George N. Morang, 1923.

Steffen, Lisa. *Defining a British State: Treason and National Identity, 1608–1820.* New York: Palgrave, 2001.

Steiner, Bruce E. *Samuel Seabury 1729–1796: A Study in the High Church Tradition.* Athens, OH: Ohio University Press, 1972.

Stewart, Frank Henderson. *Honor.* Chicago: University of Chicago Press, 1994.

Stewart, Steven J. "Skimmington in the Middle and Northern Colonies." In *Riot and Revelry in Early America,* edited by William Pencak, Matthew Dennis, and Simon P. Newman, 41–86. University Park: Pennsylvania State University Press, 2002.

St. George, Robert Blair. *Conversing by Signs: Poetics of Implication in Colonial New England Culture.* Chapel Hill: University of North Carolina Press, 1998.

―――. "Reading Spaces in Eighteenth-Century New England." In *Gender, Taste, and Material Culture in Britain and North America, 1700–1830,* edited by John Styles and Amanda Vickery, 81–105. New Haven, CT: Yale Center for British Art/Yale University Press, 2006.

Stockley, Andrew. *Britain and France at the Birth of America: The European Powers and the Peace Negotiations of 1782–1783.* Exeter, UK: University of Exeter Press, 2001.

Styles, John, and Amanda Vickery, eds. *Gender, Taste, and Material Culture in Britain and North America, 1700–1830.* New Haven, CT: Yale Center for British Art/Yale University Press, 2006.

Taylor, Alan. "'The Art of Hook and Snivey': Political Culture in Upstate New York during the 1790s." *Journal of American History* 79, no. 4 (1993): 1371–96.

―――. *The Civil War of 1812: American Citizens, British Subjects, Irish Rebels, and Indian Allies.* New York: Vintage Books, 2010.

―――. *The Divided Ground: Indians, Settlers, and the Northern Borderland of the American Revolution.* New York: Vintage, 2007.

―――. "The Late Loyalists: Northern Reflections of the Early American Republic." *Journal of the Early American Republic* 27, No. 1 (2007): 1–34.

Tebbenhoff, Edward H. "The Associated Loyalists: An Aspect of Militant Loyalism." *New York Historical Quarterly* 63 (April 1979): 115–44.

Thomas, Courtney Erin. *If I Love My Honour I Love Myself: Honour among the Early Modern English Elite.* Toronto: University of Toronto Press, 2017.

Thomas, Keith. *The Ends of Life: Roads to Fulfillment in Early Modern England.* Oxford: Oxford University Press, 2009.

Thompson, E. P. "Rough Music Reconsidered." *Folklore* 103, no. 1 (1992): 3–26.

Tiedemann, Joseph S. *The Other Loyalists: Ordinary People, Royalism, and the Revolution in the Middle Colonies, 1763–1787.* Albany: State University of New York Press, 2009.

Tillman, Kacy Dowd. *Stripped and Script: Loyalist Women Writers of the American Revolution.* Amherst: University of Massachusetts Press, 2019.

Troxler, Carole. "Loyalist Refugees and the British Evacuation of East Florida, 1783–1785." *Florida Historical Quarterly* 60, no. 1 (1981): 1–28.

―――. "Refuge, Resistance, and Reward: The Southern Loyalists' Claim on East Florida." *Journal of Southern History* 55, no. 4 (1989): 563–96.

Upton, L. F. S. "The Claims: The Mission of John Anstey." In *Red, White, and True Blue: The Loyalists in the Revolution,* edited by Esmond Wright, 135–47. New York: AMS Press, 1976.

―――, ed. *The United Empire Loyalists: Men and Myths.* Toronto: Copp Clark Publishing, 1967.

Van Buskirk, Judith L. *Generous Enemies: Patriots and Loyalists in Revolutionary New York.* Philadelphia: University of Pennsylvania Press, 2002.

Van Doren, Carl. *Secret History of the American Revolution: An Account of the Conspiracies of Benedict Arnold and Numerous Others, Drawn from the Secret Service Papers of the British Headquarters in North America.* New York: Viking Press, 1941.

Van Schaak, Henry Cruger. *The Life of Peter Van Schaack, LL.D.: Embracing Selections from His Correspondence and Other Writings during the American Revolution, and His Exile in England.* New York: D. Appleton, 1842.

Van Tyne, Claude Halstead. *The Loyalists in the American Revolution.* 1902. Bowie, MD: Heritage Books, 1989.

238 BIBLIOGRAPHY

Vickery, Amanda. "An Englishman's Home Is His Castle? Thresholds, Boundaries and Privacies in the Eighteenth-Century London House." *Past and Present,* no. 199 (May 2008): 147–73.

Vincent, Thomas Brewer. "Keeping the Faith: The Poetic Development of Jacob Bailey, Loyalist." *Early American Literature* 14, no. 1 (1979): 2–14.

Waldstreicher, David. "Why Thomas Jefferson and African Americans Wore Their Politics on Their Sleeves: Dress and Mobilization between American Revolutions." In *Beyond the Founders: New Approaches to the Political History of the Early American Republic,* edited by Jeffrey Pasley, Andrew W. Robertson, and David Waldstreicher, 79–103. Chapel Hill: University of North Carolina Press, 2004.

Walker, James W. St. G. *The Black Loyalists: The Search for a Promised Land in Nova Scotia and Sierra Leone, 1783–1870.* New York: Dalhousie University Press / Holmes and Meier, 1976. Reprint, Toronto: University of Toronto Press, 1992.

Ward, Harry M. *Between the Lines: Banditti of the American Revolution.* Westport, CT: Praeger, 2002.

Waring, Joseph Ioor. *A History of Medicine in South Carolina, 1670–1825.* Columbia, SC: South Carolina Medical Association, 1964.

Welsh, Alexander. *What Is Honor? A Question of Moral Imperatives.* New Haven, CT: Yale University Press, 2008.

West, Patricia. *Domesticating History: The Political Origins of America's House Museums.* Washington, DC: Smithsonian Institution Press, 1999.

White, Herbert H. "British Prisoners of War in Hartford during the Revolution." *Papers of the New Haven Historical Society* 8 (1914): 255–76.

White, Richard. *The Middle Ground: Indians, Empires, and Republics in the Great Lakes Region, 1650–1815.* New York: Cambridge University Press, 2011.

White, Shane. "'It Was a Proud Day': African Americans, Festivals, and Parades in the North, 1741–1834." *Journal of American History* 81, no. 1 (1994): 13–50.

Whitfield, Harvey Amani. *North to Bondage: Loyalist Slavery in the Maritimes.* Vancouver: University of British Columbia Press, 2016.

Wilson, Kathleen. "Rethinking the Colonial State: Family, Gender, and Governmentality in Eighteenth-Century British Frontiers." *American Historical Review* 116, no. 5 (2011): 1294–322.

Wilson, Lisa. *Ye Heart of a Man: The Domestic Life of Men in Colonial New England.* New Haven, CT: Yale University Press, 1999.

Wilton, Carol. "'Lawless Law': Conservative Political Violence in Upper Canada, 1818–41." *Law and History Review* 13, no. 1 (1995): 111–36.

Winsor, Justin. *History of the Town of Duxbury, Massachusetts, with Genealogical Registers.* Boston: Crosby & Nichols, 1849.

Wise, S. F. *God's Peculiar Peoples: Essays on Political Culture in Nineteenth-Century Canada.* Ottawa: Carleton University Press, 1993.

Wood, Gordon S. *The Radicalism of the American Revolution.* New York: Vintage Books, 1993.

Wright, Esmond, ed. *Red, White, and True Blue: The Loyalists in the Revolution.* New York: AMS Press, 1976.

Wrong, George M. *The Chronicles of Canada.* Vol. 4. Toronto: Fireship Press, 2009.

Wyatt-Brown, Bertram. *The Shaping of Southern Culture: Honor, Grace, and War, 1760s–1890s.* Chapel Hill: University of North Carolina Press, 2001.

———. *Southern Honor: Ethics and Behavior in the Old South.* New York: Oxford University Press, 1983.

Yazawa, Melvin. *From Colonies to Commonwealth: Familial Ideology and the Beginnings of the American Republic.* Baltimore: Johns Hopkins University Press, 1985.

Young, Alfred F. "English Plebeian Culture and Eighteenth-Century Radicalism." In *The Origins of Anglo-American Radicalism,* edited by Margaret Jacob and James Jacob, 185–212. London: Allen & Unwin, 1984.

———. *The Shoemaker and the Tea Party: Memory and the American Revolution.* Boston: Beacon Press, 1999.

Zeichner, Oscar. *Connecticut's Years of Controversy, 1750–1776.* 1949. Hamden, CT: Archon Books, 1970.

———. "The Rehabilitation of Loyalists in Connecticut." *New England Quarterly* 11, no. 2 (1938): 308–30.

Zimmer, Anne Y. *Jonathan Boucher: Loyalist in Exile.* Detroit: Wayne State University Press, 1978.

Zuckerman, Michael. "Tocqueville, Turner, and Turds: Four Stories of Manners in Early America." *Journal of American History* 85, no. 1 (1998): 13–42.

INDEX

Adams, John, 44, 114, 148

Adams, Samuel, 113

African Americans. *See* Black Americans and slavery

Aitchison, William, 37

Allaire, Anthony, 55

Allecock, Joseph, 35

Allen, Ethan, 53, 59

Allen, James, 33, 42

American Antiquarian Society, 151

American Indians. *See* Indigenous peoples

American Journal, 101

American Revolution, Loyalists in. *See* political death of Loyalists in revolutionary America

André, John, 71

anger: appropriate and inappropriate expressions of, 80–82; mentality of Loyalists postwar, 154–55, 157, 176

Anishinaabe, 94

Anstey, John, 117

Antonio's Revenge (Marston), 199n17

apologies and disavowals: political rebirth and reintegration of Loyalists after war, 150, 152; recantations by Loyalists during war, 28

Arnold, Benedict, 71

Articles of Confederation, 147

Asgill, Charles, and Asgill affair, 102–3

Associated Loyalists, 101–2, 103

attainder, 9, 10, 42–43, 147

Bailey, Jacob, 46, 80

Bailyn, Bernard, 176

Ball, Elias, 150

Baltimore *American Journal,* 101

Bancker, Evert, Jr., 100, 122

Bassett, Henry, 27

Baxter, Simeon, 83–84, 104

Baxter, Stephen, 28

Bayard, William, 12, 45–46, 47

Beebe, Abner, 36

Benét, Stephen Vincent, 180

Bennington, Battle of (1777), 55, 129

Billop, Christopher, 71–72

Bird, Ann Pamela Cunningham, 151

Bishop, Silvanus, 139

Black Americans and slavery: claims of Black Loyalists against British government, 205n31; Dunmore's Virginia proclamation freeing enslaved persons fighting for British, 11, 89–90; Election Day/Pinkster festival, election of Philip Skene's enslaved servant as governor at, 67, 197n54;

{241}

242 INDEX

Black Americans and slavery (*continued*)
honor culture in revolutionary America
and, 14; households of resettled Loyalists,
enslaved persons in, 161, 162–63; Loyalists, Black Americans as, 11, 16, 35, 89–90,
154, 163, 177; Loyalists disguising themselves as slaves, 46; popular prejudices,
Patriot exploitation against Loyalists of,
16, 23, 29, 32, 35, 78, 89; in revolutionary
battles, 90; shackling Loyalist prisoners,
16, 23, 35, 44, 71–72, 73; Sierra Leone, free
Black Loyalists settling in, 163; social
death of, compared to political death,
19; treatment of plebian versus patrician
bodies, 34
Blackburn, John, 80
Bliss, Jonathan, 157, 165
Bliss, Mary, 165
Board of Associated Loyalists, 101–2, 103
Boston Evening-Post, 23, 29, 36, 77–78,
143–44
Boston Gazette, 30, 35
Boston Weekly News-Letter, 44
Botsford, Amos, 47, 121, 122, 138, 157, 159, 163,
165, 168–70, 178
Botsford, Sarah Chandler, 163, 165
Botsford, William, 168–70
Boucher, Jonathan, 7–10, 12, 112, 113, 123, 135
Boudinot, Elias, 60, 71–72
Bowman, Joseph, 72
branding, 35–36, 144
Brannon, Rebecca, 140, 149–50
Brant, Joseph (Tyendinaga), 96, 97, 98
Breen, T. H., 31
British/Britain: consumer products, British,
Patriot suspicion of, 31; Dunmore's
Virginia proclamation freeing enslaved
persons fighting for, 11, 89–90; Loyalist
identity, British reception of, 134–35; mis-
management of war, Loyalists blaming

Britain for, 105–6, 108–12, 122, 124–34,
136; prosecution of war by, Loyalist
involvement in, 85–87, 89–94, 105. *See
also* claims of Loyalists against British
government
British Legion, 91, 93, 95
British Prison-Ship, The (Freneau), 53
Brown, Thomas, 12, 28, 29, 88, 105
Brown, Wallace, 90
Browne, William, 19, 142
Buford, Abraham, 93
Burgoyne, John, 14, 55, 85, 86, 108, 124, 125,
128–34, 136, 207n70
Burke, Aedanus, 147
Burke, Edmund, 96, 115
Burr, Priscilla Lothrop, 99
Butler, John, 78, 94–96, 143, 181
Butler, Walter, 96–97, 98, 105, 180
Butler, Zebulon, 95
Byles, Belcher, 167
Byles, Betsey, 167
Byles, Mather, Jr., 45, 111–12, 138, 158, 163–64,
167
Byles, Sarah Lyle, 163–64
Byrne, Barnaby, 46
Byrne, Jane, 46
Byron, George Gordon, Lord, 81

Calhoon, Robert M., 79, 177
Canada: exiled Loyalists resettling in,
137–42, 152–60; Late Loyalists in, 166;
literary portraits of Loyalists in, 181–82;
Mackenzie insult of Loyalist families and
Types Riot (1826), 173–76; slaveholding
in, 162–63; Unity of Empire (U.E.)
designation in, 159, 173; Upper Canada
Rebellion (1837), 175
Canniff, William, 181–82
captivity and parole, 49–75; battlefield
captures, 54–57; escapes, 50, 63, 65, 69, 71,

74, 75; exchanges of prisoners, 56, 65, 75; executions, 51, 55, 58, 62, 71, 72, 75, 102–3; extradition to home state, 51, 194n5; genteel privileges in, 49–52, 54–55, 57–58, 75; gentlemanly performance and appeals to honor culture under, 60–64; ill treatment and disrespect in, 59–60, 65, 66–69, 71, 73; inconsistent treatment of Loyalists in, 51, 194n4; Indigenous peoples, treatment of Loyalist captives collaborating with, 72–74; Loyalist violations of Patriot paroles, as honor issue, 49–51, 58–60, 64–66, 75; Patriot prisoners in British hands, 53–54, 56–57, 70, 71, 73; political death, defined as, 51; prison ships, 53, 71; retaliatory treatment of prisoners, 52, 54, 55, 63, 70–75; scholarship on, 53–54; shackling Loyalist prisoners, 16, 23, 35, 44, 71–72, 73

Carleton, Guy (later Lord Dorchester), 31, 92, 96, 103, 132, 133, 155, 173

Catholics/Catholicism, 16, 29, 32, 89

Cayuga, 94

Chandler, Joshua, 112

Chandler, Thomas Bradbury, 177

charivari, 24, 32–33, 38

Chastellux, Marquis de, 98–99, 103–4

Cherry Valley massacre (1778), 96, 104, 180

Chipman, Ward, 156

Chipman, Ward, Jr., 170

Chopra, Ruma, 20

"Civis," in *Boston Evening-Post,* 77–78

claims of Loyalists against British government, 106–7, 115–24; by Black Americans, 205n31; Compensation Act, 115, 116; Loyalist Claims Commission, 34, 35, 115–18, 135, 136; narratives submitted to claims commission, 107, 118–24; process of pursuing, 106–7, 114–18; witness testimonies supporting, 121, 206n50; by women, 116, 205n31

Clark, George Rogers, 72

Clarke, John, 102

Claus, Daniel, 98

Clausewitz, Carl von, 5

Clinton, George, 147

Clinton, Henry, 55, 62, 64, 80, 87, 99, 102, 103, 203n94

Colden, Cadwallader, Jr., 12, 16, 23, 44–45, 51, 58–64, 66, 70, 74

Cole, Albert, 58

Colonial Advocate, 173

Committees of Inspection, 31, 33

Compensation Act, 115, 116

Condon, Ann Gorman, 160–61, 166

confiscation of property: buying back/replacing property after war, 149, 151; claims against British government for, Loyalists pursuing, 106–7, 114–18; dishonoring acts of, 10, 41–43, 46; prewar debtors, postwar pursuit of, 137–38; recovering property after war, 150, 151; Treaty of Paris on, 110, 114–15, 137–38, 147

"Congratulation, The" (Odell), 85

Congress. *See* Continental Congress

Connecticut: confiscation laws, 43; treason statute, 194n5

Connecticut Courant, 16, 29, 68, 94, 99, 110

Connecticut Gazette, 33, 36, 65, 69, 88, 92

Connecticut Journal, 50, 59–60, 110

Connecticut Supreme Court on political death, 187n50

Connolly, John, 118, 119, 120, 121–22, 123

Constitution, U.S., attainder prohibited by, 10, 147

consumer products: British goods, Patriot suspicion of, 31; Prohibitory Act, 100

Continental Army, 20, 55, 56–57, 80, 95

Continental Congress: captive Loyalists and, 56, 57, 65, 67, 74, 194n5; dishonoring acts and, 41–42, 44; Loyalist identity and, 109,

244 INDEX

Continental Congress (*continued*) 110, 114, 120, 131; political rebirth of Loyalists and, 2, 7, 147, 151; public day of fasting proclaimed by, 7; revenge by Loyalists and, 83, 87, 94, 98, 102–3

Convention Army captives, Saratoga, 54

Cooper, James Fenimore, 81

Coriolanus (Shakespeare), 81

Cornplanter (Kayéthwahkeh), 94

Cornwallis, Lord, 55

corpses, affixing notes to, 102

Cottreau-Robins, Catherine, 162

coverture, 41

cowardice, imputations of, 26, 77, 78, 91, 104, 129

Coyne, James Henry, 181

Crary, Catherine, 93

crowd actions, 23, 24, 27–29, 32–37, 44, 189n17

Cunningham, Patrick, 151

Daily Advertiser, 164

Dejean, Philip, 73

De Lancey, James, 78, 92, 105, 162

De Lancey, Oliver, 91, 92

De Lancey, Peter, 1–4

De Lancey's Cowboys (Loyalist Westchester Refugees), 92–93

Denning, William, 62

DePeyster, Frederick, 149

"Devil and Daniel Webster, The" (Benet), 180

Dibblee, Fyler, 47

Discourse on Brotherly Love, A (Seabury), 82–83

dishonor. *See* honor and dishonor

dishonoring acts, 9–10, 23–48; attainder, 9, 10, 42–43, 147; bodies and appearances, attacks on, 23–24, 33, 34, 35–36; charivari, 24, 32–33, 38; crowd actions, 23, 24, 27–29, 32–37, 44, 189n17; folk custom, insults drawn from, 25, 32–33, 36; gentlemanly status, attacks on, 12–14, 23–24, 48–49; houses ransacked, 37–39, 176; Loyalist identity, construction of, 45–47, 122; Loyalist responses to, 25–29, 33–34, 46–47; marginalized groups, association of Loyalists with, 15–16, 17, 23, 25–26, 32, 35; press reportage on, 29–32; rape and sexual insult, 39–40; "Rogue's March," 8, 178; skimmington, 38; social ostracism and social connections, 43–45; tarring and feathering, 25, 27, 28, 36–37, 38, 45, 176, 178; Upper Canada Loyalists adopting tactics of, 176; violence, dishonor as form of, 17–19. *See also* confiscation of property

Ditz, Toby, 13, 16

divorce, 164–65

Dodge, John, 73

Dorchester, Lord. *See* Carleton, Guy

Drew, Mr., 33

Drums along the Mohawk (Edmonds), 180

Duché, Jacob, 43

duels: customary conduct of, 2; De Lancey/Haley duel (Charleston, SC, 1771), 1–4; equals, only between gentlemen regarded as, 4, 175; rarity of, in colonial America, 2, 4, 26; revenge differentiated from, 82; war as duel on larger scale, 5

Duer, William, 61

Duer family, 170

Dunbar, Jesse, 34

Dunmore, Lord, 11, 89–90, 120

East Florida, ceded to Spain, 111

Edmonds, Walter D., 180

education of Loyalist children, 166–70, 213n77

Election Day/Pinkster festival, 67, 197n54

Elegante (trading ship), 100

Elliot, Andrew, 86, 105

enslaved persons. *See* Black Americans and slavery

Errington, Jane, 166

Essex Gazette, 19

Eustace, Nicole, 47, 81

executions, 51, 55, 58, 62, 71, 72, 75, 102–3

extradition of captives to home state, 51, 194n5

Fair American, The (privateer), 100

family. *See* social and family connections

Family Compact, 173, 175

Faneuil Hall, Boston, 23, 28

Federalists, 151, 166

Ferguson, Patrick, 87

Ferling, John, 54

Florida, ceded to Spain, 111

folk custom, insults drawn from, 25, 32–33, 36

Fowler, Captain, 92

Franklin, Benjamin, 42, 64, 65, 113–14

Franklin, William: captivity of, 51, 52–53, 64–66, 70, 71, 74, 75; Huddy execution and, 103–4; revenge sought by, 77, 78, 87, 101, 103–4, 105

Fraser, Hugh, and family, 122

Frederic, Harold, 104, 180

French, Christopher, 59, 66–70, 71, 197n60

French involvement in American Revolution, 85, 87, 103

Freneau, Philip, 53

Gage, Thomas, 70

Galloway, Joseph, 10, 80, 108–9, 112–15, 117–18, 124–28, 133, 142

Gardiner, Sylvester, 46

Gates, Horatio, 55, 122

gender. *See* women and gender

gentlemanly status: attacks on, 12–14, 23–24, 48–49; captivity and parole, genteel privileges in, 49–52, 54–55, 57–58, 75; captivity and parole, gentlemanly performance and appeals to honor culture under, 60–64; duels only between gentlemen regarded as equals, 4, 175; education of Loyalist children and, 166–70; of literary Loyalists in U.S. and Canada, 180, 181–82; Loyalist exiles' concern with, 161–62; polite culture, rise of, 26, 80–81; spies not accorded, 70–71; Joel Stone's claim to, uncertainty about, 159

George III (king of England), "funeral" for (1776), 9

Georgia Gazette, 28

Germaine, George, Lord, 56

German Flatts raid (1778), 98, 151

Gilpin, Thomas, 59

Girty, Simon, 94, 180

Glassie, Henry, 37

Glover, Amelia, 144–45

Gore, Obadiah, Jr., 95

Grant, Isaac, 57

Gray, Harrison, 138

Gray, William, 170

Great Bridge, Battle of (1775), 35, 90

Guire, Peter, 35–36, 144

Hadden, Sally, 138

Haldimand, Frederick, 96, 128, 132–34, 206n50

Hale, Nathan, 71

Haley, John, 1–4

Hamilton, Alexander, 32, 147–48, 149

Hamilton, Henry, 72–74

Hamlet (Shakespeare), 81

Hancock, John, 57, 113, 138

Harvey, Alexander, 1

Haudenosaunee, 94–96, 129

246   INDEX

Hayward, Thomas, 1

Health, William, 58

hegemonic masculinity, 186n33

Hewatt, Alexander, 112

Hickey Plot to assassinate George Washington, 49, 50

Hierlihy, Timothy, and family, 122

histories of war by Loyalists, 107, 112–15

Holland, Samuel, 159

Holton, Woody, 89

honor and dishonor: body, reading (dis)honor through presentation of, 23–24, 33, 34; in captivity and parole, 50–52; defined, 15; democratization and redefining of, 15–17; fluidity of concepts of, 50–51; honor culture in revolutionary America, 11, 13–17, 21, 25, 178–82; Loyalist Claims Commission on, 115; Loyalist identity, honorable construction of, 16–17, 105, 106, 135–36; paroles, Loyalist violations of, 49–51, 58–60; Patriot portrayals of Loyalists as lacking honor, 88–89; polite culture, rise of, 26, 80–81; political death as loss of honor, 7–11, 177–78; political rebirth and, 139–40, 170–71; primal honor, 26, 77, 80, 82, 104; revenge and, 77, 78, 80, 81, 82, 104–5; Root's and French's dueling articles on true and false honor, 68–69; Types Riot and, 175–76; violence, dishonor as form of, 17–19; war, violations of rules of, 70; war altering perception of, 4–5; Winslow's diatribe on returning Loyalist refugees and, 152–54. *See also* captivity and parole; dishonoring acts; duels; gentlemanly status

Hoock, Holger, 17–18

Hopkins, Rene Stone, 38–39, 137, 168

Hopkinson, Francis, 10

houses ransacked, 37–39, 176

Howe, Richard, 87

Howe, Robert, 70

Howe, William, 29–30, 54, 56, 58, 65, 87, 108, 124–28, 136, 142

Huddy, Joshua, 102, 103, 142

Hulton, Ann, 27, 33

humility, in Loyalist claims narratives, 119

Humphrey, Ashbel, 44

Hutchinson, Thomas, 30, 38, 123

identity of Loyalists. *See* Loyalist identity

imprisonment. *See* captivity and parole

Independent Gazetteer, 203n104

Independent Ledger, 203n94

Indigenous peoples: *The Last of the Mohicans* (Cooper), 81; Loyalist alliances with, 11, 35, 70, 72, 94–98, 129, 143, 181; Patriot alliances with, 97–98; popular prejudices, Patriot exploitation against Loyalists of, 16, 23, 25, 35, 78, 94–98; revenge associated with, 81–82; treatment of Loyalist captives collaborating with, 72–74. *See also specific peoples*

Ingersoll, Thomas N., 17, 148

Inglis, Charles, 76, 83, 86, 104, 156, 158

In the Valley (Frederic), 180

Izard, Ralph, 3, 4

Jacobites/Scottish Highlanders: claims for losses in Jacobite rebellions, 115–16; as Loyalists, 154; Loyalists viewed as, 16, 29, 89; in revolutionary battles, 90

Jarvis, Munson, 122

Jarvis, Samuel Peters, 174–76, 181

Jarvis, Stephen, 144–46

Jarvis, William, 174

Jarvis family, 162

Jasanoff, Maya, 115, 205n31

Jay, John, 61, 148

Jefferson, Thomas, 73, 74, 153, 168

Jeffersonians/Jeffersonian Republicans, 151, 166

Jessup, Edward, and family, 122, 206n50
Johnson, John, 23, 40, 159–60
Johnson, Joseph, 1–2, 3
Johnson, Mary Watts, Lady, 23, 40
Johnson, Samuel, 15, 82
Johnson, William Samuel, 151
Jones, Brad A., 20
Jones, T. Cole, 54, 80
Jones, Thomas, 23, 59

Kann, Mark, 161, 211n53
Kayéthwahkeh (Cornplanter), 94
Kerber, Linda, 41, 161
Kettle Creek, Battle of (1779), 55
King's American Legion, 80
King's American Regiment, 149
King's Mountain, Battle of (1780), 55, 93
Kingston, Lieutenant Colonel, 130
Kyd, Thomas, 199n17

Lamothe, William, 73
Lander, J. R., 42
Last of the Mohicans, The (Cooper), 81
Late Loyalists, 166
Laurens, Henry, 146, 148, 150
Lenape, 94
Leonard, Daniel, 38
Leonard, George, 76, 91, 99, 101
Letters to a Nobleman on the Conduct of the War in the Middle Colonies (Galloway), 125, 126–27
lex talionis, 80
Lippincott, Richard, 102, 103, 142–43
literary depictions of revenge, 81–82, 199n17
literary portraits of Loyalists: in Britain, 134–35; in Canada, 181–82; in United States, 180–81
Livingston, James, 62
Livingston, Robert R., 42, 44–45, 47, 62
Livingston, William, 70, 71

Lockwood, Millington, 47
Longstreet, Captain, 60
Loring, Elizabeth, 29–30
Loring, Joshua, 29–30, 122, 142
Loyal Associated Refugees, 76, 85
Loyal Fencible Americans of Worcester, MA, 29, 89
Loyalist Claims Commission, 34, 35, 115–18, 135, 136
Loyalist identity, 20, 21, 106–36; British mismanagement, blaming loss of war on, 105–6, 108–12, 122, 124–34, 136; claims against British government, pursuing, 106–7, 114–18; defeat and loss, coping with, 106–8; dishonoring acts contributing to, 45–47, 122; exile, postwar Loyalists living in, 142, 154–60; honor, reconstructing, 16–17, 105, 106, 135–36; narratives submitted to claims commission, 107, 118–24; Patriot leadership, denigration of, 113–14, 135–36; political death contributing to, 20, 21; self-depiction and self-image, 106, 107–8, 111–12, 119–24, 136, 152, 181–82; Starke's The Poor Soldier and British reception of, 134–35; Vesuvian mentality of, 154–55, 157, 176; writing and publishing about, 107, 112–15, 118–24
"Loyalist puzzle," 176–77, 180, 182
Loyalist revenge. See revenge, Loyalists seeking
Loyalists, political death of. See political death of Loyalists in revolutionary America
Loyalists, political rebirth of. See political rebirth
Loyalist Westchester Refugees (De Lancey's Cowboys), 92–93
Ludlow, Gabriel, 157
Lymans, Daniel, 121

Mackenzie, William Lyon, 173–76
MacKinnon, Neil, 156
MacLean, Allan, 143
Malcolm, John, 27
Mandeville, Bernard, 82
Manigault, Peter, 3–4
marginalized groups, Loyalists associated with, 15–17. *See also* Black Americans and slavery; Indigenous peoples; Jacobites/Scottish Highlanders; women and gender
Marks, Nehomiah, 121
marriages of exiled Loyalists, 163–65
Marston, Benjamin, 33–34
Marston, John, 199n17
Mason, Keith, 154
Massachusetts: amnesty act for Loyalists, 142; confiscation laws in, 41, 43
Mathews, David, 49–52, 74, 197n60
McCall, Hugh, 88
McCurdy, John Gilbert, 211n53
McKay, Samuel, 59–60
McKenna, Katherine, 213n77
McRae, Jane, 129
merchants, Patriot suspicion of, 31
Middleton, Thomas, 199n17
Mifflin, Thomas, 45
Miller, James, 28
Mills, Ambrose, 55
mob actions, 23, 24, 27–29, 32–37, 44, 189n17
Mohawk, 96, 97
Moody, James, 12, 52, 70–71, 85, 118, 119, 120, 122, 123–24, 162, 178
Moore, Jonathan, 151
Moore's Creek Bridge, Battle of (1776), 90
Morris, Gouverneur, 50, 60
Moseley, Isaac, 123
Mount Vernon Ladies' Association, 151
Murray, James, 23, 28–29

Nase, Henry, 80
Nelson, William H., 79
"Neutral Ground" surrounding New York City, 92, 104
neutrality, claims of, 61, 63
Newgate Prison, Simsbury, CT, 54
New Jersey, attainder in, 43
New Jersey Gazette, 97
New York: Committee for Detecting and Defeating Conspiracies, 45, 49, 60–62; Committee of Correspondence, 58; confiscation laws, 42; neutrality, criminalization of, 63; oath of allegiance to State of, 60, 61, 63–64
New York City: "Neutral Ground" surrounding, 92, 104; political reintegration of Loyalists in, 149
New York Gazette, 91, 92, 93
New-York Journal, 9, 31
Niagara Falls, 143
North, Lord, 112

O'Brien, G. Patrick, 165
Observations on the Fifth Article of the Treaty with America (Galloway), 114–15
Odawa, 72
Odell, Jonathan, 84–85, 132, 157, 162
Oliver, Peter, 37, 38, 98, 112, 113–14, 118
Oliver, Thomas, 43, 44
Oneida, 97–98
Onondaga, 95
Origin and Progress of the American Rebellion (Peter Oliver), 37, 38, 98
Otis, James, 114

pacifists and pacifism, 59, 83, 147
Paine, Thomas, 31, 32, 78, 168
Paine, William, 151
Paris, Treaty of (1783), 105, 109–11, 114–15, 137–38, 144, 147–48, 170

INDEX 249

Parker, James, 87, 98

Parker, William, 37

Parkinson, Robert G., 15–16

Parliament, 27, 78, 84–85, 96, 100, 108, 109, 114–16, 124, 139, 146

parole. *See* captivity and parole

Parsons, James, 1

Patterson, Colonel, 58

Patterson, Orlando, 14, 19

Peltonen, Markku, 26

Penn family, 146

Pennsylvania: confiscation laws, 43; Test Acts, 147

Pennsylvania campaign (1777–78), 128, 142

Pennsylvania Evening Post, 30, 89

Pennsylvania Gazette, 81

Pennsylvania Ledger, 90

Perkins, John, 81

Peters, John, 12, 31, 55, 96, 106, 114, 118–20, 123, 124, 128–34, 178, 207n70

Peters, Samuel, 47, 112–13, 121, 174

Petition of 55, 155–56

Pfister, Francis, 207n70

Phillips, Ralph, 45

Phillips, William, 74

"Phocion," Alexander Hamilton writing as, 147–48

Piecuch, Jim, 93

Pinckney, Charles Cotesworth, 1

Pinkster/Election Day festival, 67, 197n54

Pitt, William, 96, 117

polite culture, rise of, 26, 80–81

political death of Loyalists in revolutionary America, 7–22, 176–83; captivity and, 49–75 (*see also* captivity and parole); defined, 8–9; dishonoring acts demonstrating, 9–10, 23–48 (*see also* dishonoring acts); gentlemanly status, attacks on, 12–14, 23–24, 48–49; honor culture and, 11, 13–17, 21, 25, 178–82 (*see also* honor

and dishonor); levels of violence involved in, 17–19; limits to, 19–21; as loss of honor, 7–11, 177–78; Loyalist identity, constructing, 20, 21, 106–36 (*see also* Loyalist identity); marginalized groups, Loyalists associated with, 15–17 (*see also* Black Americans and slavery; Indigenous peoples; Jacobites/Scottish Highlanders; women and gender); neutralization of Loyalist threat via, 11; Patriot victory, centrality to, 21–22; rebirth following, 137–71 (*see also* political rebirth); revenge for, 46, 76–105 (*see also* revenge, Loyalists seeking); social death of slavery compared, 19; white male propertied persons subject to, 9, 11–12

political rebirth, 137–71; apologies and disavowals of loyalism, issuing, 150, 152; business and trade relationships, 165, 166; community resistance to, 137–39, 142–46; education of Loyalist children in United States, 166–70, 213n77; exile in Canada/Britain, Loyalists choosing, 137–42, 152–60, 170–71; honor and, 139–40, 170–71; households, families, and children, Loyalist governance of, 160–70; marriages of exiled Loyalists, 163–65; notorious Loyalists unable to return, 142–44; Patriot arguments in favor of, 147–48; prewar debtors, pursuit of, 137–38; return/reintegration into American society, 137–42, 146–52, 170; slaves of resettled Loyalists, 161, 162–63; social/family connections and, 137–39, 144–45, 149–50; Treaty of Paris allowing for, 137–38, 144, 147–48; Vesuvian mentality of Loyalists and, 154–55, 157, 176; Winslow's diatribe on returning Loyalist refugees, 152–54

Pollard, Robert, 70

Pollock, Linda, 139, 152

250   INDEX

poor, the, as Loyalists, 11

Poor Soldier, The (Starke), 134–35

Porteous, John, 27, 100, 151–52

Pougher, Richard, 203n95

Poyas, James, 150

press: postwar Loyalist writings, 107, 112–15, 118; reportage on dishonoring acts, 29–32; revenge, Patriot spin on Loyalist acts of, 77–78, 87–90, 92–97, 99, 101–2; revenge justified by Loyalists in, 76, 84–85, 91–94, 96–98. *See also specific papers, pamphlets, and journals*

primal honor, 26, 77, 80, 82, 104

prison. *See* captivity and parole

privateering, 98–104

Prohibitory Act, 100

"Prologue to the Tragedy of the Revenge" (*Royal Pennsylvania Gazette*), 85

Providence Gazette, 101

Quakers, 59, 147

Queen's Loyal Rangers, 55, 85, 128, 129

Queen's Rangers, 91, 144

racialized tropes, 15–17. *See also* Black Americans and slavery; Indigenous peoples

Ramsay, David, 2, 77, 88, 93

rape and sexual insult, 39–40

Rawlyk, G. A., 166

religious dissent, Loyalist identification of war with, 112–13

Republicans, Jeffersonian, 151, 166

Restoration (flagship), 76

retaliatory treatment of prisoners, 52, 54, 55, 63, 70–75

revenge, Loyalists seeking, 46, 76–105; anger, appropriate and inappropriate expressions of, 80–82; Black Loyalists ransacking Patriot property, 89; British

prosecution of war, Loyalist involvement in, 85–87, 89–94, 105; debates about propriety of, 76–77, 82–87, 104, 105; desire for revenge, 76, 80; honor, relationship to, 77, 78, 80, 81, 82, 104–5; Indigenous peoples, Loyalist alliances with, 94–98; irregulars and privateers, 98–104; justified by Loyalists, 76, 84–85, 91–94, 96–98, 104; literary depictions of revenge, 81–82, 199n17; Patriot spin on Loyalist acts of, 77–78, 87–90, 92–97, 99, 101–2, 104; restraint in, importance of, 80–81, 85–86; scholarship on, 79–80; sermons for and against, 76–77, 82–84

Revenge, The (Edward Young), 81

Revenger's Tragedy, The (Middleton), 199n17

Revolutionary War, Loyalists in. *See* political death of Loyalists in revolutionary America

Reylander (Loyalist), 35

Richardson, John, 82

Rivington, James, 45, 76

Roberts, William, 45

Robie, Mary Bradstreet, 165

Robie, Thomas, 165

Robinson, Beverly, 165

Robinson, Beverly, III, 170

Robinson, John Beverly, 175

Robinson, Mathew, 38

Robinson, Nancy, 165

Robinson Family, 174

"Rogue's March," 8, 178

Root, Jesse, 66, 68

Rose, Jacobus, 62

Rowland, Mrs., 99

Royal Commission on the Losses and Services of the American Loyalists. *See* Loyalist Claims Commission

Royal Gazette, 54, 72, 100, 152–53

Royal Pennsylvania Gazette, 85, 91

INDEX 251

Ruggles, Timothy, 37, 48, 162
Rush, Benjamin, 147
Rutledge, Edward, 148
Rutledge, John, 1
Ryerson, Egerton, 181
Rysdorp, Rev., 45

Sabine, Lorenzo, 79, 178
Saratoga campaign (1777), 54, 55, 87, 124, 128–34
scalpings, 72, 96, 98, 151
Schieffelin, Hannah Lawrence, 26, 73, 97
Schieffelin, Jacob, 45, 72, 74
Schivelbusch, Wolfgang, 80, 108, 109
Schuyler, Philip, 40, 58, 96–97
Scottish Highlanders. *See* Jacobites/Scottish Highlanders
Seabury, Samuel, 37, 76, 83, 104, 177
Seneca, 94, 96
Serle, Ambrose, 26, 54
Seven Years' War, 125
Sewell, Jonathan, 38
sexual insult and rape, 39–40
Seymour, Moses, and wife, 50
Shakespeare, William, 81
Shawnee, 72, 120
Sherwood, Justus, 207n70
Short History of the War in America, A (Galloway), 127–28
Shy, John, 79
Siege of Corinth, The (Byron), 81
Sierra Leone, free Black Loyalists settling in, 163
Silliman, G. Selleck, 20
Simcoe, Elizabeth Posthuma, 159
Simcoe, John Graves, 91, 159, 167
Simpson, James, 80, 101
Six Nations, 98
Skemp, Sheila, 103
Skene, Philip, 57, 60, 197

skimmington, 38
slavery. *See* Black Americans and slavery
Smith, Adam, 18
Smith, Claudius, 102
Smith, Paul H., 90, 91
Smith, Richard, 102
Smyth, John Ferdinand Dalziel, 51, 85–86
social and family connections, 19–20; dishonoring acts and, 44–45; education of Loyalist children, 166–70, 213n77; households, families, and children of resettled Loyalists, 160–70; marriages of exiled Loyalists, 163–65; political rebirth and, 137–39, 144–45, 149–50
social death compared to political death, 19
social ostracism, 43–45
Society for the Propagation of the Gospel in Foreign Parts, 158
"Song for St. George's Day" (Odell), 84
Sons of Liberty, 33, 181
South Carolina: large number of Loyalists from, 11; omnibus clemency act (1784), 151; political reintegration of Loyalists in, 149–51
Spain, Florida ceded to, 111
Spalding, A. D., 45
spaniel insult, 32
Spanish Tragedy, The (Kyd), 199n17
spies: gentlemen, not regarded as, 70–71; women as, 192n68
Spooner's Vermont Journal, vii
Sprigg, Osborne, 7–8
Stamp Act crisis (1765), 38
Stansbury, Joseph, 87
Starke, Mariana, 134–35
State of the Expedition from Canada, The (Burgoyne), 130–31
Stewart, Charles, 80
Stewart, Frank Henderson, 15, 82
St. George, Robert Blair, 38

Stone, Joel: death of, 168; dishonoring acts perpetrated on, 38–39, 46; education of children, 167–68, 170; Loyalist identity and, 111, 118, 120, 121; marriage, collapse of, 164–65, 167; political death and rebirth, 10, 12, 137–39, 159–60, 162, 166, 178; revenge, Loyalists seeking, 100

Stone, Leah Moore, 164–65

Stone, Mary, 167, 168, 170

Stone, Rene. *See* Hopkins, Rene Stone

Stone, William, 167–68, 170

Stow, Edward, 38

Stuart, James, 117

suicides, 47, 118

Swift, Patrick (William Lyon Mackenzie), 174

"Tammany," Winslow writing as, in *Royal Gazette,* 152–53

Tarleton, Banastre, 91, 93, 98

tarring and feathering, 25, 27, 28, 36–37, 38, 45, 176, 178

Theory of Moral Sentiments, The (Adam Smith), 18

Thomas, Erin, 14

Tiedemann, Joseph, 148–49

Tillman, Kacy, 177

Tocqueville, Alexis de, 14–15

tomahawk, murder of Loyalist Indigenous people with, 72

Tories in revolutionary America. *See* political death of Loyalists in revolutionary America

treason, 41, 48, 51, 75, 166, 180, 194n5

Trumbull, Jonathan, 49, 58, 60

Tryon, William, 77, 87, 99, 120, 203n94

Tyendinaga (Joseph Brant), 96, 97, 98

Types Riot (1826), 173–76

United States: Articles of Confederation, 147; Constitution, attainder prohibited by, 10, 147; education of Loyalist children in, 166–70, 213n77; Federalists and Jeffersonian Republicans in, 151, 166; literary portraits of Loyalists in, 180–81; political rebirth of reintegrated Loyalists, Patriot arguments in favor of, 147–48

Unity of Empire (U.E.) designation, 159, 173

Upper Canada. *See* Canada

Upper Canada Rebellion (1837), 175

Van Buskirk, Judith, 56, 149

vandalization of houses, 37–39, 176

Van Schaak, Peter, 43, 151

Van Tyne, Charles Halstead, 79

vengeance. *See* revenge, Loyalists seeking

Vengeance (privateer), 100

Vickery, Amanda, 37

violence, dishonor as form of, 17–19

Virginia: Dunmore's proclamation freeing enslaved persons fighting for British, 11, 89; small number of white Loyalists from, 11

Wacousta (Richardson), 82

Wallabout Bay prison ships, Brooklyn, 53

Ward, Harry M., 79

War of 1812, 166, 173

Washington, George: Asgill affair, 102–3; Boucher and, 8, 9; on captives and captivity, 56–59, 64, 65, 70–74; gentlemanly accoutrements of, 47; Hickey Plot to assassinate, 49, 50; William Howe on, 126; Lady Johnson complaining to, 40; on Loyalists, 8; Moody claiming to capture dispatches of, 123; Mount Vernon, preservation of, 151; on revenge, 86; "Rules of Civility" copied out by, 27

Watson, George, 44

Wattles, Charles, 121

Waxhaws, Battle of (1780), 93–94, 95

INDEX   253

Wells, Benjamin, 89

Welsh, Alexander, 182

Weston, Captain, 33

West Point, 70–71

Whigs, 1, 2, 20, 30, 39, 53, 55, 72, 77, 78, 101, 128, 146, 149, 176, 178

White, Philip, 102

Whitfield, Harvey Amani, 163

Whitworth, Nathaniel, Jr., 44

wig-snatching, 23, 28–29

Williams, Ezekiel, 49, 57, 60

Williams, Israel, 31

Winslow, Edward, 76–77, 85, 105, 152–54, 156–57, 159, 165, 166

Winslow, Mary, 165

women and gender: captive disguising himself as woman to escape, 69, 197n60; coverture law and women's legal identity, 41; hegemonic masculinity, 186n33; households, families, and children of resettled Loyalists, 160–70; Loyalist Claims Commission and, 116, 205n31; Loyalist kin, women treated as extensions of, 19, 38–41, 46; Loyalists, women as, 11, 177; marriages of exiled Loyalists, 163–65; popular prejudices, Patriot exploitation against Loyalists of, 16, 25–26, 29–30, 32; rape and sexual insult, 39–40; republican motherhood, 161; spies, women as, 192n68; Winslow's diatribe on returning Loyalist refugees, 153

Woodford, William, 35

Wooster, David, 57

Wyandot, 94

Wyatt-Brown, Bertram, 77, 140, 150, 179

Wyoming, Battle of (1778), 94–95, 104, 143

Yale University, 169

"Yankee Doodle," 67

Yorktown, Battle of (1781), 109

Young, Edward, 81

The Revolutionary Age

The American Liberty Pole: Popular Politics and the Struggle for
Democracy in the Early Republic
SHIRA LURIE

European Friends of the American Revolution
ANDREW J. O'SHAUGHNESSY, JOHN A. RAGOSTA, AND
MARIE-JEANNE ROSSIGNOL, EDITORS

The Tory's Wife: A Woman and Her Family in Revolutionary America
CYNTHIA A. KIERNER

Writing Early America: From Empire to Revolution
TREVOR BURNARD

Spain and the American Revolution: New Approaches and Perspectives
GABRIEL PAQUETTE AND GONZALO M. QUINTERO SARAVIA, EDITORS

The American Revolution and the Habsburg Monarchy
JONATHAN SINGERTON

Navigating Neutrality: Early American Governance in the Turbulent Atlantic
SANDRA MOATS

Ireland and America: Empire, Revolution, and Sovereignty
PATRICK GRIFFIN AND FRANCIS D. COGLIANO, EDITORS

Printed in the USA
CPSIA information can be obtained
at www.ICGtesting.com
CBHW020226210524
8864CB00002B/69